STANLEY KUBRICK
and Me

STANLEY KUBRICK

and Me

THIRTY YEARS AT HIS SIDE

Emilio D'Alessandro
with Filippo Ulivieri

Translated from the Italian by Simon Marsh

Arcade Publishing • New York

First English-language Edition

Arcade Publishing books may be purchased in bulk at special discounts for sales promotion, corporate gifts, fund-raising, or educational purposes. Special editions can also be created to specifications. For details, contact the Special Sales Department, Arcade Publishing, 307 West 36th Street, 11th Floor, New York, NY 10018 or arcade@skyhorsepublishing.com.

Arcade Publishing® is a registered trademark of Skyhorse Publishing, Inc.®, a Delaware corporation.

Visit our website at www.arcadepub.com.
Visit the author's website at www.emiliodalessandro.com.

10 9 8 7 6 5 4 3 2

Library of Congress Cataloging-in-Publication Data

Names: D'Alessandro, Emilio. | Ulivieri, Filippo, 1977- author. | Marsh, Simon, 1960- translator.
Title: Stanley Kubrick and me: thirty years at his side / Emilio D'Alessandro with Filippo Ulivieri; translated by Simon Marsh.
Other titles: Stanley Kubrick e me. English
Description: New York: Arcade Publishing, 2016.
Identifiers: LCCN 2015050645 (print) | LCCN 2016002578 (ebook) | ISBN 9781628726695 (hardback) | ISBN 9781628726718 (Ebook)
Subjects: LCSH: Kubrick, Stanley. | Motion picture producers and directors—United States—Biography. | D'Alessandro, Emilio. | BISAC: PERFORMING ARTS / Individual Director (see also BIOGRAPHY & AUTOBIOGRAPHY / Entertainment & Performing Arts). | BIOGRAPHY & AUTOBIOGRAPHY / Entertainment & Performing Arts.
Classification: LCC PN1998.3.K83 D3513 2016 (print) | LCC PN1998.3.K83 (ebook) | DDC 791.4302/33092—dc23
LC record available at http://lccn.loc.gov/2015050645

Cover design by Laura Klynstra
Cover photo courtesy il Saggiatore S.p.A.

Printed in the United States of America

To Christiane,
and to all of those who,
like us,
truly loved Stanley

CONTENTS

STANLEY KUBRICK
and Me

1

GOOD MORNING,
I'M STANLEY KUBRICK

IN THE HAWK FILMS office, an enormous white phallus reflected the light from the ceiling. To one side stood two young men, staring at it motionlessly.

It was half-past nine in the evening. Outside it was raining. I was cold and wanted to go home. I'd been driving around London for more than eighteen hours, only to find that the last urgent delivery I had to make was a big porcelain phallus.

"Hey!" I said, startling them. "Give me a hand with this thing, will you?" We took it out to the Minx, but as we feared it wouldn't fit in the trunk. We put it on the front seat. The end protruded from the front window. "I don't suppose you have a blanket, do you?"

From the Associated British Pictures Studios at Borehamwood, I drove towards Thamesmead, a modern area on the right bank of the Thames. The black ice slowed me down, and it took me more than an hour and a half to reach my destination. Nobody else in the company had accepted the delivery. They all said it was too risky in such bad weather. But my training as a race-car driver had prepared me to deal with any road conditions. "Steady, not greedy," as my mentor used to say.

The bundle beside me bounced up and down as if it were alive. What damn film could it be for?

When I arrived, another two young men were waiting for me. They opened the car door, removed the contraption, and told me to wait: I was going to have to return it. Off they went, carrying it like a baby in arms, and then they brought it back to me without saying a word. I was bewildered. Not only by the peculiar load, but also by the excessive suspiciousness surrounding the entire episode. I got in the car and drove back to Janette's house. When I met my boss, Tony, at midnight, I confirmed the two weeks' holiday I'd asked for and wished him Merry Christmas: 1970 was drawing to a close, and I hadn't had a day off for nearly two years.

My holiday at my parents' home in Sant'Angelo passed quickly. When I returned to England, there was a note waiting for me on the desk at Mac's Minicabs. It said that Hawk Films had phoned every day since I left, asking specifically for Emilio D'Alessandro to make new deliveries. At the end of the note it said: ASK FOR MR. HARLAN.

Mac's Minicabs had practically rescued me. After losing my job because of the strikes in the sixties, I'd spent weeks on end in the unemployment office waiting for something to happen. I had faith that all those jobs I'd done during my ten years in England would count for something. That writing *gardener, orderly in a clinic, assistant cook in a hospital, mechanic, factory worker, petrol pump attendant,* and *racing driver* on a piece of paper would make a good impression on a potential employer. Instead, every evening I trudged home demoralized. My wife and I had tried just about everything. We had even rented out the house and moved down to my brother's place in Wales, but it hadn't made any difference. After six months, there was just five pounds left in our savings account, not even enough to do the shopping. If I didn't find a job within a week, I wouldn't be able to feed my children or pay the mortgage: the house would be repossessed.

MAC'S MINICABS, DRIVE WHEN YOU WANT, EARN AS MUCH AS YOU WANT, WORKING THE HOURS YOU WANT! That's what the ad said. I'd spent the last small change in my pocket at the newsagent's on a cheap job magazine for the hopeless. The other ads weren't any better, and at least this one had something to do with my greatest passion: cars. I had nothing to lose, so I phoned and made an appointment the same day at their offices in Borehamwood.

The Minicabs manager, Tony McDonagh, showed me in and explained that the job was for a private taxi driver without fixed working hours. Borehamwood and nearby Elstree were home to the British National Studios, the film studios of Metro Goldwyn Mayer and EMI Films, nicknamed the British Hollywood. Mac's Minicabs had an exclusive contract with some of the companies there and provided transport for managers, executives, and actors. The minicab company got the customers, and at the end of the week the drivers handed over a percentage of the takings. The more I worked, the more I would earn. "Twenty-four hours a day, if you like," said Tony. I didn't need to have any special licenses or documents, just a normal driver's license. My references as a Formula Ford driver had caught Tony's eye. He immediately handed me a contract and offered me the job.

"At a higher weekly commission rate we rent limousines if you want to deal with important customers," he said as he took me to their parking lot.

"No," I said immediately, knowing that I couldn't afford to give them a higher percentage, "I'll use my own car," and I winked at the run-down Ford Capri I'd bought in Cardiff.

It was a Friday, the weekend was just around the corner, and people were getting ready to spend the evening in restaurants, pubs, or cinemas. Tony gave me the address of my first customer; I invited them to get into the Capri and took them to their destination. In addition to the fare, I got a ten-shilling tip. By the end of the evening, I realized I'd earned what for me was an unbelievable amount of money.

I went home, went upstairs, and found Janette already in bed. I undressed quietly so as not to wake her, but without turning over she whispered, "What's the time? How did it go?" "Fine," I answered, moving closer and putting my arms around her. "It went really well. You can sleep peacefully now, really."

Tony's exclusive contracts included legal and production paperwork, so some days I transported envelopes full of contracts, checks, and production documents. I waited in luxurious center-city waiting rooms for the signed documents to be returned to me. Hawk Films was probably one of these companies, though I can't say I really remembered all their names.

Jan Harlan, a slim, well-dressed man with thick brown hair and a mustache, invited me in and asked me to take Maria, his wife, and the children to the airport. During the next few days he kept asking for me and left Tony a list of jobs for me to do. The deliveries were all subject to the maximum discretion. It wasn't easy to understand what Hawk Films actually did—*shooting film* or *shooting people*—but I wasn't worried. I needed the work. Once, I did manage to see something different from the usual to-ing and fro-ing: the front door of a white house out in the sticks beyond Well End had been left ajar, and I caught a glimpse of nearly a dozen cats chasing each other and rolling playfully on a brown carpet. Almost immediately a member of the crew hurriedly shut the door.

Hawk Films specifically requested that each job be completed on time, *without failure*. There was always a deadline, a delivery time. I had to respect this and was allowed at the very most fifteen minutes' leeway. After my meeting with Mr. Harlan, I didn't have any direct contact with them: each morning, the secretary at Mac's Minicabs gave me a list of the tasks that had been dictated to her over the phone. Every time I went back to the office, there were more jobs to do. One day, though, someone from the Hawk Films office called and asked to speak to me personally.

"Are you interested in working in the movies?"

"The movies? No, I drive cars," I replied, without really having understood the question.

"Very well," was the reply. Not another word.

"I'm interested in working," I said, in an attempt to fill the awkward silence. "Twenty-four hours a day if necessary."

"Exactly, that's just what we're looking for. Someone who doesn't stick to the timetable!" said the voice with a laugh. "How would you like to work for us? And I mean just for us?"

A few days earlier, John Wayne had asked me exactly the same thing. Sitting there on the backseat of the Hillman Minx, just like he was on the screen. With his thin lips and slot-like eyes, he looked at me silently from the cinemascope of the rearview mirror. After days of unfaltering silence on the road between Shepperton Studios and Pinewood, John Wayne finally opened his mouth and asked me to work just for him. The offer did make me think: acting in films meant that he would be constantly on the move, from one set to another, especially in the Mexican deserts where they filmed westerns . . . There was the risk that it wouldn't turn out to be a steady job, and a steady job was what Hawk Films, with their permanent base in London, were offering me. I glanced at him in the mirror and without turning around said no, that I wouldn't accept. Dozens of times I'd seen him shoot the bad guy point-blank, but inside the Minx he just said, "I understand," and looked away.

"That's fine by me," I answered the voice on the phone, "but I still have a contract with the minicab company."

"We'll take care of all that," said the voice. "We'll reach an agreement with them about your contract."

And that was it. In spring 1971 I started working for Hawk Films, from six in the morning until dinnertime. Of course, there were breaks and time to relax, but whenever the phone rang I had to be ready straightaway. It was hard work, but I felt good. I was about to turn thirty, and I had a steady job again.

One day a couple of months later, Mr. Harlan sent me to Abbots Mead, a house beyond the outskirts of northeast London. It was halfway along Barnet Lane, a tree-lined road that ran alongside the parish of Elstree and Borehamwood.

There was a closed metal gate with no bell. I tried pushing it, and it opened slowly. I parked the car in the gravel courtyard under the branches of two large trees. I rang the bell, and a rather tall lady with a big smile opened the front door. She introduced herself as Kay, a secretary.

"Are you Emilio?" she asked. "Do you know who you're working for?"

"Yes, for Hawk Films."

"There's someone who would like to meet you. He'll be here in a moment."

A few minutes later, two golden retrievers came through one of the doors in the corridor followed by a brisk-looking man of about forty.

"Good morning," he said, holding out his hand.

"Good morning," I replied. We shook hands. He was slightly taller than me and had an impressive, curly black beard. He looked like Fidel Castro.

"I'm Stanley Kubrick," he said, looking me in the eye.

There was a moment of silence. Maybe I was expected to say something. I didn't say anything, apart from: "And I'm Emilio D'Alessandro."

Without letting go of my hand, he took a press clipping from his pocket.

"Is this you?"

It was an old article from 1968 describing my career as a Formula Ford driver.

"Yes, it's about me," I answered.

"Do you drive like that on the roads, too?"

"No, you must be joking! Only when I was on the circuit."

"Do you respect the speed limit and road signs?"

Was it a trick question?

"Of course," I replied, "I have to respect the highway code. Any infraction would be reported on my racing driver's license, too. I would lose points, and my score affects my rating. I even have to be careful where I park."

A smile appeared through his beard. "I have a Mercedes 280 SEL automatic. Do you think you can handle it without a problem?"

"It's a car that does half the work for you. I think I can manage the rest."

"Let's try, then. Why don't we have a night out with my family at the Royal Opera House and you drive us?"

He took his leave and went back into his room, followed by the dogs. Before he closed the door, I caught a glimpse of a cat yawning and stretching on the desk. I smiled.

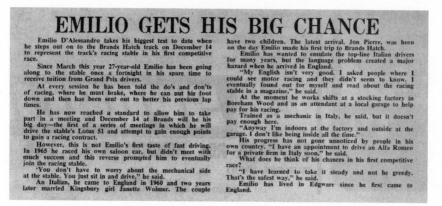

EMILIO GETS HIS BIG CHANCE

Emilio D'Alessandro takes his biggest test to date when he steps out on to the Brands Hatch track on December 14 to represent the track's racing stable in his first competitive race.

Since March this year 27-year-old Emilio has been going along to the stable once a fortnight in his spare time to receive tuition from Grand Prix drivers.

At every session he has been told the do's and don'ts of racing, where he must brake, where he can put his foot down and then has been sent out to better his previous lap times.

He has now reached a standard to allow him to take part in a meeting and December 14 at Brands will be his big day—the first of a series of meetings in which he will drive the stable's Lotus 51 and attempt to gain enough points to gain a racing contract.

However, this is not Emilio's first taste of fast driving. In 1965 he raced his own saloon car, but didn't meet with much success and this reverse prompted him to eventually join the racing stable.

'You don't have to worry about the mechanical side at the stable. You just sit in and drive,' he said.

An Italian, he came to England in 1960 and two years later married Kingsbury girl Janette Wolmer. The couple have two children. The latest arrival, Jon Pierre, was born on the day Emilio made his first trip to Brands Hatch.

Emilio has wanted to emulate the top-line Italian drivers for many years, but the language problem created a major hazard when he arrived in England.

"My English isn't very good. I asked people where I could see motor racing and they didn't seem to know. I eventually found out for myself and read about the racing stable in a magazine," he said.

At the moment he works shifts at a stocking factory in Boreham Wood and as an attendant at a local garage to help pay for his racing.

Trained as a mechanic in Italy, he said, but it doesn't pay enough here.

"Anyway I'm indoors at the factory and outside at the garage. I don't like being inside all the time."

His progress has not gone unnoticed by people in his own country. "I have an appointment to drive an Alfa Romeo for a private firm in Italy soon," he said.

What does he think of his chances in his first competitive race?

"I have learned to take it steady and not be greedy. That's the safest way," he said.

Emilio has lived in Edgware since he first came to England.

The article from 1968 that Stanley had found goodness knows where.

The secretary explained to me that this man, Stanley Kubrick, was a famous American film director who had been living in England for some years. I had never heard of him. Those days I never went to the cinema. I didn't have time. I'd driven a great many actors, actresses, and producers, but that's as far as my knowledge of the world of film went: handshakes and tips. I only ever got to see actors in the flesh.

"Are you pleased that you've met him?" asked the secretary.

"Well," I blurted out, trying to think of something polite to say, "I'm pleased that he's an honest and respected person. That means he'll treat me well, too."

That evening, when I returned to Abbots Mead to take Mr. Kubrick and his friendly, smiling wife, Christiane, to the Royal Opera House, I apologized for not having recognized him. Cars, not cameras, were my world. I wouldn't even know how to hold a camera. His wife laughed out loud at what I said, and he told me that it wasn't in the least bit important.

Two hours later, after the performance, Mr. Kubrick asked me if I wouldn't mind taking an extra passenger. He moved aside to let a young, very elegant lady get in. He introduced her to me as Gwyneth Jones, adding, "She is a famous opera singer." Understandably, he probably imagined that I had never heard of her before.

"We need to stop at a restaurant, if you don't mind waiting for us while we have something to eat. It's the Mumtaz. Do you know where it is?"

"Halfway down Park Road. I've been there before."

"What's the food like?"

"Actually, I meant that I've taken clients there. I've never been inside, but from the outside, I'd say it looks like a good place."

"Okay . . . but don't you need a map?" he added. "My chauffeur always has a map in his hand."

"If you don't know the streets of London after two years as a taxi driver, you'd do well to emigrate!"

The next day Mr. Kubrick asked me to take him to the American Embassy in Grosvenor Square to renew his passport. Then we went to Wardour Street, to the London offices of Warner Bros., the American company that financed his films. I was about to get into the Mercedes again, but Mr. Kubrick stopped me: "Do you mind if we go in yours?" Before I had time to reply that the Minx was a just a supermini and nowhere near as comfortable as the Mercedes, he was already on the backseat.

Kubrick looked around in silence while I drove. After a few minutes, he said, "It's a nice car. Is it new?"

"No, I bought it secondhand. It's at least three years old. It's got a fair amount of miles on the clock."

"It looks new; it's in better condition than my Mercedes. Do you look after it yourself?"

"Yes, but it doesn't take much—just a damp cloth now and then to get rid of the dust."

"The Mercedes isn't this clean when it comes back from the carwash. Does everything work?

"So far . . ."

There was another long silence.

"Why do you drive so carefully?"

He expected a Formula Ford driver to be more aggressive—all screeching tires and whizzing around corners. I explained that this had been one of the most important lessons I'd learned at the Brands Hatch Motor Racing Club course: if you take a corner too fast, when you steer the car you risk skidding. "Imagine that you've got a glass full of water in the middle of the hood," Tony Lanfranchi told us. "When you turn the corner, the water can tilt, but not so much that it spills. If you get water on the hood, you've made a mistake."

It was Tony who had taught me everything I knew about car racing—he was a wonderful driver. He knew how to corner instinctively and had tried to teach me to do it. "Get the front wheels on the edge of the curb and then forget about the bend, think about the next one so that you can be sure to arrive there with the shortest possible trajectory. You need to anticipate—your brain needs to be one curve ahead of your body." And then he'd said, "Learn to feel the way the car vibrates if your tires are losing their grip. Anticipate there as well. Like the way a doctor finds an illness before it becomes apparent, you have to understand that you're skidding even before you actually skid."

Was I disturbing Kubrick by talking so much? My enthusiasm and nostalgia had carried me away. However, in the rearview mirror I could see that he was listening carefully and looked interested, so I added that Tony had also been an advisor on John Frankenheimer's film *Grand Prix*. He'd also driven all the single-seater cars, going flat out to give the director the most spectacular shots possible.

"What's that noise when you brake?" he asked. He'd noticed a squeaking sound coming from the wheels.

I enjoyed answering questions like this, because I could never talk about cars to Janette. She got bored immediately.

"It must be a stone stuck between the brake disk and the cover."

I stopped at the first lay-by, got out, and gave the wheel a gentle kick.

"Is it dangerous?"

"No, don't worry."

The next time I braked, the wheel didn't make a sound. "How did you know that?"

"It's happened before. It does that sometimes."

He didn't say anything else until we pulled up in front of the embassy. He asked me to park in a road nearby and wait. I waited for

him for nearly three hours, and when he came back to the car he was
rather annoyed. "A complete waste of time!" he grumbled. "Can you go
and get my documents next time? I'll give you a signed proxy."

When we arrived at Abbots Mead, the courtyard was swarming
with busy secretaries and assistants. Kubrick showed me to a shed on
the left side of the courtyard and stopped in front of two Volvos—a
146 "bought recently," and a yellow 240 "that only Christiane uses."
He pointed to a Ford van and a Volkswagen minibus parked a little
farther down the shed. These both belonged to Hawk Films and were
used to get to the set or transport materials or equipment. A Volkswagen pickup with a tarpaulin covering the trailer served the same
purpose.

There was an off-white Land Rover parked on the other side. It
came from the set of his latest film, where it had been used as a police
car. There were still blue lights on the roof. He told me his wife used
it to get around locally. He finished by saying, "Could you clean them
all? I'd like them to be like yours. But you'd only need to clean the
inside of the Mercedes."

I liked driving that wonderful car. It was comfortable and quiet.
The first time I got in it, I had been amused by the choice of seat belts.
They had a harness similar to racing car belts that went from the shoul-
der right down to the groin.

On our next trip to London, Kubrick sat in the back again and
spoke even less than the previous time. I didn't say anything either,
leaving him to read his documents. Only after we had been driving for
many miles did he observe that even though his Mercedes was an automatic, he didn't notice any difference compared to my Minx.

"That's because I'm using the same foot," I replied.

"I feel less relaxed with other people's feet."

"I'll leave you with Andros," he said when we returned to Abbots
Mead, and he disappeared quickly into a small room built on the side
of the house. A young man with the same black, tousled beard, but
with a shrewder look about him, appeared in front of me and introduced himself as Andros Epaminondas, Kubrick's personal assistant.

"He's gone to the dubbing room," he explained. "We're in the process of finishing a film." He showed me to the small square building beside the courtyard entrance. "I'll show you our headquarters," he chuckled, and as we went upstairs to the second floor he told me he was from Greece. He was twenty-seven and had a passion for cinema. Despite continual protests from his family, he had decided to work in filmmaking. I had experienced much the same resistance to my interest in race-car driving. He spoke about himself in an open, cheerful way, and I took to him immediately.

"This is where I spend most of my time, and usually on the phone," he said pointing to his desk. "Jan's, the secretary's, and the accountants' rooms are over there. Then there are some other rooms we use for storing stuff. Stanley prefers to work at home, but there isn't enough room for everyone in the house and the Lodge, so he's rented the Chantry. That's the building you saw on the left before you came through the gate."

Andros had been working with Kubrick for over a year. He confided in me that he had learned all the various tricks behind the management of Abbots Mead. He told me about rooms being emptied and filled, removal vans and vacated locations. He made the Kubrick home sound like a factory. "If we need an empty room," he added, "we put everything in a container and take it to the warehouses we rent in Bullens near Borehamwood." I'd heard Andros say "storage room" at least ten times, and I was asking myself how they could possibly have problems storing things with all that space.

When we went back downstairs to the courtyard, he told me that Christiane used the ground floor of the Lodge for her painting. She spent a lot of time there, painting the plants and flowers that were grown in the greenhouses, as well as local rural landscapes. This was her territory: surrounded by canvases and the smell of tempera, and by the classical musical and lyric opera that kept her company. I spotted three golden retrievers dozing in the shade under the trees in the garden. "That's Teddy and Lola and their mother, Phoebe. We've got cats, too." He rattled off such a long list of names that I couldn't keep up with him. "Always remember that you must never leave Freddie and Leo alone together. They fight so violently that they invariably wreck the place. There's a room on the second floor of the house especially for them. They take it in turns: one in the room, the other in the garden. Yes"—as he finished, he looked at me seriously—"I'd say that that is the most important thing of all."

At seven the next morning, Andros was waiting for me on the first floor of the Lodge with a cup of American coffee. He handed me a pile of envelopes to take to London. When I came back, I was to use the Mercedes to drive some of Kubrick's collaborators. Even though production of the film was finished, he still called a number of people to the house, and it was my job to drive them. My day was pretty much the same as it was when I worked for Hawk Films and knew only Jan Harlan, though receiving my list of tasks was now more amusing. Andros took every opportunity to make wisecracks and joked about almost everything, laughing heartily.

For some days I carried out the tasks Andros gave me, then one morning I saw Kubrick again. "Emilio, I have to go to London." No sooner had he said this, he was already in the car. Unlike the actors and directors I'd driven in the minicab, Kubrick didn't wait for me to open the door for him. He was actually so quick that he got to the car before I did. More and more frequently, he chose to get in the Minx rather than the Mercedes driven by his elderly chauffeur, Leslie. Kubrick still didn't say much when he was in the car. He read various documents and took notes in a notebook, which he always put swiftly back in the inside pocket of his jacket. When he did open his mouth, it was always to ask some question out of the blue.

"You've tried lots of different jobs," he said one afternoon. "Which one is your favorite?"

"Racing cars is my passion; the rest are just jobs. Hopefully, I'll be able to race again soon. I miss the circuit at Brands Hatch."

He fell silent for a moment.

"Can you promise to continue working for me?"

"Sure, if things continue this way, with plenty of work and a check at the end of the week."

He didn't return to the subject until we were on our way home, when he asked me if I belonged to a union. There was a tone of hope in his voice. For me, hearing the word "union" formed a knot in the pit of my stomach. He didn't wait for me to answer and explained that he needed an assistant who wasn't bound by the English workweek, from eight to six. "It's a waste of time to stop work at six. There's still half a day to make use of," he said simply. "I need you to be there when I need you," he explained, "even if that could mean in the evening, after dinner. And when I'm shooting a film, I need to be able to rely on my assistants, always." He emphasized this last word by saying it slowly. Suddenly, he became talkative; adding that the person he was looking for had to be able to help him with a variety of tasks. He had to be a driver, courier, secretary, manager of the car pool, and so on. This didn't really fit the job definitions of the English unions, who had a way of categorizing work excessively. This segmentation meant that to complete what he saw as one job, would, according to the unions, require several people. He saw this as another enormous waste of time. "When we're working together, I'll need to hand you notepads, notes, cameras. . . . I need to be able to put a notebook in your pocket without thinking that this violates union rules. If it were up to them, I shouldn't even lay a finger on you."

"I understand," I said when he stopped talking. "If helping means sticking to finicky rules, it's not much of a help, is it?"

"Precisely. Don't be taken in by what the trade unionists say. I'll give you everything you'll ever need."

In the silence of the car, I thought how wonderful it would be if what Kubrick had said was true. I was never going to believe the trade unionists again, that was for sure. When the wave of strikes in the sixties reached the hosiery factory in Borehamwood where I worked, my colleagues assured me that the unions would protect us and that we had nothing to worry about as far as our wages were concerned. The all-out strike went on, and I found myself alone in the midst of all those euphoric people, thinking what at the time seemed obvious to me: *We're not working, we're not making hosiery, so there's nothing to sell, no money is being made, and we won't get paid.* In fact, the factory closed. There were endless debates on television, but I didn't have much of an education and it was too complicated for me. I couldn't understand who was in the right: Labour, who supported the strike, or the Conservatives, who opposed it? The workers who were protesting for better pay and shorter working hours, or management, who produced figures and statistics to show that this simply wasn't feasible? The only things I was sure about were how angry I was at having lost my job and with it the future I'd been building a little at a time, and how ashamed I felt to go back home and look Janette in the face. At the end of those months of hardship, she gave me a plate of soup and left me to eat alone at the table. When I asked her if she'd given Marisa and Jon something to eat, she answered, "Yes, of course," elusively. "And what about you? Have you had something to eat?" I asked. "Yes, don't worry," she answered immediately, but I knew it wasn't true—she always answered this question with her back to me. The desperation, the helplessness, and the stagnant odor of poverty that filled our home—I'll never forget any of that.

"Emilio, give me a hand moving this stuff!" Andros was waving to attract my attention. He was in the storeroom behind a pile of trunks. I'd loaded up plenty of sacks of cement and odds and ends when I was working in Sant'Angelo. Manual work was certainly no problem for me. However, instead saying thank you, he started to make fun of me: "Come on, you lazy bastard! Didn't you say you liked work?" he grumbled through his mustache. But the look in his eye gave him away, and he laughed at the surprised expression on my face. Andros couldn't help teasing you—when I called to wake him up in the morning, he told me to get lost and hung up on me. When I got to Abbots Mead, he was already there and ready to offer me some coffee. "Let's see what Uncle Stanley has to ask of us today."

If I was a courier and driver, then Andros could best be described as the filter between the office and the outside world. He spent all day on the phone weaving a close-knit web of contacts that allowed him to track down anyone Kubrick needed in five minutes. Whatever the problem was, he always knew who to contact. He organized appointments, asked for expert advice, and made sure that everything ran smoothly. When I wasn't off taking Kubrick somewhere, he took care of me too and taught me how things worked at Abbots Mead.

"Don't wait forever for something to be delivered. Jump in the car and go and pick it up yourself. Don't let me see you walk empty-handed. Stanley is watching you. You can't see him, but he is."

"Who is he, God almighty?"

"In a certain sense." He nodded earnestly.

Another time he said, "If a machine's broken, figure out how it works and try to repair it yourself while you're waiting for the technician. If you manage, when he arrives send him home. That way you've helped him save time, too."

— BASIC TRAINING —

1. If you open it, CLOSE IT!
2. If you turn it on, TURN IT OFF!
3. If you unlock it, LOCK IT!
4. If you break it, REPAIR IT!
5. If you can't fix it, CALL IN SOMEONE WHO CAN!
6. If you borrow it, RETURN IT!
7. If you use it, TAKE CARE OF IT!
8. If you make a mess, CLEAN IT UP!
9. If you move it, PUT IT BACK!
10. If it belongs to someone else, GET PERMISSION TO USE IT!
11. If you don't know how to operate it, LEAVE IT ALONE!
12. If it doesn't concern you, DON'T MESS WITH IT!

Abbots Mead code of conduct.

The old proverb "If you want something done well, do it yourself" is true. The Abbots Mead version went: "If you want something done, do it."

Andros's introductory course included a seminar on the animals living in the house: "You must be very careful with them; very, very careful." While we were both struggling to push Freddie into his cage so that he and Leo could swap places, Andros told me about the time that the cat had climbed to the top of one of the trees in the courtyard in front of the house. He had started to meow loudly, and even though Andros had begged the cat to be quiet, Kubrick heard, came running, and went into a total state of panic. "You have no idea what a balls-up that was," he confided. "Stanley kept on saying, 'Call the fire brigade! Call the vet! Call Christiane!' as well as just about everyone else who had ever been to Abbots Mead." Andros not only had to call the fire brigade but also had to help them get Freddie down with the aid of a ladder.

"But that was the wrong thing to do," I said, laughing. "You should have left Freddie up the tree. He would have come down on his own soon enough."

"Sure," he answered ironically, "I'd really like to see you tell him: 'Don't worry, Stanley, the cat will come down when he feels like it.' There's nothing doing when animals are involved. Absolutely nothing doing."

As we were crossing the courtyard on our way back to the office in the Lodge, Andros stopped in front of the door of a shed. "Can you drive lorries, too?" He opened the door, and in the half-light I could make out a solid, robust-looking yellow lorry with very large wheels and unusually high ground clearance.

"The yellow submarine?" I said jokingly.

"It's a fucking Unimog!" explained Andros, in that colorful way he had. "Mercedes designed it for the military. It's difficult to drive because it's got sixteen gears and a steering wheel so stiff that you need four hands to turn it!"

He started it up, and the roar of the engine was like the London Symphony Orchestra. Andros had discovered it himself. It had belonged to a landowner, who had bought it from NATO to use in the country, only to sell it soon afterwards because it used too much fuel. Stanley loved anything military, and so he bought it without really thinking about what to use it for. Andros suggested that since it was compact, it would be good for moving heavy loads on the set. But nobody was able to drive it, so it had been shut away, gathering dust in Abbots Mead like an old trophy.

That morning I cleaned it inside and out, brushed away the cobwebs, and lubricated the engine. Mechanically, it was in good condition; it was just really dirty. I ran my hands across the rounded bodywork and the solid, wrought-iron bumpers. I couldn't wait to start the engine and drive it. The incredibly robust chassis was made of iron girders the size of rail tracks joined by huge bolts. It was suspended nearly a meter from the ground and gave the impression that you could quite easily drive it up a flight of stairs. The air vent protruded from the roof like a mushroom, which meant that even with half the vehicle underwater the engine would keep on working.

"I hope you can handle it, because Stanley just adores it," said Andros.

"You'll see. In a few hours we'll bring it back to life."

I climbed up into the cabin. There was room for two on the hard metal seats. The space between them was full of levers and buttons. When I started the engine, everything began to vibrate and clatter loudly: the cabin was made of iron and there was no soundproofing. It sounded as if I had switched on a pneumatic drill.

First, I found reverse and then first gear. The Unimog moved slowly. Stanley heard the roar of the engine and phoned Andros in the Lodge. "Who's driving the Unimog?"

"Emilio."

"But does he know about the gears and how to go?"

"If he didn't know, he would have already demolished Abbots Mead."

"That is my jewel!" said Stanley about his beloved Unimog.

"Well, in that case he must use the Unimog at least once a week, and give him a set of keys for himself."

Sitting in the cabin driving down Barnet Lane, it felt like I was flying. You needed to double-declutch to avoid grinding the gears: two taps on the clutch and one on the accelerator. It was possible to use only some of the sixteen gears: starting in fourth, changing to sixth, then ninth and so on—three at a time. The lowest gears were for when the Unimog was used without a driver. You could lock the steering wheel, put it in first or second, and the vehicle would go on its own. It was useful if you had to cross a river for example: the Unimog would just keep going, slowly and relentlessly, like a giant metal turtle.

Suddenly, I heard a sharp sound and the Unimog started to jolt violently. The gears were jammed. I pulled over to the side of the road, called Andros, and asked him to ring for a tow truck. When I got back to Abbots Mead, Kubrick asked me what had happened.

"Since I couldn't change gears, my first thought was that the clutch plate must have broken."

"Is that serious?" he asked me, a little worried.

"No, you just have to replace it. It's quite common when a vehicle hasn't been used for some time."

The Mercedes mechanics took the Unimog away and sent a report of the repairs. Kubrick read that the iron springs that held the clutch disc in place had broken; they'd been eaten away by rust. "How did you know that?" he asked, and I told him that in the past I'd been a mechanic in Cassino. My job there was to deal with very old cars that often had problems of this kind. "Can you take care of the maintenance of all the cars?" he asked, and went back into the editing room without giving me time to answer.

"When you ask me to drive you somewhere," I asked Kubrick one morning, while we were on our way towards London, "do you want me to dress formally, to wear a tie?" I hadn't received any instructions on this point, and yet there seemed to be an instruction manual for every-

Just arrived in Stanley's office.

thing at Abbots Mead. I looked at Leslie in his elegant dark suit and white gloves, and I asked myself if I was breaking some unwritten law.

"Good Lord, no! Dress the way you want!" he suddenly implored. This was one of the first nice things I heard Stanley say. Working as a taxi driver, I'd had to wear a jacket and tie. The opportunity to dress casually was a relief. When I worked with him I wore a white shirt and dark trousers. I was well-dressed but not formal. Most importantly, it wasn't a uniform. "I see that someone's been influencing your choice of clothes," his wife, Christiane, commented. "Please keep shaving; otherwise it won't be long before I can't tell you apart!"

My first impression of Christiane was of a woman who was kind and straightforward, not in the least bit interested in formalities. That evening in the car, I saw her smile at the amusing things her husband said. In the days that followed, she behaved in just the same way, regardless of whether we met in passing in the courtyard or if she was asking me to take her to London in the white Mercedes. She wore very comfortable, colorful clothes, full of pockets that she filled with brushes, tubes of tempera, and other things for painting. I thought that this perfectly reflected her character. Unlike her husband, who always sat in the back so that he could spread his paperwork out on the seat, Christiane always sat next to me. She never made me feel like a driver, not even at the beginning. She opened the door for herself, turned on the radio, and started chatting.

She revealed to me that she was a foreigner in England, too. She and her brother, Jan, were born in Germany and had grown up there. She had lived in Germany until she met Stanley in Munich while he was shooting a film. I exchanged confidences by telling her about how I'd met my wife at Christmas lunch at a friend's house. Janette was seventeen. She had short, neatly combed hair and a witty smile that didn't quite fit with the attractive shyness in her eyes. I'd been watching her for a while, and when she did finally look at me, she gave me a friendly smile: the movement of her lips seemed to spread right across her face, screwing up her eyes and bringing color to her cheeks.

By the time we got to dessert I was hopelessly in love. A few days later I invited her out for a walk in Canons Park. After a whole afternoon of me trying to say something interesting despite my nervousness and poor command of English, Janette asked me to take her home on my Lambretta. At each crossroads she whispered which road to take in my ear and held me tighter and tighter around the waist. A year later we were married.

Christiane liked London a lot, too. She had lived with Stanley in New York for a few years but felt the city was too chaotic. Subsequently, they moved to England for reasons connected to the production of her husband's films. They both loved the peacefulness of the area north of the city, with its tree-lined roads, wide sidewalks, and well-trimmed hedges. It was the ideal place to bring up children. The state schools were excellent, and Katharina, Anya, and Vivian had settled in perfectly. I replied that Marisa was six and Jon four. It was too early to be worrying about their academic careers. In the meantime, Janette had enrolled them in the elementary school nearest to our house on Farm Road.

2

EITHER YOU CARE
OR YOU DON'T

THE FILM BEING MADE at Abbots Mead was called *A Clockwork Orange*. Shooting had finished, but there were still a few small things to straighten out. While Stanley worked with the promotional team in the Chantry, I went to Malcolm McDowell's house. Malcolm was the star of the film, and Stanley had decided to give him one of Phoebe's puppies. It was a golden retriever that Stanley had named Alex, after the character Malcolm played. Together with the dog came detailed instructions about how to look after it, including which shop to buy food from since the supermarkets were not to be trusted. At that time, Malcolm lived in a flat on the Bayswater Road in Notting Hill. Stanley's trusted dog food supplier was a wholesaler in Stokenchurch, the other side of High Wycombe, about forty miles or so to the west. Malcolm was clearly in difficulty when it came to following the complicated instructions for how to look after the puppy, so once a month, when I went to buy sacks of food for his dogs, Stanley told me to buy a sack for Malcolm's dog, too. "When you go, make sure you deliver the food to him in person. That way you can go in and see how the dog is. Check to see if he's eating well, if he has water, ask if he's getting enough exercise, if he's getting taken for walks on the grass. . . ."

The flat was in a block with no garden and only a concrete courtyard, so there was nowhere for the dog to roll on the grass unless Malcolm took him "at least once a day," as Stanley had asked, across the road to Hyde Park. Increasingly impatiently, Malcolm made a point of telling me that he *was* taking Alex to the park. "And tell Stanley, please, will you!"

I also helped to dismantle the sets and locations. As Andros had foreseen, most of the stuff was stored in Abbots Mead and only transferred to the warehouses when there was absolutely no room left at all. While moving all these things around, I couldn't help noticing that most of Christiane's and the other artists' paintings were of erotic subjects. I even found myself handling some female nude sculptures and other strange objects. The phallus I'd transported the previous year was clearly in good company.

I don't think everyone took this film the right way. It was, let's say, rather particular in nature, and at the beginning of 1972, after *A Clockwork Orange* had been screened successfully in London for a few months, the papers were filled with fierce controversy. The film was accused of inciting violence among young people, and for over a year it was blamed for just about every episode of violence that happened in England. I couldn't grasp the seriousness of it. How could they possibly have blown things out of proportion like this? I was convinced that Stanley was worrying too much; and he worried more and more. After all, I asked myself, who was he? In the end he was just a director who had made a film. How come everyone had suddenly gone off their heads?

Stanley couldn't understand, either. The way the press framed it, anyone who saw the film

Pablo Ferro was an eccentric guy who had been hired to edit the trailer of A Clockwork Orange. *Stanley adored him and said he came up with ideas so original that nobody else could possibly ever have thought of them.*

automatically wanted to do the same things the protagonist did. The whole thing left me bewildered. After all, as I told him when he asked me what I thought, you don't see a western and then go out, buy a pistol, and start shooting in the pub!

I realized things were getting really tense when, in the mail I picked up every day, Stanley found a letter with a death threat. It was written using letters cut out from newspapers. "Never touch these letters again," he said, "and don't say anything about it to Christiane!" Andros and I found more and more intimidating letters: threats, drawings of bombs, and insults aimed at Stanley and his daughters. On several occasions, we had to call the police and ask them to check whether ticking or vibrating parcels were explosive or dangerous. From that day on, I handled only mail from known senders. The post office sent all the rest directly to Borehamwood police station.

Stanley didn't understand the particularly "English" nature of the problem, either. The film had had a positive impact everywhere else. It's true that it had provoked a lively debate and more than a little controversy in the press, but nowhere had it caused such a hostile reaction as in London and throughout the country.

In the end, the police asked Stanley to intervene, and in 1974 he decided to withdraw *A Clockwork Orange* from British distribution. Regardless of whatever had really caused the uproar, banning the film worked. The threats stopped, and things gradually got back to normal. Stanley told me that he thought of the film as medicine; that was exactly the word he used. And when he realized that the medicine didn't work, he took it off the market.

The secretary who had first met me at Abbots Mead left her job just after production work on *A Clockwork Orange* had finished. In 1972, before starting out on his next film, Stanley hired a personal secretary named Margaret Adams.

When I met her for the first time in the lodge, she was talking into two phones and typing in a way that sounded like bursts of gunfire. Though only twenty-eight, Margaret had plenty of experience. She was the perfect choice. Even though she was a tiny little woman, she was full of energy; it was hard to imagine where it all came from. She spent all day at base camp in the Lodge, dealing with administration, documents, registers, and tons of paperwork. She gave a new meaning to the word "secretary," because she didn't only deal with documents regarding film productions, she took care of Stanley's "secret" family matters, too.

I got on well with Margaret immediately. "Come in, put the kettle on," she said cheerfully every morning, inviting Andros and me to sit down and have a coffee while we organized the day ahead. It wasn't long before we were a perfectly efficient trio. All three of us cared about getting things done properly. I'd experienced the individualism of motor racing, and now, with them, I was discovering how good it felt to be part of a team: if Margaret was busy photocopying, Andros would answer the phone; if Andros had to rush over to Borehamwood Studios for something, I took care of the office or, more often, offered to go instead of him. When Margaret was too busy to stop for lunch, I would pop round to her flat to feed the cats. Stanley didn't complain about me being half an hour late, because I had to feed the cats. On the contrary, he made sure I went to feed Wishbone and Rosemary and that I always gave them fresh fish and nothing else. Actually, more often than not, while I was out, he asked me to run an errand for the film somewhere near Kew Bridge, where Margaret lived.

We were like a perfect production line with no need for maintenance. Things worked even better than they did when I first arrived at Abbots Mead: I would go to appointments with an excellent introduction from Andros and Margaret. I was always treated in a polite, kind, and respectful way by secretaries and receptionists. However, when I went to the administration department of a film production company for the first time, they wouldn't let me in. In those places, the receptionists had orders not to let in anyone who was not formally dressed. But when they got to know me, they paid no attention to my appearance. I even turned up scruffy and covered in oil from working on the cars, but when I said, "No, please let me in. I phoned earlier. I'm

Emilio D'Alessandro, and I'm here on behalf of Stanley Kubrick!" they answered, "Oh, of course. I'm terribly sorry."

It was the name that opened doors. Not the tie.

I realized how important it was for us to be recognized everywhere as representatives of Stanley Kubrick. We had to deal with a huge number of people, and if that meant explaining who we were over and over again, we would have wasted precious time. And time was precious; Andros explained to me that the only way to win the daily race against time was to do our best to be "kind," so that we could ask small favors in return. Every Christmas I spent two days delivering lavish gifts, mainly cases of whiskey, to dozens of offices in London.

The workload at Abbots Mead didn't decrease when *A Clockwork Orange* was finished. Actually, I realized that it didn't really make much difference whether we were making a film or not. The first thing to deal with was the mail. Every morning, when I left Farm Road, I went to the post office at Borehamwood, where I found at

Andros and me at my son Jon-Pierre's First Communion party.

least a sack full of letters for Stanley. Just after a film was released, there were as many as three sacks. Margaret was the first to sort the mail, separating what looked interesting from what was clearly trash. If the sender was unknown, the letter was put to one side for further investigation. What Margaret didn't filter out was then passed on to Andros. He made a second selection, and what remained was given to me to take to the house, but only after it had been sorted by addressee.

Then we looked through the documents and research results that arrived from people hired by Hawk Films. We sorted them, organized them, and delivered the results to Stanley, often with additional notes in the margins. We were like a funnel, gathering material and sending it to just one place: to Stanley. He had hired accountants as well as other secretaries and bookkeepers, but nevertheless you could always hear him say, "Check this, Margaret," or "Andros, check this," sometimes followed by Andros saying, "Margaret, check this again."

We read car insurance contracts, paid installments and various bills, did research into new technical developments, and requested product catalogs. Then we drew up reports comparing the prices of televisions, projectors, photocopiers, lights, typewriters, lenses, and portable recorders. We also had to prepare documents for the lawyers and accountants, deliver them, then go and fetch them again. We found out which library had the books Stanley was looking for and took the ones he'd finished with back to the London Library. We often had to apologetically return books late that he hadn't even opened. We made photocopies of books that couldn't be borrowed. We took Stanley to do the shopping in Borehamwood. We took him to villages where he'd found houses or places that might be suitable for a scene in an upcoming film. Then the next day, if Stanley really had decided to film there, we went back to the village to sort out all the red tape associated with filming. We made a note of who we had talked to so that there was always someone we could contact for information. We returned to a potential location day after day to measure the hours of sunlight for outdoor shooting. We even measured the widths of the roads so that we knew which trucks and trailers we could rent and use without getting stuck at the first crossroads.

You name it, we did it. We did masses of things every day, with absolute precision and a totally free hand. Quite simply, we were there to deal with Stanley's needs, whatever they might be. He made a request, we responded to it, he checked, and then he made another one. Ours was a vast organization, it was far-reaching yet simple, and it really was easy. Stanley's effective working method, put into practice with Andros and Margaret's meticulousness, was an unbeatable combination.

Working like that was wonderful, and it made me feel proud, but only for six days a week; because on the seventh, disaster inevitably struck. Day after day, lots of small mistakes mounted up: an apparently unimportant delay, a small mistake in a document, a missed phone call, a lost order, and the system got stuck. It was cyclical, regular as clockwork, a balls-up a week. "Oh fuck it! This is the day!" Andros would declare with a heavy heart, letting his arms fall with disappointment. There were weeks, though, when the disaster didn't happen, and that was nothing short of a miracle.

Stanley was our employer, and what he said was not to be questioned. Whatever he wanted had to be done. If he needed a document within a couple of hours, it had to be ready on time. If he called home on Saturday evening because something urgent needed doing, we went back to Abbots Mead. Saturday, Sunday, day, night, Christmas or Easter, it made no difference: the three of us were always at his disposal.

Mind you, our devotion was not unquestioning. If a request didn't seem reasonable to us, or if we thought it might not be the right solution to the problem, we told him. Normally, Stanley refused alternatives to his ideas with passionate disapproval and sharp reasoning that wore out any would-be critic. The way he readily accepted suggestions from Margaret and Andros was a clear indication of how much he trusted us.

STANLEY: "No."

MARGARET: "Yes, actually."

STANLEY: "Okay."

Easy.

The only other person he trusted like this was Julian Senior, the head of advertising and publicity at Warner Bros., Europe. I first met Julian in the courtyard outside the house, and I realized immediately that never a day passed without him dropping in on Stanley. Before *A Clockwork Orange* was released, Stanley and Julian had discussed every detail of the promotional campaign: posters, photographs for magazines, even Pablo Ferro's trailer. Julian's visits didn't become less frequent when the film was finished. Like Andros, Margaret, and me, Julian was consulted for matters that were beyond his competence. Thanks to his high-ranking

Stanley and his phone were inseparable.

position, he knew about all the ongoing Warner Bros. productions as well as those in other companies. Stanley was just dying to know which directors were working on what projects. He was curious about their choices of actors, technicians, and studios, too.

Julian must have violated secrecy agreements more than once when he told Stanley the latest news from the studios, but I can swear that this worked one way only: Stanley trusted Julian implicitly and knew he would never betray his confidence. Julian would give him an objective opinion on anything and would do everything he could to solve any kind of problem. Julian was the king of the scoop; the film expert. He was the missing piece of the puzzle, the fourth member of our team. He was the one who made it possible for Stanley to interact with the world of cinema.

Of course, being a key member of Stanley Kubrick's team could be hard at times. "I can't make it this evening, I'll drop by tomorrow. What difference does it make?" said Julian, trying in vain to slip free of Stanley's net. "No, I'm not coming this evening," he would say, trying to put his foot down, "because I'm sure that what I say to you tomorrow will be exactly the same thing I said to you yesterday!"

There was no need to get angry. Stanley expected twice as much of himself as he did of anyone else. When, thinking back, you realized that he was almost always right, and when you understood that everything he asked you to do was for a reason, and the reason was to do the job in the best possible way, you couldn't feel resentment; you just had to admire him. "Either you care, or you don't." That was how he answered one evening when, even though we were exhausted, he kept on giving us work to do. No, we couldn't turn a blind eye today, because "Either you care or you don't. That's all there is to it, Emilio."

Stanley was that simple: he cared about his work and his family, and that was it.

When I went to pick him up from Fleet Street after a meeting with his lawyers, he started grumbling about how affluent law firms were: "Those people are going to ruin the country. Their offices are full of valuable wood, expensive ornaments, and huge paintings. What do they need all that for? All I need is a desk, a chair, a pen, and a coffee machine; nothing else." While I was working for British Hollywood, I had the chance to see how many famous people are spoiled by money and luxury, and it is not unusual for them to become arrogant and rude, too. Stanley was one of the few celebrities who were still in touch with the real world. Instead of taking Christiane or one of his assistants to dinner in a famous restaurant full of VIPs so that he could be photographed on the way out, Stanley preferred to have food delivered to Abbots Mead where he could dine comfortably in the living room. When I asked him why he never went to any of the fashionable parties his colleagues went to, he replied, "They always talk above their heads."

I think the way Stanley managed his assistants was wonderful. If he had something to say to me, Andros, or Margaret, he did it in private. We were called to his office one at a time, and he explained how a certain task was to be done or how we should deal with a particularly delicate situation in the future. He liked to have a clear relationship with the people who worked for him. He knew that everything revolved around him but wasn't in the least bit interested in throwing his weight about. If he had been, all he would have had to do was line us all up in his office every morning, give us orders, and listen to us reply, "Yes, sir!" all together. But nothing could be further from the truth. "Don't call me sir. I don't need that," he said to me during one of the first trips we made together. "Call me Stanley."

Stanley's system of rules had been devised to ensure that Abbots Mead worked perfectly. All we had to do was follow them to the letter. I realized this practically immediately when he advised me never to trust hotel receptionists or the concierge when I was delivering documents. I should always place them in the hands of the person they were addressed to. He did everything he could to avoid problems arising. And he didn't care for idle chat: after telling us what we had to do, he would just leave notes on our desks about routine tasks.

Stanley didn't waste anything. But he wasn't bothered about saving, either. He woke up at ten or eleven, sometimes at midday, and he went to bed very late so that he could take full advantage of the opening times of Warner Bros.' offices in America. Andros, Margaret, and I started work early in the morning, while Stanley was still asleep. We dealt with the tasks he had left us just a few hours earlier before he went to bed. When he woke up, everything was done and we started all over again. It seemed like a never-ending cycle, because it was.

We had all received a kit with everything we needed. Mine was a briefcase with all the maintenance and insurance documents for the Mercedes and the other cars, as well as every other document I might need while I was running errands. Taking a traveling office everywhere you went reduced the risk of having to go back to base and waste time. Stanley did the same, stuffing his jacket pockets with pens, photocopies, sheets of paper, recorders, and tapes.

My pockets were full, too. I carried two notepads, a small one and a large one, two pens (one was a spare), and my day timer, which was a datebook with a weekly planner on each page. There I wrote names, office addresses, appointments, telephone numbers, and the prices of various things. The notepads were chosen to fit in the breast pockets of my shirt. Stanley had been very clear about shirts: I was to use only shirts with two breast pockets. In the right pocket I kept the notepad, notes he gave me, and receipts. In the left one I kept cash, my driving license, and other ID. The pockets had to be button-down so that nothing would fall out if I bent over. He also asked me to make sure I always had five hundred pounds in my wallet to cover any expenses I incurred during the working day. If I spent any money, I had to go

In front of the gate at Abbots Mead.

home and replace it so that I'd always have five hundred pounds in my pocket.

The equipment for the car consisted of a first aid kit, a flashlight, a lighter, and more pens here and there. We also carried three thirty-meter ropes just in case we came across an injured or abandoned dog (tie up the dog, take it to a vet, then back to Abbots Mead, and find a reliable person to give it to). There was also a muzzle to use if the dog was nervous, and for the same reason, thick leather gloves, too. The gloves also came in handy if we found a particularly angry cat.

We had to make sure that the office never ran out of photocopy paper. There was also a supply of notepads and notebooks as well as countless ballpoint and fountain pens. Stanley was mad about fountain pens. He had several different ones and just loved dipping them in his bottles of ink when he was writing. He was so keen on his Parker pens that he even tried to convert me to them by giving me one in a luxury gift box.

"Stanley, why are you giving me this? I don't even know how to use it. I'm much happier with a Biro."

"No," he answered, putting the box back in my hands, "you've got to accept it."

I had no choice, but I kept it in a drawer at home and continued using twenty-pence ballpoint pens. But a simple thank-you was never enough for Stanley. A few weeks later he came back with another shiny wooden box; this time it had Montblanc written on it. Inside, there was a pen and pencil set with two Biros. "Now you can use whichever one you like."

"Stanley, somebody will steal them! Why do you give me these expensive presents? I don't need them."

"Then keep them at home. Marisa and Jon can use them to do their homework."

All the things Stanley asked me to do inevitably took up a great deal of time, and this had negative consequences for my family life. Janette spent entire days without even seeing me: I left home just after six and didn't come home until dinnertime and, increasingly often, even later. "I'm sorry Janette, but Stanley . . ." I tried to explain, but my empty chair at the dinner table at Farm Road spoke for itself.

She told me that since we'd made it through that rough patch a few years earlier, there was no longer any need to devote every waking moment to making money. I explained to her that it wasn't about money. I hadn't been working for Stanley for long, and I wanted to prove to him that I was up to it. Furthermore, how could I ask for more time off when Andros and Margaret worked as hard as I did? "But don't they have anybody to go home to?" Janette asked with bewilderment. "Yes, Andros has got two kids too, but he hasn't told me the secret yet: how to keep the peace in the family."

Janette took care of Marisa and Jon. She loved art and used to take them into town to the theater or the cinema on weekends. She always said that you never could tell what a child was going to be capable of so it made sense to get them interested in as many different things as possible. Marisa went to dance classes and Jon learned the guitar, but when she sent them both to Italian lessons after school, I knew that things were okay in the D'Alessandro household once more.

3

THE *BARRY LYNDON* ADVENTURE

TOWARDS THE END OF 1972, loads of people I had never seen before started to arrive at Abbots Mead. Every morning, in the courtyard outside the house, there were more people than there had been the day before.

Unbeknownst to me, the *Barry Lyndon* adventure had already begun.

Stanley's production office was Stanley's house and vice versa. There wasn't a studio or an office where people working on the film could be received. Everything happened at Abbots Mead. Anyone involved would wake up, hop in the car, and drive to Stanley's house.

I said hello to everyone, but I didn't know anybody's name. As soon as I had memorized a few, all the people changed. I saw them running here and there, and I asked myself if I was doing the right thing. I was still getting the hang of the job. I'd been with Stanley for a year, but *Barry Lyndon* was the first production I'd taken part in.

Earlier that day, Margaret and I had crossed paths in the courtyard: "Emilio, come and let me introduce you to a fellow countrywoman of yours," she said. In front of the gates stood Milena Canonero. She smiled, shook my hand, and said hello in Italian. She was petite and slender and had been working on the film for some time. I had hoped she would give me some advice, but she disappeared immediately into the comings and goings that were part of the production process. One afternoon I met her again. "You're working on the film, aren't you?" I said to her in Italian, taking advantage of the fact that other people wouldn't understand what we were saying. Her advice was reassuring: "It's easy. Stanley doesn't like people who waste time. If you get on with it, everything will be just fine. Sorry, but I really must be going."

And off she ran, but to where?

"Emilio, come here, you lazy bastard!" Andros was calling me. Okay then: time to get a move on. The new batch of arrivals had meant that space in Abbots Mead was running out, so Stanley decided to have a small warehouse built in the courtyard in front of the house. Officially, it was a garage for the cars, but it was really used as an art department. We put a board on the left-hand wall, and added a large white draftsman's table and a pantograph. Andros added the finishing touch in the form of a box of Montecristo cigars and went back to the Lodge. Milena went across the courtyard again. "I saw you with Andros. Well done, let him be your guide," she said without stopping. "It's not easy to keep up with him. Andros is a phenomenon," I replied, running after her, "and so is Margaret."

"Excellent teachers!" Milena laughed.

"What do you do?"

"I'm a costume designer, with Ulla. We're working on the look of the film with Barbara, the makeup artist, and Leonard, who's the hairdresser. Then there's Ken; he's taking care of the sets."

"I can't put names to faces. Which one's Ken?"

"The one with the cigars."

There was an elegant gentleman who left every morning driving a white Rolls-Royce surrounded by a thick cloud of smoke. For days, he had been piling up dozens of books on the tables in the warehouse and sticking maps of England and charcoal sketches on the walls. Okay. He must be Ken Adam.

The warehouse shelves were filled with lenses and other photographic equipment. This all belonged to an angular, well-mannered guy called John Alcott. He was the director of photography Stanley had chosen. The three of them seemed to work well together. There was mutual respect: they all thought carefully about the other two's remarks before saying anything. While the courtyard was frenetic, time in the art department seemed to pass more slowly. This was partly due to the thick spirals of smoke from Ken's cigars and Stanley's cigarettes. What's more, John's thoughtful character was in perfect harmony with Stanley's desire to keep everything under control: he expressed his opinion on technical matters, suggested solutions, but never imposed them and never made a decision without speaking to Stanley first.

Since Stanley was always busy, it wasn't easy for them to find time to discuss things all together. Ken and John left Stanley notes and comments on the board. Much in the same way, they were often away taking photos or doing research, so Stanley replied by leaving them notes, too. Sometimes entire conversations consisting of hypotheses, questions, comments, and answers formed chains of notes across the board. The garage walls quickly filled with diagrams and photos of English villas. There were so many books heaped everywhere that it was difficult to find a way through them.

Nearly every day, before coming to see Stanley, Ken drove his white Rolls-Royce to the London Library, where he ransacked the antique books department looking for information about eighteenth century aristocratic houses. The film was set in the eighteenth century, and it was Ken's job to create a photographic archive of historic English houses and country landscapes around London. Stanley had also given Ken the task of evaluating the impact of filming in these places. He had to calculate the size and volume of the equipment and decide whether or not the floors could bear the weight of cameras and lighting rigs. He also had to make a note of any antique pictures or furniture that needed to be protected, and, if necessary, come up with an ad hoc way of doing that.

Sometimes Ken was so busy that I offered to go to the library for him. Then Milena would call me. "Emilio, Ken said you're going to London." She continued in Italian: "Give me a hand, will you? Go and pick up the feathers for this hat. I ordered them from a place in the city center. Margaret told me that you used to live in the country. That's great. Can you make sure that the feathers are from real cockerels or pheasants, like the ones you used to see? If they look fake, just leave them there." She gave me a note with the address of the shop and details of the order she'd made over the phone. As I was getting into the car, she stopped me. "Emilio, I really think you're going to make it."

"What?"

"You're doing just fine."

At Radlett Airfield, a long line of Volkswagen Type 2 vans came and went all day. The disused airport had been built in the thirties by Hadley Page Ltd. The little control tower was falling to bits. It was a mass of shattered glass, rubble, cracked tiles, and broken window frames, but the low, spacious hangars were in good condition. Stanley had spotted them and, since both the Abbots Mead garage and all the rooms in the house were full, he secretly used the hangars to store the costumes for *Barry Lyndon*. Radlett was perfect. It cost less than a studio, it was enormous, there were no opening or closing times, and it was peaceful. It gave Stanley the chance to move work away from home; it became a sort of extension of Abbots Mead.

The Volkswagen vans were one of the production company's first investments. Stanley bought thirty-two of them. That way he could be sure that there were always a couple free at any time, so nobody would have to wait for one to become available before leaving on a job. For each van, Margaret had photocopied a map of the area with the routes to follow clearly marked.

In no time at all, the hangar was turned into a costume shop. There were dozens of sewing machines lined up on long tables. Here Milena worked on the costumes for *Barry Lyndon*, with a petite girl from Copenhagen named Ulla Brit Soderlund.

An army of dressmakers sewed the material that Milena and Ulla had cut using tracings from period dresses. For more than two months, the hangar echoed to the metallic sound of sewing machines. The costume department worked like a production line: Milena and Ulla chose models from books, they cut the material accordingly, and the dressmakers put together a prototype for Stanley's approval. If he said, "Yes, that's fine," dozens and dozens of copies of the dress were made for the walk-ons.

There was still some space left, so Stanley used Radlett for the makeup department and the office where actors were met for the first time, interviewed, and auditioned. He had the hanger divided up, and each section was fitted with lockable doors. In the end, he had successfully transformed Radlett Airfield into a film studio.

A year had already passed, and there was still no film. Stanley and his team were still planning, studying, and getting organized. All this dredged up the memory of what my Italian teacher had said to me at Cassino secondary school during a visionary lesson about the directors of Cinecittà, the famous "Cinema City" studios in Rome: "A serious film producer takes care of everything; even the tiniest details. It's just as difficult and as hard as working the land." Stanley must have been one of these rare producers. He was leading a team of artists who, starting from scratch, were trying to create an entire world. From shoes to wigs, from carriages to buildings, everything was done with a degree of care and accuracy that I would have thought only God was capable of.

Stanley had taken on another secretary to help Margaret with paperwork for the production. Her name was Patricia Pennelegion. She was my age but was already considerably experienced. It was easy to understand when someone had made a good impression on Stanley, because they were allowed access to some of the offices that were usually locked. However, Pat's dog, Fergus, hadn't made the same good impression on Lola, Teddy, and Phoebe, who started to growl as soon as they saw him in the courtyard. Part of the Lodge was fenced off, so I had to put Stanley's dogs in first, and then Pat's, in this sort of pen. They took turns, like the cats: a maximum of two hours each, and of course, I had to check that everything was okay every half hour.

Stanley considered managing the animals one of the many production problems and was imperturbable in his search for a solution. It wasn't surprising that one of the first jobs given to the *Barry Lyndon* set builders was to add a second gate to Abbots Mead. This smaller, inside gate was meant to stop the cats and dogs escaping, which they often did, thanks to all the comings and going to and from Barnet Lane. In vain, Stanley had put up a sign: PLEASE, CLOSE THE GATE. He had put other signs on the main gate, the Lodge, the garage door, practically everywhere. Not even an exasperated CLOSE THE GATE, BY ORDER! in large letters outside the gate had worked. Stanley was irritated by the fact that people kept ignoring the sign, so he sent the set builders to his house again. This time they surrounded the house with wire netting so that the animals definitely couldn't escape into the road. Now we could really get down to work on *Barry Lyndon*.

"Hello, how can I help you?"

My mind went blank. I looked at the hotel receptionist, but I couldn't remember the name.

"An American actor . . ." I said, to buy a bit of time.

"It is our privilege to have many American actors among our guests," he replied.

"He's a famous one . . ."

He batted his eyelids. "Why don't you take a stroll around the block? It might help you remember." He gestured towards the door with his chin.

I left with my tail between my legs. "Tell Emilio to go to the Westbury Hotel and pick him up," Stanley had said to Andros, "and make sure that he's made a note of the name and address." The name seemed so familiar to me that I ignored Stanley's orders. "He's on TV every day in *Peyton Place*, no way am I going to forget," I had said to Andros. For five minutes, I tried to bring it back, but without success. Admitting defeat, I decided to call the Lodge. "Fuck me, you forgot it!" exclaimed Andros. "I told you to write it down! It's Ryan! Ryan O'Neal!"

I had learned my lesson: always write absolutely everything on the notepad Stanley had told me to keep in my shirt pocket. I learned another thing that day, too: you can tell how pleased an American is to meet you by how firmly he shakes your hand. Ryan was a good-looking guy with a thick head of hair and blue eyes. He smiled enthusiastically, gripped my arm, and tightly squeezed my fingers. But the handshake that worried me most was his bodyguard's: Greg Hodell was a two-meter tall Viking with a blond mustache.

The production company had a new Rolls-Royce for chauffeuring actors, but Stanley asked me to pick Ryan up in his Mercedes, to spend the whole day with him, and to do my best to grant his every request. I didn't find this as difficult as Stanley had made it sound. Taking Ryan shopping in Saville Row, or to lunch in the most fashionable restaurant in Belgravia was a great pleasure. We spent all the time in the car joking with each other and laughing. In the evening, I left him at the Royal Albert Hall, where the production company had booked him a luxury apartment. Then I went back to Stanley to reassure him that his star had settled in to London quite nicely.

For the next few days, the mornings were spent at Radlett for the costume fittings and the afternoons at the Londsdale Club, in the center of London, where Ryan was learning to fence.

It was there that our idyllic existence came to an end. Even if he hadn't starred in *Love Story*, Ryan was physically the kind of man that would turn any woman's head. His face was everywhere: on TV and in the kiosks in the center that sold posters with a great close-up shot of him. Ryan did everything he could to keep a low profile, but one morning a girl recognized him in the street, and in just a few minutes he was surrounded by a hoard of screaming fans. Greg intervened immediately. He grabbed Ryan by the shoulders and shielded him from the girls: "Get to the car!" I started running toward the Mercedes. Behind me Greg made his way like a snowplow through the crowd. He was clutching Ryan tightly. Ryan's feet barely touched the ground. He threw Ryan into the car, jumped in, and slammed the door. "Put your foot down!" he ordered. I grabbed the steering wheel and saw Brands Hatch in front of me, but my adversaries were passersby and taxis along the roads that crossed Sloane Street. When I slammed on the brakes and screeched to a halt in front of the Royal Albert Hall, Greg was smiling with relief. Ryan was as white as a sheet. "Emilio, wherever did you learn to drive like that?" he stuttered.

"Stanley, today was a disaster." That's how I started my daily report about Ryan. Stanley listened carefully, but at the end, all he said, without turning a hair, was, "I'm sorry they frightened you." Greg's wisecracks about scantily clad girls in summer, and Ryan's enthusiasm for my career as a racing driver weren't enough to keep my spirits up. Obviously, they were far more used to this kind of thing than I was.

I had no intention of driving like a maniac through the streets of London again. If Stanley didn't want to relieve me of my duties as Ryan's driver, then per-haps somebody else could. The next time Ryan asked a question about racing cars, with Andros's

Ryan O'Neal in his dressing room in Radlett during a makeup session with Barbara Daly.

help I brought Margaret's Mini into the conversation. I explained that it was exactly the same model used in the film *The Italian Job* for the spectacular car chases in the city. We managed to get Ryan so excited that the only way to calm him down was to buy him an orange Mini, which the production company did the very same day. With child-like enthusiasm, Ryan jumped into the car and raced out into Barnet Lane, spraying the gravel in the courtyard everywhere as he went. Greg scratched his head: "How the hell am I going to get inside that thing?"

The incessant search for suitable film locations spread like ripples in a pond after a stone has been thrown in. Ken went farther and farther away from Abbots Mead until he reached Ireland. The hills and historic buildings around Dublin seemed indispensible, especially as much of the story was set in the Irish countryside. Stanley had no choice: he had to leave England.

In the summer of '73 he planned the vast removal operation. Each production department was given a couple of vehicles to move all their material, and Stanley chose someone to be responsible for the whole process. Christiane and the girls were responsible for the dogs: an entire carriage on the train to Dublin was booked for Phoebe, Teddy, and Lola. Margaret was to look after the seven cats. She stayed in Abbots Mead to keep base camp operational.

There was an incredible amount of material to move: ten cameras, lenses, filters, dozens and dozens of lighting rigs and lamps, hundreds of costumes, and reels of film. Once everything was packed and loaded, actually transporting it all didn't take long, because Stanley decided to move everything at once to waste as little time as possible. One after the other, semi-trailers, trucks, vans, and buses drove through the gates of Abbots Mead and Radlett in the direction of Dublin. When the tail of this huge serpent on wheels left, its head was already halfway there. Most of the equipment and material was loaded onto the semis, but Stanley asked each department to take the bare essentials for two or three days' work with them in their minibuses. That way they could get started as soon as they arrived in Dublin.

Christiane's yellow Volvo full of painting materials was taken to Dublin. A driver took Stanley's white Mercedes there, too. The Unimog we'd brought back to life after years of disuse was converted into a *camera car.* The inside of the loading area was insulated and water-proofed with rubber seals. This meant that all three doors, the back door and the two side ones, were air, light, and humidity proof. We put up some shelves inside for rolls of film, lenses, and other photographic material. Since I'd been given the job of transporting the cameras, a member of the production team drove the Unimog to Dublin. He seemed rather daunted by the prospect, so I gave him a sort of crash course in how to manage the beast. I tried to reassure him: the Unimog was big, but tame. "When you don't know what gear to change to, stop and start again from fourth!" He climbed up into the cabin and set off for Dublin at the amazing speed of 50 miles per hour.

Jan Harlan was traveling, too. He was responsible for the economic aspect of the film and had to keep a careful eye on all the expenses, the budget, as well as numerous bills, salaries, and invoices. Once filming started, he would have to make sure that Stanley always had the latest figures. This meant the balance: the budget allocated for the film minus the production expenses. Warner Bros. had sent a couple of bookkeepers as well to make sure that everything was done correctly. They were loaded onto one of the buses for Dublin, too.

Jan left with his wife and children. So did Andros and the production assistants. I watched the courtyard at Abbots Mead empty out and wondered what Stanley had in store for me. Should I have suggested a radical change like this to Janette and the kids?

"No, you're in charge of transport."

Stanley and the others were near Dublin, and Margaret couldn't leave Abbots Mead, so someone had to make sure the two locations kept in touch efficiently.

My first trip in a rented Ford van was with some photographic equipment. There was a well-equipped studio in Dublin, but Stanley wanted to use his own cameras. After that, I spent a week collecting private mail from the Borehamwood post office. I took the post together with some sealed envelopes that Margaret had given me, and headed north.

Everyone was staying at the Ardree Hotel in Dublin. Stanley had booked adjacent rooms, all on the same floor. He didn't like the idea of using two-way radios for important messages because he was afraid that someone could listen in. He knew this was possible because he could hear the police and London Airport with his radio equipment at Abbots Mead. It made more sense to knock on the door and discuss things face to face. The previous week, I had gone round the hotel to pick a room for him. He asked me to "Choose the one that would be best for your family." Then I had to take all the bare essentials there, which meant sheets, soap, towels, toilet paper, etc. When I tried to tell him that there was no need to worry because the hotel staff would take care of these things, he replied calmly: "Just to be on the safe side."

It took only a few days for all the employees of the production company to arrive in Ireland. Everyone who had started work on *Barry Lyndon* was to be involved right until the end. Stanley didn't close down any aspect of the operation, though he did reduce the number of workmen on the payroll in order to save as much as possible. The vast production machine that had gradually gained momentum in Abbots Mead and Radlett kept on working. It consisted of dozens and dozens of cogs: some small, some large, but all of them important. Each one was a necessary working part of the engine that was Stanley Kubrick.

I took a variety of documents to Ireland: authorization from the lawyers to start work on the film, the payroll ledgers that the accountants had prepared, and the insurance contracts drawn up by Margaret. I took a few vanloads of furniture and props that had either been rented or commissioned in London. On the way back, the vans were full of material that was no longer needed in Ireland and could be stored in the warehouses in England. I even had to take dozens and dozens of boxes of candles. Stanley and John had decided to use these to light the indoor night scenes; they wanted to use spots and other electric lighting as little as possible.

I traveled by land, sea, and air. The plane took about an hour plus check-in time. By car or van meant taking the ferry, so it took all morning or afternoon. By train, it took just as long, though it was much more comfortable—I could have something to eat and relax; it was like being in a hotel room. However, it was a luxury I didn't often get the chance to enjoy, because everything became increasingly urgent. The worst trips were those by sea. When I embarked from Calais on January 19, 1960 to immigrate to England, I saw the sea for the first time in my life. It was a terrible journey: the ferry seemed too small, overloaded with people, and dangerously out of control. I'd made all that effort just to come and die here, in the middle of a storm, without even knowing whether I was in England or France. When Stanley told me he wasn't prepared to trust the ferry company to take good care of a dozen boxes, I started gasping for breath. I spent the three-hour journey clinging to the handrail with my eyes closed, deafened by the sound of the waves crashing against the windows, and praying that I would touch dry land again.

At Heathrow Airport, I used open tickets, which meant I could take the first available flight. Margaret had managed to negotiate favorable conditions with the airlines thanks to the large number of bookings that Hawk Films made. Anyone who spent time in Heathrow during the autumn of 1973 would have heard this announcement: "Emilio D'Alessandro to contact the office." The announcement was made every fifteen minutes, along with others giving news of delays or which gate to go to. I knew it meant that I had to contact Margaret. It was her idea: I would hear it as soon as I reached the check-in area and knew that I had to get in touch with the Lodge straightaway. On my way to the gate, I went past the airport staff notice board. Among their messages were notes Margaret had left for me by phone, with details of where to pick up various material and whom to contact when I got there. I tore these notes off the board, stuffed them in my pockets, and hurried along. These were special privileges obtained using the Lodge's tried and tested system: gifts made to whoever was in charge.

The same strategy was used with the customs ports in England and Ireland. It didn't amount to much, but it made an enormous difference: a telephone call the day before to make sure there was still space available, slipping a fiver to someone who let us get aboard a ferry that was already full . . . If we hadn't done this, it would have taken ten years to finish *Barry Lyndon*. The production of the film was constantly hanging by a thread, which was the efficiency of the transport system. Even the slightest delay, just one day caused by a misunderstanding at customs or a missed plane, meant that a hundred people would be standing around doing nothing, and that was outrageously expensive. What was the odd five pounds, a handsome tip in those days, compared to five thousand pounds saved by respecting the schedule?

After weeks of traveling back and forth, Stanley tried to get me to stay with him in Ireland: he wanted me to move there, like Andros had done, and leave Margaret to cope on her own at Abbots Mead. Stanley had no doubt already thought of answers to any objections I could raise, like how to break it to Janette or the problem of finding

Stanley busy directing a scene. Christiane looks on, feeling the cold.

a school in Ireland for the children. But it wasn't necessary: Margaret solved the problem for everyone. Quite simply, she said to Stanley, "If you take Emilio, I'll go." She was alone at Abbots Mead and not only did she have to take care of the production office, but also maintenance of the house, the cats, the post, the plants, and goodness knows what else. She didn't even go home. She slept in one of the guest rooms on the first floor. She had even agreed to leave her cats alone on condition that I, and not some stranger, went into her house to feed them. She reminded Stanley of all the changes she had already accepted, and though he was used to having everyone follow him everywhere he went, he realized that even he could go too far. Margaret explained her position firmly and rationally, and Stanley conceded that she was right.

So I kept on traveling. I'd spent such a lot of time going through customs that I'd become a familiar face, so much so that at times I was waved through without having to queue for all the red tape. I turned up with every imaginable type of luggage; from suitcases to folders held under my arm; from wooden chests, to entire vanloads. They laughed it off while wondering what the hell I was doing. All I ever said was that I worked for a film production company. I never mentioned Stanley's name.

Our friendly relationship with the customs officers came in handy when a lorry transporting muskets disappeared somewhere between London and Dublin. The troupe had been idle for two days. Without rifles it was impossible to film the battle scene. Stanley was doing everything he could: he'd sent out people and phoned customs; for hours he had been pestering a clerk at the Irish Ministry of Defence whose job was to deal with just this kind of thing.

I didn't know anything about it. I'd had the load embarked at Fishguard, an English port in Pembrokeshire, using the five pound tip trick. I wasn't worried once the ferry had actually left; they could hardly send it all back when it arrived in Rosslare, could they? When I reached the Irish coast, one of the customs officers called me. As he approached, I could see he had a suspicious look about him. A lorry load of rifles had been there for two days. "The driver said they were for a film being made near Bray," said the officer, cautiously.

"That's right," I confirmed. "Just like everything else you've seen me with in recent weeks."

"We need a document signed by someone from the production company certifying that these really are props."

The customs officer's cautiousness was due to the hostile political climate at the time. The confrontation between the Irish Republican Army and the British government meant that they couldn't be too careful: a lorry full of rifles, albeit period rifles, was still a lorry full of rifles.

"Haven't you got a document that declares that the rifles aren't real weapons?" he asked.

"I only transport personal items for the director, nothing else."

"Haven't you at least got something that says you work for Hawk Films? That way I can put that an employee of the production company vouches for the rifles."

I showed him the document Margaret had prepared for me. Stanley had implored me to keep it with me at all times.

Hawk Films Ltd.
PO Box 123
Borehamwood, Hertfordshire

August 22, 1973

To whom it may concern.
This is to certify that Mr Emilio D'Alessandro is an employee of Hawk Films Limited and has been authorised to accept goods, or other property in the name of Hawk Films.

For and on behalf of
HAWK FILMS LTD.
M. E. Adams
Secretary

The customs clerk stamped the authorization and released the lorry. When I arrived at the Ardree Hotel, I asked Andros to explain why the lorry had been impounded, but he didn't know what had actually happened, either. He didn't even know where the lorry was. I called Stanley and told him that I had come across his muskets and that they had been cleared through customs. "Then what the hell is the clerk at the ministry there for?" Stanley burst out. It was no surprise that he was angry. He'd found the guilty party. "What the hell is he there for?" he repeated. "Then Emilio, who has got nothing to do with it, turns up and gets the rifles through customs. . . ."

"Stanley, I was just passing through Rosslare with your packs of coffee! It's a good thing the customs officer recognized me and called me over."

"Thanks, Emilio," he said, calming down and putting his hands on my shoulders. It was as if I had saved him. "What the hell is he there

A break on the set. From left to right: Stanley, Leonard Rossiter, Ryan O'Neal (on Stanley's chair), Gay Hamilton, and Godfrey Quigley.

for?" He started grumbling again. "Andros, fire him. Wait a couple of days, then thank him and tell him we don't need him anymore because we've finished the scenes with weapons."

IRA threats had an effect on every trip I made. The airport police checked every flight to Ireland from top to bottom. We were often grounded because of a bomb scare. The Air Lingus flights went smoothly, but there were always setbacks with British Airways. Mind you, I looked on the bright side: it took the police nearly an hour to check the plane and luggage, so I could relax in my seat and grab some sleep. After the first few times, I stopped noticing the open plane door and the freezing cold air that drifted into the cabin. When the alarm went off at the Dublin airport, it was even better: the departure lounges there were really comfortable.

Inevitably, once when my luggage was thoroughly checked at Heathrow Airport, the packages I was carrying set off the alarm and suddenly I was surrounded by policemen. I saw all the other passengers drop their bags and run away noisily. One policeman came up to me and asked me what was in the packages. "Coffee grains," I replied. Stanley always bought his coffee at the Algerian Coffee Store on Old Compton Street. He wouldn't drink anything else. So I hardly ever made a trip without a five-pound pack of the stuff. On that occasion, Margaret had given me two, and one had set off the alarm. The police became more and more insistent and apprehensive. "I'm telling you, it's coffee! You see me come through here every day. By now you know who I am: what do you expect me to be carrying?" They called the bomb disposal squad, who brought a strange looking robot with them. The robot had a long arm, which reached out towards the box. It touched the bottom of it, presumably drew a conclusion of some kind, then extended its metal arm, cut open the cardboard, and put its hand inside. It pulled out a round, plastic object and all the policemen and passengers burst out laughing.

"What is it?" I asked, a bit confused.

"What do you mean, 'What is it?' It's a condom!"

"And what's a condom?"

I'd never seen one before. When I got to the set, everyone knew what I'd been carrying and I was greeted with a roar, as if I was some kind of hero. They told me that the guys from the production team had talked to one of Stanley's assistants, who had talked to another assistant, who had talked to yet another assistant, until their request had finally reached Andros, who had taken care of it with Margaret's help. Ireland was a Catholic country, and you couldn't buy condoms anywhere, so Margaret had bought a box of them in London and had disguised it as a pack of coffee. At least apparently, the pack contained film production material, so Hawk Films paid for delivery.

"You are free to go," the airport policeman dismissed me, smiling maliciously.

"Listen," I replied, a bit irritated, "do you really honestly think two kilos of those things could be for me?"

I was just about to leave for Dublin, when Margaret stopped me: the entire production team was coming back to Abbots Mead immediately. I didn't understand much about Stanley's work, but I did know that they weren't even halfway through the shooting. Margaret explained that the previous evening, just a few hours after I'd left to take the last flight to London, they had all hurriedly packed everything ready to come back to England. I found out that the IRA had threatened the production team and had demanded that they leave immediately. It was nearly Christmas, and this, together with the fact that shooting had been going on for a long time without a break, was used as an excuse to stop the news leaking out: leaving in such a hurry was made to look as if it were simply a break to celebrate New Year.

On reflection, in the months leading up to this, there was a different atmosphere: there were more and more alerts at the airport, which now made me uncomfortable whenever I traveled by train, plane, or ferry, as these were all possible targets for a terrorist attack. I once took an Irish taxi that had bullet holes in the seats. When I noticed this I realized how serious the situation really was. I even spoke to Margaret about my fears: what if they found out I worked for Kubrick and attacked me as a way of getting to him? What if they targeted one of us to attract the attention of the media?

The same thoughts were probably going through Stanley's mind. I don't know what they said to him that evening. Did they threaten him directly, or did they send a letter to the production company? Either way, I know all too well the effect it had on him, Christiane, and all the rest of us in the family. I realized that a lot of people stopped acting normally when they heard the name Stanley Kubrick. A few months later, when *A Clockwork Orange* was withdrawn from distribution in England, it became apparent that the impression I'd had of Stanley up to then was a bit limiting, given that people took him and what he said in his films so seriously.

I thought that coming back to England would mean traveling much less and a chance to organize my time better. I was wrong.

Filming of *Barry Lyndon* started again in February 1974 about a hundred miles southwest of London, where there were a number of suitable houses that meant Stanley could finish his film. Neither Salisbury nor the other small towns in Wiltshire were ready for a film production. The arrival of Hawk Films was a sort of invasion: the production staff booked all available accommodations in the area, from hotels to makeshift rooms for rent above pubs and restaurants.

Like when we were filming in Ireland, Stanley left Margaret at the Lodge and I went back and forth between Abbots Mead and the film locations. It was nowhere near as far to go as the previous year, but that was of little consolation. Since it took me less time, I could get in more trips each day than before. And it wasn't easy. Work had only just started on the M3 motorway, so I had to use busy main roads for most of the journey. It never took me less than three hours to reach Stanley. There were no more trains or planes, and the delivery schedule became entirely my responsibility, come rain or shine, fog or gusts of wind. The hours of rest I managed to get while waiting to travel to Dublin were gone. There were no more hitches or setbacks I could take advantage of; there was just the Mercedes or the van, and a race against time.

Location scouting: the granary near Glastonbury.

Without train or plane timetables to stick to, it made more sense for me to set off whenever something needed to be moved to or from the location. While I was waiting to leave, I had my first ever chance to watch Stanley at work on the set. He didn't seem to mind me looking around behind the cameras. Actually, he seemed to encourage me to spend time among the technicians and actors. "Have a look, but don't say you work for me," he said. "Just tell them you're the production company's courier." That way, everybody would carry on normally, and he could make sure that they were all working hard.

Anyway, I never overheard anything worth telling him. Everyone said that Stanley never stopped work and wasn't easy to please, but he already knew that perfectly well. However, being demanding didn't mean that he wasn't eager to look after his troupe's every need. He made sure that their accommodations were comfortable, that everyone was happy with the catering, and that the assistant director answered any questions that the members of the troupe might have. I had the distinct feeling that he went out of his way for everyone not to make sure that they worked hard, but because he was convinced that other people's requirements were just as important as his own. It was as if the needs of the people he'd hired were one of the many, equally important issues that he as producer of the film had the task of dealing with.

But the actors I drove to meet Stanley for first-time interviews near Salisbury didn't agree.

"So, what's Stanley Kubrick like?" asked Hans Meyer, a German actor I'd picked up at the airport. "Is it true what they say?"

"What do they say?" I asked curiously.

Very discreetly, Hans confided in me: the press depicted him as an arrogant, overbearing director with quite a few strange ideas in his head.

"I wouldn't know. I haven't been working for him all that long," I answered cagily.

"So, how's it going?"

"Well," I admitted. But Hans didn't seem all that convinced. "The only thing I can tell you for certain," I added, "is that I'm incredibly busy and I practically don't have any free time anymore."

"Ah, that's good. Anyone who works hard is a good person," Hans concluded, unwinding at last.

The next day I took an actor named Leon Vitali to Glastonbury, where Stanley was deciding whether or not a granary was a suitable location. Leon raised the subject again.

"Do you know Stanley Kubrick?" he said, after a long silence that simply oozed apprehension. "What's he like?"

The Stanley I knew was completely different from the one described by the actors' half-baked remarks. Ryan, the only actor I had really got to know over the past few months, had never asked about Stanley or his character. I thought that there must have been a misunderstanding of some sort. How could someone seem so radically different depending on the person who was describing him? When I saw Andros, I asked him for an explanation.

"Why is everyone afraid of Stanley? They say they read stuff in the papers . . . but what's written in the papers?"

"A load of shit."

One day Stanley asked me to go to Heathrow to pick up Marisa Berenson, the leading actress. He told me again and again to be "as polite to her as you possibly can." He added, "She mustn't have lunch. We've arranged a buffet in her honor for when she gets here." When I asked Margaret how I would recognize Marisa at the airport, she said I couldn't go wrong: "Emilio, look for a tall, beautiful, well-dressed woman and that will be Marisa."

At Heathrow I kept looking and looking at the people who came through from arrivals. I was holding a notice that read: MARISA BEREN-SON. After what had happened with Ryan, I thought it might be a good idea. Suddenly, I realized that the notice was useless. I spotted a girl who was moving differently from all the others. It was almost imperceptible, but she was more elegant, more suave. She stood out from the crowd without any apparent effort. Marisa was just as Margaret had described her: tall and very beautiful. I was so fascinated by the sight of her that I didn't realize she was heading straight for me with a huge smile on her face. She might have been given a physical description of me, too: "Emilio D'Alessandro, short and ugly."

Being beautiful didn't stop her from being easygoing. I'd only just met her, and I didn't feel in the least bit intimidated or embarrassed. Actually, I found her smile reassuring, despite the fact that my plain white open-collared shirt seemed noticeably inappropriate alongside her flowing dress as it swayed in time with the elegant way she walked.

We had no trouble making conversation on the way to Wiltshire. I thought I would have to speak in English, but Marisa, who was soon on first-name terms with me, answered one of my questions in perfect Italian. She said she'd learned the language from her mother, who had Roman origins. She asked about my family and why I'd called my daughter Marisa like her. "I don't know. We just thought it was a nice name," I answered. She laughed enthusiastically and put a hand on my shoulder.

"Emilio, can we stop and get something to eat? I'm hungry."

"It might be better if we just kept going," I suggested.

"I'd rather stop for a snack if you don't mind."

Who was I supposed to obey, Stanley or Marisa? What had he said? Be as polite as you possible can . . .

"I once stopped to eat in a place a bit farther down the road," I ventured, "but it's hardly a first-class restaurant."

"You stopped to eat there; that's good enough for me."

I slowed down and drove the Mercedes along a country road until I reached a makeshift forecourt in front of a place popular with lorry drivers. Without hesitating, Marisa got out of the car and nodded to me to follow her. The tinkling of the bell as we opened the door was the last thing she heard. Everyone turned around to look, and the room fell completely silent. A few seconds later someone was unable to resist the temptation to let out one of those wolf whistles that usually hailed the arrival of a beautiful film star. I prayed that Marisa had a sense of humor. She said nothing, passed in front of me and headed for a free table. While she was eating her salad, Marisa started talking enthusiastically again. She told me about her work as a model, about her sister, who was a fashion photographer, and her Italian grandparents. When we left, there was another loud whistle.

But that wasn't all. A roar of admiration that made even me blush followed it, and Marisa's lips moved to form a shy smile.

During the rest of the journey, Marisa revealed that she too was apprehensive about meeting Stanley. She asked me what I thought, and I reassured her by saying that from what I'd seen so far, Stanley seemed like a really good person. I told her about his characteristically calm tone of voice, and how it was easy to work for him because he always made what he wanted perfectly clear and never played games by asking for one thing when he really wanted another. You simply had to do what he asked, that's all there was too it.

"The things I've read . . ." she started to object, but immediately changed her mind. "No. Maybe you're right. You need to meet a person face to face to understand what they're like."

When we arrived in Salisbury I told the assistant director that Marisa was here and that the lunch in her honor wouldn't be necessary because we'd stopped along the way. "Where, exactly?" he asked, surprised that someone had changed one of Stanley's plans. "In one of those lorry driver places," Marisa replied quickly before I could say anything. She reached out to shake Stanley's hand. He was taken by surprise, his expression changed, and he greeted her rather coldly. Later, when we were alone, he asked me incredulously: "How is that possible? Even the most humble walk-on makes a fuss about lunch, and Marisa settled for a greasy spoon in the middle of nowhere?"

When filming was in full swing, I sometimes made more than three trips a day between London and the set. I started traveling at dawn and finished in the middle of the night. I wasn't much help to Margaret, because I never stayed in the Lodge long enough to do any work. After a few weeks going back and forth between Abbots Mead and Salisbury, Stanley suggested again that I stop traveling and stay with him and Andros on the set. It was the end of my life on the road. There would be no more precious nights spent at home with the family. Margaret tried to negotiate with Stanley as she had done when we were in Ireland, but this time he was not going to give in. I found myself in a sticky situation, caught in the crossfire between Stanley and Margaret, and of course Janette, who wasn't at all happy about me moving to Salisbury. I didn't know what to say to any of them so I just kept repeating that the only thing for sure was that I couldn't be in two places at once. Andros tried to act as a go-between, but obviously Stanley got what he wanted.

Emilio,
In case Andros calls you before I surface. Stanley definitely wants you in Salisbury and as he always gets what he wants I

have no choice but to say okay. I guess you are his driver. Obviously the choice is up to you but I want you to act as though I didn't exist, okay?

You'll be able to make a much better deal and will be using the Mercedes—and it could only mean better things. At least you won't have to drive up and down the M3 all day and every day.

Love,
Margaret

During filming in various elegant English country manors, I had the chance to see how all the hundreds of beeswax candles I'd transported in cardboard boxes were put to use: it was beautiful to see the actors moving in the flickering light of those tiny flames while the rustling of the sumptuous costumes made by Milena and Ulla filled the rooms of period furniture. If you watched the scene in silence, it was easy to lose any sense of time.

After a few takes at Wilton House, we moved to the area of Bath, where we filmed at Longleat House and then at Petworth House, where Stanley had set the first meeting between Ryan O'Neal and Marisa Berenson at a gambling table. Stanley had hired David Berglas, a famous illusionist, to teach the actors how to handle cards. While I was waiting to go back to London, I bumped into him wandering around the set. Neither of us had much to do while we were waiting for Stanley to give us instructions, so we passed the time chatting. David told me that Stanley was totally absorbed by his conjuring tricks. So much so that David had to do them over and over again while Stanley tried to discover how they worked. But he couldn't. So he bombarded David with questions. Understandably, David wanted to keep his secrets, even if it was Stanley Kubrick asking for explanations. Rather amusingly, this had been going on for weeks. "If Stanley is interested in something, he really is interested, eh?" remarked David. And he was right. "That's a very astute observation," I said, and explained to David: "When something new comes along, first he wants to know *if* it works, then when it works, he wants to know *how* it works. And when he knows how it works, he wants to know *when* it might not work. You can talk for hours about a thing with Stanley."

Filming had been going on for about a year. It was the first film I was involved in, so I judged how things were going by the atmosphere among the technicians. From what I heard, the producer-director of *Barry Lyndon* was clearly exaggerating. While I was walking past the set I heard more and more nervous comments and complaints. The troupe dreamed of having at least a weekend off, a break from Friday evening to Monday morning so they could spend some time with their families. From their point of view, this was a perfectly reasonable request, but for Stanley it was unthinkable: if the set was ready and the troupe was there, why wait until Monday? Why waste two days of work? That's what he said when I went to tell him about the increasing discontent. Stanley was completely undaunted. There was no point whatsoever in waiting. If you really needed a rest, it would make much more sense to take a month off when the film was finished.

The constant variations to the production plan were another cause for complaint: the assistants got the set ready, took up their positions, and then all of a sudden they received orders to dismantle everything because Stanley had arrived declaring that he wanted to film a completely different scene. Then there were days when everything was ready, but Stanley couldn't make up his mind to start filming, so everyone had to wait around until he decided what to do. It was not my place to ask questions. However, since I spent a lot of time with Stanley, I was in a privileged position compared to the others. I was often there when he and John Alcott discussed something together, or during the endless telephone calls he made from his office. I began to realize that there was nothing arbitrary about the waiting or sudden changes of plan. Stanley had quite simply seen something that didn't correspond to the idea he had for that scene, so he preferred to wait until everything was exactly as he had originally conceived it.

The reason was usually something to do with the weather, especially when filming outdoors. Stanley had to cope with variable atmospheric conditions, particularly when he was working in Ireland, but it was a problem in the south of England, too. The distinctive feature of Stanley and John's approach to photography was absolute precision. For the indoor scenes, this could be achieved only after hours of fine-tuning and adjustment to the lighting. It was even harder to attain outdoors: all it took was one passing cloud to completely transform the look and feel of a shot, making it incompatible with previous takes. Stanley asked for an up-to-date weather forecast every day and adapted his schedule accordingly. When we were in Ireland, he ignored the local weather forecast and put his trust in reports from the London Met Office, which he considered more reliable. Unfortunately, meteorology at that time was about as scientific as getting someone to climb to the top of a pole and squint at the horizon. Rogue clouds appeared above Stanley's head, forcing him to stop, to bring forward, or postpone filming.

Stanley had foreseen this. He had even had a clause put in the financing contract stipulating that he didn't have to spend his own money in the event of bad weather. Stanley had taken care of all kinds of things; he was ready to deal with unexpected problems, human error, and the forces of nature. He had done everything a man could do to safeguard himself and his employees, but his employees didn't realize this and asked themselves what the hell he was waiting for. I could have calmed them down by explaining all this to them, but Stanley didn't tell anyone what happened in his office. Not even the department heads knew why they had to change their plans. I asked myself this question: would knowing the reason for these changes and delays make up for the lost minutes or hours? I understood why Stanley behaved the way he did. I also understood those who kept on complaining.

After five months in England, Stanley announced that he was satisfied and stopped filming. Work on the film, which had spanned the Irish countryside near Dublin and the whole of the south of England, was suddenly concentrated in Abbots Mead. The various departments were closed, personnel were dismissed, and Stanley was left alone with the editor and sound engineers. They worked in the garage next to the greenhouse. Some months earlier, while we were in Ireland, it had been soundproofed and transformed into a cutting room complete with a Moviola and audio mixers.

Stanley spent the whole day there. He was even more concentrated on the film than he was when he was shooting. Nobody was allowed to disturb him, not even the Warner Bros. managers. Andros filtered all calls. Only Julian was allowed to speak to Stanley.

The music being chosen for the soundtrack filled the air at Abbots Mead. Stanley listened to it in his office on the first floor when he was having a break, while Christiane and Jan played it on the stereos in the Lodge. The walls shook, quite literally. Most of the time I was out running errands, but Margaret had to stay there all day. When I got back, she rolled her eyes upwards in desperation and put her hands over her ears.

Like every other aspect of *Barry Lyndon*, the choice of music was the result of lengthy research. For years, Stanley had been listening to tapes and LPs of classical and Irish folk music. Christiane and Jan helped him. They had grown up surrounded by music because their mother, Ingeborg Harlan, was an opera singer who was famous in Germany. Stanley constantly asked his wife and brother-in-law which records made a particular impression on them. This was the first test, and the records they chose were put to one side and listened to again. "Have you heard this? Do you think it's right for this scene? In your opinion, does it need something louder?" When Stanley was concentrating, he didn't realize that he could be tedious: "Stanley, please, stop it! Just let me paint my pictures!" Christiane exclaimed, exhausted by these never-ending questions. So Stanley turned his attention to Jan: "Have you found out who the director of the orchestra is? Do you know where he lives? Have you got any other performances of this piece?"

Instead of booking expensive recording studios, Stanley sought out churches or theaters where it was possible to record an orchestra.

For *Barry Lyndon*, he found a church in Richmond, Surrey. He also used the Barbican Centre. It hadn't yet been officially opened, but the concert hall was functional. "Perfect!" ordained Stanley. "It's bound to be available and will be cheaper, too!"

The sound effects were recorded at Bushey Studios, an old film studio that at the time had excellent audio recording facilities. Once I had to go to the studio for something, and I found the sound engineers intent on clattering coconut shells and running around on sand they had spread all over the studio floor. They were recording the sound of the horses' hooves because the live recording wasn't good enough. It was amazing what they could do: they seemed completely crazy, but then I looked up at the film on the screen and as if by magic I heard real hooves. A horse without a horse.

Three years had passed since Stanley started work on *Barry Lyndon*. Three years of work before the projector could finally illuminate what had been, up until that moment, just an idea in Stanley's mind. Three years for three hours of film.

The first projector to come into contact with the film was in the private screening room at Abbots Mead. Andros was in command and took care of changing the reels, while the family sat on the divan and chairs. Katharina, Anya, Vivian, Jan, and his wife Maria were all there. And so was Christiane, of course. She was in the front row, as it were. When the film was over, she stopped to talk to Stanley. They discussed every scene: Stanley cared a great deal about his wife's opinion and listened very carefully. Christiane complimented him at length; she loved the film. She said it brought back the pure beauty of the places they had lived in during the shooting. The atmosphere of all that work in Ireland had somehow permeated the film itself; it was all there: the sumptuous costumes, the crystal clear photography, the motionless elegance of the actors, and the romanticism of the music. Everything was perfectly in place and contributed to the final result, which she found extremely beautiful and moving. *Barry Lyndon* satisfied the painter in her. She talked about it for days.

This extremely positive reaction might have worsened Stanley's disappointment when the film did so poorly at the box office. Despite favorable reviews, the public didn't seem drawn to *Barry Lyndon* in America. Stanley couldn't understand why and hounded Julian. After three years of hard work, it wasn't easy for him to accept that filmgoers didn't share the passion he'd put into it. On the other hand, reactions in Europe were excellent. The film was a huge success in France and Italy. I was pleased that my countrymen had given Stanley the reaction he had hoped for.

After the film came out in December 1975, Abbots Mead went back to being, at least for the most part, Stanley Kubrick's private home. There were still clear traces of when it had been used as the Hawk Films office: a huge quantity of material cluttered the offices and there were containers in the parking area. One particular problem was the costumes. Stanley had decided to keep them because he was thinking of using them for another project he often talked about: a film about Napoleon Bonaparte.

The Abbots Mead garages were crammed full, and the storage space at Bullens was, as Andros had predicted, overflowing with the legacy of *A Clockwork Orange*. So the costumes were stored in a rented warehouse at Bushey Studios. However, there wasn't much space and Stanley thought it was poorly ventilated: Andros and I had to take turns to go there every afternoon, leave the door open, and move the costumes around ("Make sure you stay nearby, just in case someone smoking walks past and throws a match in there by mistake. . . ."). Fortunately, Andros had an idea that saved us: he got in touch with a general from the Queen's Regiment and offered to let him have his soldiers use the costumes for official parades. Stanley agreed: the costumes were hardwearing and wouldn't get damaged. Actually, using them would make them look more lived-in and not so new, thus more suitable for *Napoleon*.

When the hangar at Radlett was emptied out, the thirty-two vans were sold at a special price to the people who had used them. Stanley kept a blue-and-white one, and told me to use it for my trips to London. A red-and-white van was given to Andros, who also decided to buy the Mini Ryan O'Neal had left at Abbots Mead when he went back to America.

Finally, he gave me back the Unimog. It was no longer needed as a camera car and could be returned to the garage. I gave it a thorough service, changed the oil, cleaned the engine, and replaced the tires; after all, it had done at least a thousand miles back and forth between Salisbury and Dublin. I carefully washed and polished it, then I closed the garage doors and left it to enjoy a hard-earned rest.

4

OPEN HOUSE

ACCORDING TO MY CONTRACT with Stanley, I was paid by the day, not the hour. When I was moving from Mac's Minicabs to Hawk Films, we talked about this, and it seemed to me to be the best solution. My weekly check from Stanley was enough to take care of all my family's needs and pay the mortgage. I preferred a fixed salary because it meant I knew what was coming in each month and could plan how to deal with my expenses. Furthermore, when I was discussing this with Stanley, I didn't really know how a film director worked, and I didn't want to find myself with not much work, and so less money, when he wasn't actually making a film.

I was paid by Stanley except during filming, when my services became part of the production costs covered by Warner Bros. This got a bit awkward while we were filming *Barry Lyndon*. When I took my weekly timesheets to the administration office, the secretaries noticed that I had worked more hours than union rules allowed. "How come it says you had only had five hours free in a day? Are you sure that's right?"

"Yes, it's right." Then I added rather innocently, "Actually, I had a bit less than five hours off. I rounded down the hours I worked." They called Stanley, and in a conspiratorial tone, told him: "This person has worked too many hours, which could lead to problems." Stanley didn't waste any time: "Emilio, don't go anywhere near the unions!" After that, Warner Bros. paid me for a certain number of hours per day and Stanley drew up a separate contract and paid the rest.

I wasn't the only one who didn't belong to a union. Neither Andros nor Margaret respected the law regarding working hours, and Stanley certainly didn't. Tea break, lunchtime, weekend off—they simply didn't exist. Once we'd started a job, we kept on working until it was finished. I understood what the unions were trying to do—they wanted to safeguard workers—but I didn't feel the need for it for me. Stanley had told me that he would take care of all the people who believed in him, and that's exactly what he did.

The trouble was, I didn't even realize how many hours I spent at the Lodge. It was no surprise that Janette grumbled. "What have you got to be angry about?" I asked her, when I came home and found her waiting, visibly irritated. "A wife should get angry if her husband doesn't come home. I always come home."

But this wasn't good enough for her: "You're never here, I never see you, the children never see you!" This was what we talked about most at home. It was the same for Andros and Julian. We all had to deal with a bit of domestic tension, thanks to Stanley. "What does Christiane say about it?" Janette asked during one of our discussions on the subject. Christiane knew perfectly well how nerve-racking it could be to live with Stanley Kubrick, and just like us, she tried to defend herself. She had managed to create some personal space at home and did her best to be patient and accept her husband's total devotion to his work. No doubt she had understood that the only solution was to let him do what he wanted. He was so wrapped up in his work that he was unlikely to realize the consequences of what he was asking of himself and of those who worked for him.

At a practical level, we preferred not to talk about it. When I had to pick Christiane up in London to take her home, I arrived late. She didn't even give me a chance to apologize because she knew perfectly well why I hadn't arrived on time. Her smile said quite clearly that she didn't want to talk about it. Penny, Julian's wife, did pretty much the same. There was a sort of non-belligerent pact among the wives surrounding Stanley: they knew perfectly well that Abbots Mead had exaggerated by proclaiming itself the center of the universe, yet they pretended that everything was just fine and chatted about the children and their schools or anything else, as long as they didn't mention Stanley and his films. Janette took a detailed interest in my work, but only when we were at home. And sometimes at home there was criticism instead of questions: "Don't you think about your children?"

"It's precisely because I think about my children that I work so hard!" I answered, but it wasn't enough for her.

"Why does the work you do for Stanley have to be more important than anything else?"

"It's my job. It's what I do: I do the things Stanley asks me to do."

"Unreasonable things."

"But that's what he asks. Anyway, we're all in the same boat."

The conversation was going nowhere. Janette said that even if I worked fewer hours, I could earn enough money to support my family. I replied that it wasn't at all easy to find a job with a regular salary and most of all with a responsible boss. She must remember what we'd been through in the past.

"I just want to see more of you. I want a normal life," she said one evening after we'd barely seen each other for three days. "But what is a normal life?" I answered. "*This* is a normal life. It's when you look back and you're happy with the choices you made. It's when you can provide for you family, give them space to live and grow freely. This is a normal life, Janette, and I'm doing everything I possibly can to make it possible for you all."

Just then, the phone rang.

"God," Janette exclaimed, "he doesn't even give us time to argue!"

That evening at Abbots Mead I kept to myself more than usual. I kept thinking about what my wife had said, about her accusations. Were they accusations? I thought about her solitude, about how sad she was to see our children growing up without me. Sure, I knew all this. I'd forced it in the back of my mind, but I knew it was true. But what I said was true also. I worked hard for my family, and every morning I had the satisfaction of going to do a job I enjoyed doing. That was the trouble: even though you were breaking your back for Stanley, you felt fine. He'd created such a pleasant, loyal, transparent, simple environment that even exhaustion was enjoyable.

Janette could have left me, I remember thinking one day, surrounded by paper in Stanley's office. And yet, when Andros came to our house for lunch and we laughed until we cried about all the absurd things that happened every day at Abbots Mead, I saw the way she smiled. It was that proud smile that racing drivers' wives have when they run to embrace their husband in the pits after he has won the race.

When I got home, I found her in bed reading a book. She had waited up for me. All she said was: "So you're home. Is everything okay?" Then, as she pulled back the covers, "Come here, let's get some sleep; we both have to work tomorrow." Her formidable character had come to our aid yet again. She gave me a kiss, turned off the light, and lay down beside me.

Sometimes life makes decisions for you. You can't always choose which circuit to race on: all you can do is try to keep the car on the track, and not lose control when you come to the most difficult curves. "Let's try," Janette had said, years ago, when we were considering the offer from Hawk Films, "let's see how it goes." And now things were moving faster than ever and seemed about to overwhelm everything else. At moments like this, what you have to do is move forward. You just have to keep on going and do your best.

During those years, a series of unexpected events inextricably entwined my family with Stanley and Christiane's.

Even before we'd started filming *Barry Lyndon*, Stanley told me he'd fired his chauffeur. From that moment on, I would have to take his children to school.

I was sorry for Leslie. He was getting old, and I was afraid it wouldn't be easy for him to find another job. Sitting at the desk opposite Stanley, I confessed I was in a difficult position because I didn't want Leslie to think that it was my fault he'd lost his job. Stanley was vague about exactly why he'd fired Leslie, but he made perfectly sure that I understood he had his reasons. It had been an "inevitable deci-sion," and there was no reason for me to worry.

Until the Kubrick family left for Ireland, I spent over half an hour each morning with their daughters in the Mercedes. The girls had completely different characters. Anya was twelve and very calm and contemplative. On the other hand, Vivian, who was a year younger, was lively and never stayed still for a moment. Katharina was eigh-teen and very much like her mother, kind and serene. When they all sat shoulder to shoulder in the backseat of the Mercedes, all hell broke lose. Anya wanted to listen to classical music. Vivian's tastes were modern; she wanted rock and the latest singers. Anya wanted the volume turned down; Vivian reached over and turned it up even higher. Katharina told them both off and asked me to make them stop.

Because of her wild character, Vivian needed constant attention. She never meant any harm, but it was hard going. She was always up to mischief. Though she seemed like a tomboy, under the surface she was sweet. Whenever I told her off, she would stamp her feet, run away, and would be angry all day long. But when evening came, before she went to bed she would find out where I was, come and say sorry and kiss me good night with a mischievous grin.

I started taking them to their afternoon courses, too. Anya took singing lessons, Vivian piano and elocution, and Katharina went horse-back riding. Stanley's children spent more time with me than they did with him, and I spent more time with his children than with my own. Janette didn't see anything at all ironic about that.

One day Stanley asked me if I could give Anya Italian lessons. He had a way of surprising you with these requests by making them, quite unexpectedly, while he was talking about something else. "Most opera is sung in Italian," he said to convince me, "and she could do with some help with pronunciation."

"Stanley, I didn't even finish school. Wouldn't it be better to find a qualified teacher in London?"

"At least an hour a day . . . Will you, Emilio?"

After a few weeks correcting Anya's vowels, I had to go back to Stanley. The hour I was spending with his daughter was making everything else run late, and I risked having to constantly postpone one commitment after another. As Andros, the expert on the subject, would affirm, the theory of small setbacks that could bring down the entire tried and tested system continued to hold water.

Sylvester, one of Stanley's cats, was run over by a car in Barnet Lane. He was the second cat to be killed in front of the house. The same thing had happened to Penny not long before. When Stanley called me to his office to ask me to solve the problem, I remembered what Andros had said about Stanley and his pets and felt disheartened. I summoned up my courage and protested: "Stanley, if the carpenters from *Barry Lyndon* couldn't manage it, what do you expect me to do?"

"Try."

"It's impossible to keep the cats under control! And there's nothing around the back to stop them. They'll get out anyway. What can we do?"

"At least find a solution for the front of the house so they won't be run over by cars. Think of something, will you, Emilio?"

The carpenters had fenced off the sides of the house. They had driven big poles into the ground and nailed planks to them. The planks leaned inwards at the top of the fence. It was a good solution, but the cats used to dig their nails into the wood, climb to the top, and tumble down the other side. Perhaps if we used something else, they might not be able to get over. I replaced the planks at the top with sheets of Perspex acrylic.

A week later I heard Andros swearing in the courtyard. I went downstairs and found him, Margaret, and Stanley looking at his orange Mini. Alice, another of the Abbots Mead cats, had had her kittens right there.

"You see, Emilio? The cats can't get out anymore. Thanks."

"Well, fuck me!" replied Andros resentfully. "What do I go home with?"

"Get a minicab. Tomorrow Emilio will come and pick you up."

Stanley added that we should put two video cameras on the trees. These were to be connected to monitors in the Lodge so that Andros and Margaret could make sure nobody, including the dogs, went near the Mini and disturbed Alice.

"Who's going to take the kittens?" he said finally.

"I've already got Poika," Andros answered immediately.

"And I've got Wishbone and Rosemary," said Margaret.

"Okay then, that's decided," concluded Stanley. "Emilio can have them."

What? Who decided that? "I need to talk to Janette first," I argued, "and Marisa suffers from asthma. I don't know if—"

"Asthma isn't an allergic reaction to cats," Stanley interrupted, and then went back to his office.

Marisa and Jon called the two kittens Ginger and Rosie. Stanley told us to keep them in a closed room for at least fifteen days without letting them out. That way they would get used to it and wouldn't run away. It was a terrible idea. They completely destroyed our living room. They tore off the wallpaper and scratched all the furniture.

"Call Stanley and tell him what they've done!" yelled Janette. "And then pass him to me, because I've got something to say to him too!"

"I'll fix everything, I'm mortified, I'll fix everything!" Stanley kept repeating. "I'll send some people around to sort it all out, I promise!"

When the day came to let the kittens out, I opened the living room door. Contrary to Stanley's expectations, Ginger and Rosie ran out, flew over the fence he'd had built, and in no time at all were up the giant oak in next door's garden. Stanley's feline training theory was a complete failure: Ginger and Rosie were never tame cats and rarely spent the day indoors. They would just come home to eat and pass the rest of their time wandering around Farm Road. Cats decide for themselves where they want to live, and even if they know Stanley's theories, they choose to ignore them.

A number of sad things happened during the winter of 1973. Jack, Janette's father, had a violent heart attack and passed away. A few months later, my wife was rushed to the hospital: she was already suffering due to the loss of her father, and then she came down with a severe bout of the flu. This weakened her so much that it turned into rheumatic fever. I was confused by how quickly all this happened. I called Stanley to tell him that I wouldn't be coming back to the set because I had to take care of Janette and have our neighbors look after Marisa and Jon. Stanley interrupted me: "Don't put your friends to any trouble. Bring the kids to Abbots Mead. My house is your house."

I looked at Janette lying in a hospital bed. She seemed so distant behind the glass that sealed off her room. It upset me terribly. I counted on her for everything, and I felt lost. My parents and my brother had gone back to live in Sant'Angelo and my sister lived miles away in Wales. I was alone. Alone without her.

"Don't worry," said Stanley, as soon as I arrived back in Salisbury. "Don't worry." He repeated this to me, and like a sort of magic spell, it calmed me down. "Don't worry, go to sleep at Abbots Mead too. That way you won't have to make your own bed at home.

"Don't worry, go and stay with Janette. Andros will take care of everything else." Stanley did everything he could to take some of this terrible weight off my shoulders.

That same day, Christiane sent me a bunch of flowers with a get well soon card to take to my wife. Both she and Stanley knew just how to show affection and be supportive without making me feel awkward. It was a rare quality. When summer came and filming was over, the Kubricks came back to Abbots Mead. It was then that I realized I wasn't alone. Stanley and his wife took care of Jon and Marisa. They treated them just as they did Katharina, Anya, and Vivian. It was like one big family. When I realized this, I felt an incredible sense of relief. Without Jack, without my parents, without my brother and sister, I relied on Stanley. He was my port in a storm.

When Stanley's parents came to visit from Los Angeles, he said, "How can I take them around London when I don't know the city? You'd better take them around. Don't worry about anything else. Forget about me. I'll manage on my own or take a taxi." Before I could protest, he added: "Dedicate all your time to them. Treat them as if they were your own parents."

At the airport I saw two quite elderly but lively looking people coming towards me. Jack was very tall, and thin on top. He was elegant and yet simple in his ways. Gertie was smaller, with unruly gray hair. Stanley took after her, especially in the way they talked: calmly and with long pauses for reflection. They had the same expression, too: perceptive and prone to sudden changes that were often ironic.

I realized that Stanley was very close to his parents, regardless of the fact that they had been living on different continents for more than ten years. I knew all too well that physical distance didn't matter when it came to family ties. And it was even less important if you loved the phone as much as Stanley did—he called his sister, Barbara, in Connecticut nearly every evening. He was incredibly happy to have his parents with him and to be able to talk with them over dinner. I had never seen him smile so much.

In the days that followed, I showed Jack and Gertie around London. It gave me a chance to visit the capital as a tourist, too. It might have been true that I knew London better than Cassino, but only the streets, the one-way system, and the shortcuts.

Mama and Papa Kubrick visited the museums and art galleries and showed a keen interest in local architecture. When they asked me if the buildings we drove past were Georgian or Victorian, I replied, "You need to talk to Ken Adam!" Since I didn't know much about the history of London, I just told them about the history of Stanley's films, showing them where the actors had stayed. When I took them home in the evening, I didn't need to report to Stanley. Jack enthusiastically told him all about the day. "But where did you find this guy, eh?" he said to his son. "In an old newspaper cutting," Stanley replied, laughing.

Many months later, when *Barry Lyndon* was finished and Janette had recovered, I tried to find the right moment to talk to Stanley about my job. I wanted to find a way to satisfy my wife's desire for me to spend more time at home.

"You always come to me with other people's requests for more money, but never with one for yourself," he said, after I'd shown him the requests for pay raises that the housekeepers and accountants had asked me to take to him.

"Actually, that's what I wanted to talk to you about."

He stopped perusing the documents scattered around his desk and looked up.

"I never come to ask you for more money because I'm not interested in money," I said. "I mean, I am interested, but only in having enough money to take care of the needs of my family."

"And is it enough?"

"Yes, Stanley. You told me that I would never have to worry about anything, that you would have everything taken care of, and that is exactly what's happened."

"But there's something wrong, isn't there?"

"Yes, there is. Well, there's nothing actually wrong, it's . . . I don't want more money, I want more free time."

Stanley didn't answer.

"I hardly ever see the kids. They've grown up, and I didn't even notice. Sometimes weeks pass without me getting to see them."

"What has Janette said to you?"

"Just that she'd like me to spend more time with her. And there's another thing, but she didn't say this; it's my idea. I'm sure she didn't say anything until *Barry Lyndon* was finished because she knows that when we're working on a film, the normal rules don't apply. Arguing during that period would have just made things worse and would have tired me out even more, but now the film's over, we've talked and—"

"What about if I gave you a pay raise?" he interrupted.

"It's not about money, Stanley! Even if you give me more money, I won't have time to spend it. What I want is more time off; working hours that are more . . . conventional."

"That's not possible."

"You haven't even considered the idea! It's important, Stanley."

"If you never see your children, bring them here. They like it here."

"You know I'm always coming and going. I wouldn't see them anyway. Besides, we have a home of our own, Stanley. It would be enough if I could go home a bit earlier in the evening, or even just *some* evenings, so we could all sit down and have dinner together, not just see each other briefly before they go to bed. A weekend off now and then would be enough," I concluded. "Let's try to find a solution because it's very important to me."

"Um . . . Well, for the time being, accept a pay raise," he said, and went back to scrutinizing the papers on his desk.

If I hadn't paid very careful attention, I wouldn't have noticed anything different. Sometimes I got back to Farm Road early in the evening and I asked myself whether this was part of a new approach or just a coincidence: miraculously, a day with not much to do. Sometimes, I managed to take the whole weekend off, but this had happened occasionally even before I'd talked to Stanley. I remember them all, because I used to take Jon and Marisa to the country outside London for a picnic with Janette. She had stopped raising the subject, and when one Sunday, Stanley called and asked me to go round, I looked at her and asked defenselessly: "Tell me what you want me to do and I'll do it."

"You must do what you like," she answered immediately, "and in the way you've always done it."

Abbots Mead was home to my children for a while, but it was always open to friends, too. Considering the number of people Stanley knew, and the number of people who knew him, the entire world took it in turns to visit Abbots Mead: writers, TV producers, actors, film critics, novelists, scriptwriters, and directors. There were so many names that my Scandex organizer was bursting. Just to be on the safe side, Stanley wanted me and Christiane each to keep a copy. Katharina, Anya, Vivian, and even Jan had copies, too. I think Stanley could consider his address book safe from any possible kind of loss, theft, damage, fire, or other disaster.

Riccardo Aragno could often be seen in the garden at Abbots Mead. He was an Italian who had been living in London since the sixties. He worked as a scriptwriter and as a journalist for the BBC. He was exactly the type of person Stanley made friends with, mainly because of his wry sense of humor. He always managed to find the most ironic way to make fun of someone. If your witty remarks made Stanley laugh, he would be your friend forever. Added to that, he was an excellent cook. Stanley had always been sorry that I was the exact opposite of the Italian stereotype: I was neither a food connoisseur nor handy in the kitchen. Riccardo, on the contrary, was incredible. Stanley was mad about his recipes, and every time Riccardo came to Abbots Mead he was obliged to cook something. Stanley would then spend the afternoon telling me how tasty the pasta Riccardo had made for him was. "What a shame you weren't here to taste it, Emilio. It was so good!" Sure, what a shame that you'd sent me running all over the place with just one of Margaret's sandwiches in my bag, Stanley.

Stanley's friendships and work usually went hand in hand, so when *A Clockwork Orange* was finished, he asked Riccardo to take care of the translation for the dubbing of the film into Italian. Aragno had worked closely with Mario Maldesi, one of the best post-production and sound mixing engineers. After *A Clockwork Orange*, Riccardo and Mario worked together again on *Barry Lyndon*, and then on all the other films. They were both perfectionists, and this made for a successful partnership.

Stanley and Riccardo also shared an authentic passion for cameras and typewriters. They spent hours in the garden discussing different models, and when Stanley found one that Riccardo didn't have, he would phone him up brimming with childlike enthusiasm. Stanley was literally mad about typewriters. He used them to write absolutely everything and kept on buying new ones. He loved the graphic clarity of typed text and was genuinely absorbed by the machines that

ON SATURDAY EMILIO SWAP CATS BEFORE
€ VIVIAN'S PARTY ARRIVES

FEB 27 ⊠X MEMO ON WEEKEND

1. We are at Hotel Imperial, Prixcess Princess Parade, Hythe, TEL (o3o3)
                                                                  67441

2. We are registered under name of Mr and Mrs Harlan.

3. ALL CATS but Leo and Freddie should be kept out of front yard.'.'.'.
Keep kitchen window closed, and NEVER leave front door open longer than
it takes for someone to go in and out.

4. Vivian, should be especially carefull about this at party.   *Vivian if you*
                                                                 stayed deal
                                                                 with door on all
5. All dogs to be kx kept out of front yard, too.   *Your friends*
                                                     comings + goings.
6. Think ahead and be smarter thaxn the animals, if you possibly can.

7. FIRE - in case of fire, dont just let animals outdoors. Put the cats in
a car, preferrably one parked in outside fourecourt, and the dogs in
another. Then , when you can, drive the cars nextdoor to Chantry
until situation is restored. Make sure none run out.

8. TV PLUGS should be checked on all 3 color tv sets and pulled from wall .
each night.

9. Check that all doors and windows on ground floor are locked.
10. Check oven is turned off.
11. Leave smaller light on in 1st floor hall, on landing.
12. pxxtxxxx FRONT AND BACK outside lights should be put on.

13. Keep Freddie room keys on the booksehlf outside my bedroom door and
replace them, so everyone knows where they are and can get in.
There is a spare set in my txx top desk drawer downstairs office   *projection*
                                                                    room is ok

14. VIVIAN party: please keep your friends from going into my office. I dont
want to lock the door because Penny likes the room and I dont wnt to lock
xx her in. Slxxx Also, I keep them out of lodge office and ck studio, as
well as our bedrooms, etc.   Beer and wine ok, no hard liquor, please.
                                                          NO DRUMMING
15. ANDROS is to be dxxyxxkx obeyed.   *IT FRIGHTENS*
                                                          THE
16. Close food and dont leave it on sideboards for cats to lick.   *CATS*
                                                                    WHEN
                                                                    THERE
                                                                    ARE LOTS
Be good. Love.   *OF*
              DAD   *PEOPLE*
                                                                    HERE

Two memos written by Stanley.

Dec 31

Emilio

EMILIO

1.Replace the bulbs in th the ceiling of the projection cinema room. The spot bulbs (
actually they should be medium or floor flood bulbs. I suggest you look at the bulbs
and see what it sasy on them.

2.Tonite Catos Cats

I suggest you feed them as late a s posi possible, when you have them rounded up, please
lock them up as follows:

SK BEDROOM AND ANYA BEDROOM DOOR OPEN BETWEEN BUT HALL DOORS LOCKSED
Polly, Penny Jessica, plus sandbox - & water

FREDDIE OFFICE
Leave Leo there. I know it is his turn to go out but its beg better to leave him and I'll
let him out when the party is over.

SK LIB RARY NEXT TO FREDDIE OFFICE
Freddie

Note: Make sure the two doors on each side of the bathroom are closed, so that Freddie
and Leo are seperated by two doors, otherwise they will spend the evening clawing at
the carpte carpet.

Put a sandbox in the sk library flf freddie and some water

CK DRESSING ROOM (if she agrees - ask her)
Pandora, plus sandbox and water.

If she doesnt agree, put PaANDORA ON TOP FLOOR in anyas top floor bedroom, plus
sandbox and water.

MAKE SURE VIVIABN locks up FANNY into her bedroom.

BUBBLES   rolls
1. please find out th e sizes, widths, lengths, that the large bubble xabls come in . Tell
me. and then lets order some for packing.****

produced characters with the highest possible definition. His favorite models were those wide, metal typewriters like the ones in police stations in American films. Nearly all the messages he left me on the desk at the Lodge were typed, including shopping lists and instructions for running the house on those rare occasions when Christiane managed to convince him to go somewhere for the weekend. These were lengthy directives, arranged in lists, to which he couldn't help adding additional instructions afterwards with a pen. The main points were: close the doors and windows, switch off household appliances, and take care of the animals (which cats were to go in which rooms; the dogs were to be put in the rear courtyard . . .), and, of course, even what to do "in case of fire."

While the world was enjoying Stanley's new film, Andros and I went back to running Abbots Mead. I immediately realized that before I arrived, Andros had dealt with absolutely everything personally. Stanley totally relied on Andros. No task was unimportant enough to be assigned to one of the other people who worked there. I knew what Stanley was thinking: if you have found someone who can solve all your problems and do everything you ask exactly as you would like it to be done, then why ask anybody else? This was the perfect solution for Stanley, but for Andros it was becoming a considerable burden.

One of the trickier jobs I relieved Andros of was cleaning the precious Zeiss projectors that Stanley had bought in Germany when he moved to Abbots Mead. He had totally transformed the ground floor of the house, turning "that wonderful living room," as Christiane remembered it with a hint of disappointment, into a professional screening room. I first saw the projectors when Stanley showed *Barry Lyndon* to his family. I discovered that, in order to make sure the machines worked well, technicians were regularly servicing them. Now it was up to me to clean them thoroughly every two weeks so that dust didn't have time to settle on the surface. Andros provided me with a special cleaning kit. They couldn't be cleaned with just any old cloth, because the material would have moved the infinite number of tiny levers and rings and would have snagged on the toothed rollers that guided the film. A vacuum cleaner was no good either because it might vacuum up tiny screws that weren't tightened properly. I had to use a feather duster and be careful. Very, very careful. I used a damp cloth to get rid of dust that had formed on the top and on the covered side. Then I used a dry one to stop any dust from sticking to the damp surface. When I'd finished cleaning the projectors, I had to switch them on and run a reel of film to make sure they were working properly. I think they were the most precious objects that Stanley owned.

"Emilio," said Andros one day, holding a radio in his hand, "it doesn't work."

"What can I do about it?"

"Have a look at it."

"You're enjoying this, aren't you?"

"No, I don't know the first thing about electronic stuff, sorry."

I took the radio and dismantled it. I didn't really know what I was doing, but I wanted to keep Andros happy. The only thing I knew about electrical equipment was that sometimes the fuses blow, so just to be sure, I changed all of them, and the radio started working again. "Stanley! The radio's working!" announced Andros.

"Who fixed it?"

"Emilio."

"There's a television in the bedroom. Same problem."

Stanley decided to give me the keys to all his vehicles, not only his private cars, but also all the vans bought for *Barry Lyndon* that were now cluttering up the courtyard outside the house. He didn't ask me if I'd had them repaired, if I'd renewed the insurance, or if I'd had to do anything in particular to them—he behaved as if they were mine. When I went to Italy, he insisted that I use one of his Mercedes, and if I had to do work at home, he wanted me to use one of his vans.

It made no difference to me what kind of vehicle I was driving: luxury cars, ORVs, superminis, vans, military vehicles, and even a bus that was used as a traveling wardrobe for the costumes. As Christiane said, "Give Emilio anything with four wheels and a steering wheel and he'll drive it." Anyway, my favorite was still the Unimog. It didn't cause problems; it solved them.

When Christiane asked me to take her somewhere nearby to paint an English country landscape, I answered: "With pleasure, but this is my ORV!" And pointed to the Unimog. While I was loading canvases and easels, she tried to climb into the cabin, jumping on the running board and hanging on to the handle to pull herself up. I know she would have preferred the Land Rover, but the Unimog was so functional. "Don't you think it's great?" I said, as I started the engine. She shook her head and laughed amid the din it made. Nobody else could understand why Stanley and I preferred the Unimog. Ours was a love beyond their ken.

The Volkswagen minibus from Barry Lyndon *in our courtyard in Sant'Angelo. It was perfect for our trips from England: there was enough room for all our luggage plus the things we bought in Italy to take back with us.*

5

DRIVING LESSONS

ON ONE OF THOSE miraculous Sundays off, I managed to fulfill a wish that I had been forced to disregard for far too long. I went back to Brands Hatch. While I was going towards the track, I heard the voice of Brian Jones over the loudspeakers, "Guess who's coming! It's Emilio!" he shouted. It was fantastic. It felt like five minutes, not five years, had passed.

Brian was "the voice of Brands Hatch." He was the commentator for all the Formula Ford, Formula 3, and Formula 1 races at the circuit. "Good. I'm pleased to hear that you've been working hard," he said approvingly, when I told him what I'd been up to. He took me by the arm and asked immediately: "Listen, do you want to start racing again?"

For me it was a physical need. In the past, on those rare occasions when I managed to race, it was as if I'd taken some sort of medicine. I forgot about everything else; nothing existed apart from the racing car, the circuit, and the challenge of the curves. I was alone in my Lotus. Stanley wasn't there. Neither were Andros or Margaret, or Janette, Marisa, or Jon. There were no parents, wives, colleagues, errands, documents, lawyers, or insurance. Everything disappeared, and my mind became empty, free, and light. Brands Hatch gave me back my brain. It was more restful than sleep. I told Brian that I wouldn't be able to practice regularly, but he didn't seem to mind and said calmly, "Let's see what we can do."

All the records of the races had been kept in the circuit archive. There was still proof that I hadn't had an accident during my career. I made my debut in Formula Ford in March 1968. Portentously, the day before, my son, Jon, was born. We christened him Jon-Pierre after the stylish driver Yves Montand played in *Grand Prix*. I had raced against numerous other drivers but above all Emerson Fittipaldi and James Hunt. Their names were always close to mine in the driver rankings. Fittipaldi was unbeatable at Snetterton, Hunt did pretty well at Silver-stone, and I performed best at Brands Hatch. The circuit was in a valley, and so there were plenty

In my racing suit.

of hills and sharp bends, which made driving there a lot of fun.

"I know what we can do," said Brian. "If you can't practice or do the qualifying laps, we can place you on the grid according to the time you got in the previous race."

"You're the ones who make the rules, so if you can find a way to let me race, I'm happy," I replied, unable to suppress a satisfied smile.

"And we're happy, too, Emilio."

I was curious to find out whether, after all those years without setting foot in a racing car, I could still drive like I once used to. I was pleased to discover that racing is like riding a bike: once you've learned, you can pedal for the rest of your life.

Stanley followed my trips to the circuit from a distance. Then one Monday morning he sprang a request on me: I was to teach Anya to drive, "perhaps using an old car." I'd bought an Austin 1100 from a Spanish guy who worked at Borehamwood. It was an old banger, but mechanically it was impeccable. It had recently been serviced, so the brakes, lights, and engine were in perfect condition. It would do just fine.

In the attic I found one of the assessment sheets that Tony Lanfranchi had used to evaluate the drivers attending the Brands Hatch driving school. It consisted of thirty-four points—a listing of defects that had to be eliminated in order to become a safe and successful driver. I sat next to Anya and marked a cross whenever she made a mistake: 1. ONLY ONE HAND ON THE STEERING WHEEL WHEN INITIATING BRAKES; 2. COMPLETE LACK OF BRAKING BEFORE CHANGING GEARS; 13. FAILING TO ACCELERATE PROGRESSIVELY OUT; 22. INSUFFICIENT USE OF GEARS; 28. POOR SITTING POSITION; 30. POOR USE OF MIRRORS; 31. BAD PARKING; and so on.

When all three of the girls had got their licenses, Stanley, mindful of my driving, decided that his daughters should have a few lessons on the circuit. He wanted the instructors to give the girls a brief course, explaining the most common dangers on the road and the best way to deal with them. I wrote a letter to Brian to arrange everything. All the documents were filled out in my name to safeguard Stanley and his family, but I told Brian the truth without beating about the bush, and made him promise not to tell anyone.

Emilio D'Alessandro, Esq.
94 Farm Road
Edgware, Middlesex

February 15, 1978

Dear Emilio,

My apologies for the delay in replying to your 1st of February letter. Of course we shall be delighted to receive Mr. Stanley Kubrick's daughters here at Brands Hatch (you don't say how many daughters! I assume two). If they both do the Initial Trial and Stage 1 of the Skid-training exercise, the cost will be £85.00 inclusive. I am enclosing a list of dates when we are operational and shall be delighted to hear from you when would be a convenient date. My very best wishes to you.

Sincerely yours,
B. A. Jones

A few days before the course was due to start, Stanley started to approach the subject in a somewhat perplexed and circumspect manner.

"Emilio, have you seen the new Mercedes ORV?"

"Do you want to buy one?"

"It does have good road-holding, doesn't it?"

"I suppose so."

"Is it worth sending the girls to the circuit if they would be safer anyway with a car like that?"

This was one of Stanley's typical indirect questions. I understood what he was getting at.

"Well, Stanley, the course would mean a safer driver *as well as* a safe car. I still think it's a good idea."

"What's Divina Galica like?"

This was another thing typical of conversations with Stanley: he would completely change the subject without making any apparently logical connection. Divina was an athlete. She was a skier who had been very successful at the Olympics some years earlier. I had mentioned her to Stanley because she had recently started kart and car racing as a new career. She'd even managed to make it as far as Formula 1, and her Italian-sounding name had caught my eye in the papers.

"What's she like . . ." I hesitated. "She's a girl. But it doesn't make any difference as long as they like engines, drive safely, and don't cause problems for anyone else on the track. It doesn't matter whether the driver is a man or a woman. The rules are the same for everybody."

"So they're the same for Vivian, too."

So that's what he was thinking. Actually, I could just imagine her coming back from Brands Hatch wanting a racing car for herself and perhaps another five or six for her friends.

"Stanley, I don't know. I mean you know yourself what Vivian's like."

"Let's just forget about it then. It's probably better."

Perhaps Stanley could have made good use of the booking at Brands Hatch himself. Distracted as he was, he was always having accidents. The first one happened just after he'd come back to England from Ireland. He was driving the brand-new gold Mercedes 450 SEL. He found himself unexpectedly in a thunderstorm and braked suddenly when he saw a dip in the road full of water right in front of him (6. BRAKING JERKY AND VIOLENT). The car behind plowed into the Mercedes and destroyed the trunk. Sometime before this happened, there had been a lengthy debate about the seat belts in the new car. Stanley wanted the harness type fitted, even though the staff at Mercedes had told him they were difficult to unfasten. He only gave in when I explained that, at the circuit, there was always a steward with a knife ready to cut the drivers free if they had an accident. But still skeptical, Stanley insisted on examining the results of the crash tests to see how long it took the centrifugal clutch to work. All he was interested in was proving that everything Mercedes had told him was true.

The Gold Mercedes was an unlucky car. Some years later, when he was working on *The Shining*, Stanley told me that he would go to EMI Films on his own and that I was to meet him there. I'd already been waiting for half an hour when I saw the set designer coming towards me. "There's a problem. Stanley has destroyed the back of the garage with the Mercedes." When I got home, Stanley was still standing there next to the wreckage. He'd put the car in reverse instead of first. "Call Mercedes. They'll sort it out," was all he said, keeping his proverbial calm.

In addition to always being in a hurry, Stanley was constantly distracted. He always did too many things at the same time, and he behaved the same way in the car as he did in the office—he talked on the phone, read reports, reached for a pen to make a note of an idea, and dictated into his recorder. Despite this, he still had the courage to complain that his daughters didn't concentrate when they were driving. Whenever he drove me somewhere, I felt I was staring death in the face. Once, when he was driving the Porsche he'd bought at the beginning of the eighties, he went the wrong way around a roundabout in St. Albans. We found ourselves face to face with a double-decker bus that, fortunately, slammed on its brakes. The bus driver made the sign of the cross and then started to swear at us. "What's that bus doing there?" said Stanley, as if nothing out of the ordinary had happened.

Sometimes he asked questions about my driving: "Why are you cornering like that? How come the engine makes that noise when you shift down? Are you sure it's all right to do it like that?"

"Stanley, don't tell *me* how to drive. I don't come and tell you where to put the camera, do I?" I said reprovingly.

"It's just that I feel so relaxed when you're driving."

"Good. Well then don't say anything!"

But Stanley simply wasn't able to not say anything. When a series of tragic accidents hit the world of British motorsport at the end of the seventies, he even started to grumble about it more openly than Janette did. "Were there any accidents?"

"No, Stanley, there weren't any accidents. Listen, if you're not happy, next time come and watch me race."

"That's not a good idea."

He bombarded me with questions. He didn't do it because he was interested in the result of the race or because he wanted to know whether I'd won or not. He was trying to gather information that he could use against me to convince me to stop racing.

To start with, he had a go at the car I was driving. Ferraris had been involved in a number of accidents and this had been widely reported in the press. Engines that had caught fire, tires that had exploded, things like that. Stanley cut these articles out, added his comments to them, and left them on my desk: "Emilio, you see? Racing is dangerous." I wrote my answers below his remarks: "Stanley, I don't drive a Ferrari, I drive a Lotus."

Then he tried a more direct approach: "I'd rather you didn't race anymore. By all means go to the circuit, but do something else. Repair the cars or something; I don't know, just don't race."

Whenever he read in the paper that a driver had ended up off the track, he started all over again. "How did he escape that accident

A photo taken by Jon of me in a single-seater.

unscathed?" I explained that there were very rigorous safety measures, but he insisted on hearing the details: "What is there before the safety wall?"

"Sand bags," I answered. I was starting to get tired of all these questions. "And there's a layer of gravel all around the edge of the circuit to slow the cars down if they go off the track."

He adopted yet another approach: "How come those people choose to do that job?"

"It's a job like any other job, Stanley. Like yours or mine. I can assure you that driving in town is much more dangerous than driving on a race track."

"There are policemen on the streets to make sure people obey the rules."

"Maybe in the movies, yes! How often do you see a policeman jump out from behind a bush and chase after someone who's breaking the speed limit? At Brands Hatch there's a steward at every bend. They use colored flags to let the drivers know everything they need to know."

He insisted: "At that speed, a problem with the engine or the brakes could cause an accident."

Finally, when he had completely worn me out, he delivered the fatal blow in the form of a long speech explaining how the insurance companies that covered the personnel working on Stanley Kubrick's productions could protest if one of his employees was exposed to a higher than average risk factor because of his or her lifestyle. He quoted such a long list of figures, data, documents, and clauses that I gave in and promised I would give up racing. I don't know if it was just an excuse. In any case, I realized that, be it for practical reasons or personal concern, Stanley would have been happier if I had stopped. So I did. "It's hard to believe, but for once I agree with Stanley," said Janette.

Brian Jones found me a job as one of the marshals, the people responsible for the safety of the competitors, but it wasn't good enough. I was too far away from the engines themselves. After a couple of years, Brian managed to get me into the group of scrutineers. Their job is to make sure that all the technical rules and regulations are respected. We inspected the cars before the race, noted down the serial numbers on the chassis and engine, checked that the drivers' gloves and race suits were in good condition and adequately padded. We made sure their helmets conformed to standard, and so on. The most important thing was that once again I was immersed in the heady fumes of Castrolite oil.

As luck would have it, my son Jon started to get interested in racing cars just a few months before I stopped driving competitively. When he was small, I had tried taking him to the circuit, but it never worked out. He was far more interested in the sheep in the nearby fields than in watching his dad trying to win for Marisa and him. When he was about ten, his interests changed. I found him looking through the motor racing magazines I kept at home. Sometimes I managed to take him to Brands Hatch on Sundays. Jon looked attentively at the cars as I pointed and explained who the fastest driver was, who the most reckless was, and who always came last. They were my favorite Sundays.

Janette hoped he would grow up to be an engineer. I thought putting him in a go-kart might be worth a try. For his twelfth birthday, I took Jon to a car manufacturer, promisingly called Emilio Ferrari, to order a custom chassis for him. On the Sunday of his first race, while he put on his suit and helmet, Jon listened carefully to everything Mr. Ferrari said. When he was ready, I kissed him and wished him good luck. I didn't want to worry him excessively. He already had the tension of the race to deal with. I was his father; it was obvious that I was afraid. My head was reeling with dreadful thoughts: Jon would be out there with nineteen other 100cc karts on that terribly narrow circuit. Despite this, I didn't give him any advice. A driver's instinct counts more than being cautious. But when he was heading for the starting line, I couldn't help calling out "Be careful!"

Jon was great. He immediately got the hang of the kart and managed to weave his way through the others without crashing into anyone. In the end he came in seventh, which is the standard result for every D'Alessandro competing in his first race. When he ran to me and hugged me, I had tears in my eyes.

After a few races, Jon was always one of the first five to finish and often even made it onto the podium. He even won. I was really happy, and Janette hated me. However, she behaved the same way with Jon as she did with me. She didn't want to dampen his enthusiasm. All she did was ask me to keep a watchful eye and make sure Jon didn't take any unnecessary risks.

Taking Jon to the kart races was fantastic. It was our special moment—just the two of us for a whole day, with our hands covered in grease and no distractions. Father and son together, sharing something they really cared about. Even when it rained and we ended up soaked to the skin and covered in mud, everything seemed just great.

By the time I'd been working for Stanley for ten years, I'd stopped kidding myself that I was in control of my own life. I was fine. I was happy and satisfied, but I couldn't honestly say I was able to do whatever I wanted. Somehow fate overheard what I was thinking and

Checking Jon's kart, while Janette does her best to hide her feelings.

offered me a couple of tempting opportunities to change the course of my family life.

I heard that Alitalia was hiring people for the new terminal at Heathrow. I filled in the forms and I was offered a job. Now I had to decide. I went to Stanley and told him about it. He looked at me in silence for a moment, and then said: "How much are they offering you?"

"You know it's about the working hours, not the salary. I work fourteen hours a day for you; there it would only be eight. Then there would be holidays to spend with my children and Sundays off when I could go to the circuit!"

"I can pay you more than Alitalia."

"Stanley, it really isn't about money, it's about working hours!"

"No, no, no, no," he started to say, "I'll give you more time off, just stay!"

"I don't know, Stanley. I need to think about it."

I left his office and walked to the Lodge. When I got there, Andros and Margaret already knew. That's the power of the phone for you.

"I don't know if it would be worth your while to leave," started Andros.

"Ah, so now it's a conspiracy!"

And then Margaret added, "If he's promised that he'll reduce your hours . . ."

They went on like this all day. When I went back to the Lodge to pick up more things to deliver, Margaret asked, "So, are you going to stay?" Then when I was in London I got a call from Andros. After he'd given me my instructions, he added, "But are you really going to leave us? I can't believe it." After hours and hours of psychological terrorism, I let them convince me. "Let's believe his promise, Andros," I announced. "Even better, let's pretend we believe it." By then I had learned that nothing was going to change. However, seeing Andros, Margaret, and Stanley so apprehensive about my leaving had a strangely pleasant effect on me.

Some years later, there were advertisements in the press for would-be high-speed train drivers. These new trains were spreading throughout Europe. The ad also mentioned that work was about to begin on the channel tunnel between England and France. From London to Paris, then down on to Milan and Rome. I would be in Cassino in no time at all, and I would get a salary in the bargain. Without saying anything to Stanley, I sent off a letter asking to take part in the recruitment process.

I silently went into his office and handed him an envelope. He looked at me inquiringly and opened it. When he realized what it was about, he started to stutter.

"Oh no . . . No, no, no, no. No, no, no, no . . ."

"Stanley, calm down."

"Why are you doing this to me?" he said, looking up from the letter.

"I'm not doing it to you. I'm doing it to me. It's the same old story. I need free time."

"You'll have more free time, but if you take this job, you'll spend more time away from home than you do now working for me."

"No, you're wrong. There are very strict rules to safeguard the passengers. If you work five days in a row then you have five days free. Days to spend with whoever I like. I've already told Janette about it."

"Janette? Oh no . . . No, no, no, no."

"Oh yes! She doesn't think it's a bad idea either. But it's my idea, not hers."

"What can I do to stop you from leaving?"

"Give me what I've always asked for: more free time! But it falls on deaf ears. You see? You don't even remember."

"You're right . . . I promise you, I really honestly promise that I'll give you all the time off you need, weekends to spend with the family, everything; just don't leave."

He was in a terrible flap. I felt as if I was hurting him by leaving. My resolve was already beginning to falter when he said something that completely won me over: "Emilio, aren't you happy here with me and my family? If you change jobs, who knows what kind of people you will meet. Here you know us all, me, Christiane, and my daughters; you're one of the family. Why do you want to turn your back on all this?" Suddenly, I had a thought that filled me with doubt. I remembered that bitterly cold night in January 1960, when I had arrived in England. I had felt totally estranged. I was freezing and lost; I was alone and helpless in the face of events. "Why do you want to turn your back on all this?" was what my father had said, sitting on my bed before I left for London. There was the same tearful expression on his face as there was now on Stanley's. He had used the very same words, and he cared in just the same way. It was hopeless, I said to myself. I have to stay with Stanley.

He had promised to give me all the time off I wanted, and he did, for a couple of days. For a while, just one thing did actually change. If I was about to go home but Stanley needed me to go back and deal with yet another of his requests, he would get Christiane or Katharina to call my house. "Janette? It's Christiane. Is Emilio there? Could he come back? I've forgotten something." Janette looked at me heavy-heartedly. I realized exactly what was going on, took the car, and went back to Abbots Mead. When I arrived, Christiane or Katharina made up some pathetic excuse and "quite by chance" Stanley appeared, and said, "Oh, you're back! Listen, since you're here, do you think you could . . ." Yes, of course I can, Stanley. Of course I can help you.

6

THE SHINING

"WHAT DO YOU KNOW about horror films?" asked Stanley. Evidently I had surprised him when I asked him if the new film would be full of open graves, moldy skeletons, and churches in ruins. I explained that when I was driving a minicab, I often took Peter Cushing to the Hammer Films sets, which were full of coffins, crucifixes, and dead trees. I used to stop near Denham in front of an old Norman church that had been chosen as a location. It had a pointed roof with a wrought-iron crucifix on top. Peter was never waiting for me in the street when I arrived. I always had to get out of the car and look for him. I used to walk towards the cemetery at the back of the church; the moss-covered granite gravestones were made even more horrifying by the artificial fog and the occasional old well that the special effects team had added. I already knew that the garden gate was going to creak, that the church door would be heavy and damp, and that at least one of the graves would be open. I called out as quietly as I could through the fog: "Mr. Cushing? Mac's Minicabs."

"Don't worry. Stephen King doesn't write that kind of stuff." Stanley laughed as he reassured me.

"But . . . if you're about to make a horror film, what's going to happen?"

"You'll see."

Work on *The Shining* started in 1977. Stanley told me to go and get the cameras that were stored in the Schenker warehouses in Freiburg in Germany. He liked to use his own equipment when he was filming. In addition to the cameras themselves, this included lenses, viewfinders, lighting rigs, gels, and filters, as well as just about everything else. He said he preferred to own everything he needed for his work, as this helped him to reduce costs considerably. Nevertheless, I would be prepared to bet that it had more to do with the pleasure of owning his equipment and the certainty that he would find everything just as he had left it. Even though we never actually talked about it, I'm almost sure this was the real reason. I felt precisely the same way about cars: the driving seat exactly the right distance from the steering wheel for your body, and the mirrors in the correct position. These things were important; they were a fundamental link between you and the machine. Finding them just as you had left them was gratifying.

Stanley hired Diane Johnson to help him write the screenplay. She was an American writer who taught at the University of California. When I went to pick her up, I found her company surprisingly pleasant. She had an amenable expression, a friendly smile, and a clear, calm voice. She dressed comfortably and carried a big leather shoulder bag. I thought she seemed like a very sensible person. After a few weeks, Diane decided to leave the hotel the production company had booked for her and move to a friend's flat in Maida Vale. This turned out to be a wise decision, because she then spent the rest of the season working closely with Stanley on the script.

During the journey, I asked her about America. Did she know any families of immigrants from Cassino? I wondered if they'd been as lucky as I had in England. Stanley never talked much about America, just the odd phrase about his childhood in New York or fleeting remarks about the films he'd made there. Instead of satisfying my curiosity, he aroused it. On the contrary, Diane was more than happy to tell me all about the place. Like Christiane, she found American cities far too chaotic compared to English ones. She was sad to say that there it was becoming increasingly difficult, if not impossible, to get some peace and quiet, even in the privacy of your own flat. She openly admired Stanley's decision to move his family to a more peaceful country.

Stanley and Diane worked in the ground floor living room that looked out on the garden. Sometimes a journalist for the *Evening Stan-*

These were the notes Stanley left me to tell me to put the reels of The Exorcist *in the screening room. He kept the film at home for weeks and studied it carefully.*

dard named Alexander Walker came to visit. The three of them would go onto the veranda and spend the whole afternoon talking, conferring, deliberating, and analyzing. I always thought of them as three very cerebral people. They only ever stopped work to watch films in the screening room or to eat together with Christiane and the girls.

All the films they watched at home during those weeks were horror films because Stanley wanted to learn all about the genre. He thought making a horror film was lots of fun. His eyes twinkled when he came up with new ways of making the audience leap out of their seats. He and Diane talked in detail about the films they watched, and when they came up with an idea that was even more frightening and original than the previous one, they laughed contentedly.

While Stanley and Diane's brains were hard at work at Abbots Mead, at the Lodge it was more a case of do than think. Andros had been given the task of auditioning some of the actors for the cast. As he read the book, he made a list of all the minor characters and asked Margaret to call the acting agencies and have them contact the character actors who were best physically suited to the roles. To keep the project secret, Margaret simply said that Peregrine Films, the name Stanley had chosen for the production of *The Shining*, was looking for actors for a film with a contemporary setting. For the same reason, auditions never took place at the Lodge. We rented a room at the Churchill Hotel and took a couple of Lowel spotlights to light it, as well as a camera and a 16mm film camera. The actors performed a short piece of text, answered Andros's questions, and posed for two photos: a front portrait and a profile. Then they left their personal details. Stanley wanted to audition actors he already knew, too. Often, many years had passed since they had last worked together, and he wanted to see if there was anything different about their appearance or tone of voice. If the instructions he gave to Andros as we were leaving were anything to go by, the actor's voice was the most important thing for Stanley.

Philip Stone, who had already worked with Stanley on *A Clockwork Orange* and *Barry Lyndon*, agreed to do an audition. I went to pick him up at his house in Woodville Road in the London suburb of Ealing, just as I had done ten years earlier when I worked for Mac's Minicabs. In those days, Philip had to leave home at the crack of dawn to go to the rehearsals of the theater company he was acting with. I was the driver who always called him at four in the morning to wake him up. The first time I went to his house he invited me in: "I'm nearly ready. Come up for a coffee. It'll wake us both up." He opened the door for me and then went to get dressed. The kitchen was tiny and untidy. There were clothes all over the place, unwashed dishes, piles of books, and scripts in every available space. It was just how I'd imagined a London theater actor's house. Philip went over to a cupboard and took some dentures out of a glass. He started to brush them and splashed water everywhere. "Here's your coffee," he said, handing me one of the two cups that were right next to the glass. I felt my stomach heave. "Thanks . . ." I said, raising the cup a little and forcing a smile. When Philip started brushing his dentures again, I took advantage of the fact that his back was turned and quickly poured the coffee down the sink behind me.

"Sir? Are we ready?"

"Oh, yes, yes," answered Philip, putting in his dentures, "now I'm ready."

"Good morning, Emilio, come in. I'm nearly ready," said Philip at front door. *Was history repeating itself?* I went in and saw to my relief that the hall was clean and tidy. Time could change even theater actors. "Would you like a coffee while I get ready?" he called from the kitchen. "No thanks, I had one before I came out," I answered quickly.

From a production point of view, *The Shining* was completely different from *Barry Lyndon*. The film was set in a deserted hotel, so it was necessary to construct an enormous set. There would be no Volkswagen vans driving around England scouting locations. Christiane insisted that Stanley get used to working in the film company offices. *Barry Lyndon* had deprived her of her home for more than two years, so this time she had no intention whatsoever of being "evicted." There would be no art department in the garage, no meetings until late in the screening room, and no irritating noise coming from upstairs while she was trying to paint in the Lodge.

So Peregrine Films rented some offices at EMI, one of the most important studios in England. EMI was halfway between Elstree and Borehamwood and five minutes away from Abbots Mead. EMI took up more than six thousand square meters. There were seven stages and an open area at the back, so there was plenty of space to build sets. All the necessary manpower was on hand: carpenters, electricians, film editors, and sound engineers. When I drove Stanley through the gates at Shenley Road for the first time, I felt like I was going into an industrial city.

The production offices of *The Shining* were in the first building on the right just past the entrance. Stanley's office was at the very end of the corridor, after the secretaries, the bookkeeper, and Andros and Margaret's room. That's where my desk was: ready for the letters and notes that Stanley would have written to me throughout the day. Apart from Jan, who stayed at the Lodge, the only person not affected by Christiane's veto was John Alcott. Lighting, film quality, and the right choice of lens were all of the utmost importance to Stanley, so he had appointed John long before hiring anybody else, and once again he had offered him the garage at Abbots Mead to work in.

Another person who arrived earlier than necessary was Ray Lovejoy, the film editor. Ray had already worked on *2001: A Space Odyssey*, and Stanley wanted to make sure that he was available for *The Shining*, so he hired him before filming actually started. Stanley never laid a finger on a single frame until shooting was finished, so Ray spent over a year wandering around the set with little or nothing to do.

The film was set in the Overlook Hotel, and Stanley used the same approach to building the set as he had for *Barry Lyndon*: he extensively researched the architecture and furnishings of the great American hotels. In addition to studying catalogs and magazines, he sent two people to the United States: the set designer Roy Walker, who had been Ken Adam's assistant for *Barry Lyndon*, and Murray Close, Stanley's daughter Anya's boyfriend. For weeks the two of them took photographs of the most interesting hotels and compiled an album that could be referred to for the design of each room, corridor, wall, and lounge. Stanley didn't want a new hotel based on the descriptions in the novel. He wanted a replica: he wasn't going to use the photographs taken in America as inspiration; he was going to copy them.

Roy made notes of the ground plans of the hotels he visited, and with the help of his assistants, built a white cardboard model of them and drew in furniture, carpets, and sofas. When the cardboard model was approved, they made a wooden scale model. It was about a square meter in size and included rooms, corridors, stairs, the façade, and the roof. Every floor could be removed to reveal the one below; it was a bit like taking the lid off a saucepan. This model was used to test John Alcott's lighting and to try out some indoor shots: Stanley slipped a camera into the model rooms and took photos that gave him a view of the hotel from inside. It was the point of view that the film cameras would have on the life-size set.

The model was submitted for final approval to someone who worked at Timberline Lodge, which was the hotel that the exterior of

In front of the wooden model of the Overlook Hotel in one of the production offices at EMI Films. You can see part of the Colorado Lounge with the wide staircase. It is here that Jack threatens Wendy and she hits him with a baseball bat.

the Overlook Hotel had been copied from. Stanley brought him to London from America, stood him in front of the model, and showed it to him a floor at a time. Then Stanley started to interrogate him: Are all the windows there? Is there a door missing? Is that the right number of chimneys? Are the trees the same height as yours? Are the stones okay like that? And the paths? And the woodpiles? And the litter baskets?

At last the team of set constructors could get to work on the life-size Overlook Hotel. The first part they finished was the façade; it only took three months. "More people, less time" was always Stanley's golden rule. It was built on the back lot behind the studio, an area that was usually used for scenes with special effects that couldn't easily be filmed indoors. The façade was imposingly tall and perfect in every detail, from the guttering to the curtains. But it only looked real from the front. Behind there was nothing. It was just a few meters thick, a sort of huge panel. The back was sealed to protect the electrical wiring for the mock-up rooms. There was just enough space for some narrow stairs that led to the windows.

Once all available space on the back lot had been used up, the set constructors started work on the interior of the hotel. In the end they occupied four out of the seven stages. But they weren't enough, so Stanley used some empty offices and whatever space was left in the stages booked for other projects. *The Shining* was spreading through EMI like a river that had burst its banks. The biggest stage was used for the set of the enormous ballroom called the Gold Room. Another was used for the sets of the kitchen, the red bathroom, and the room for the elevator-of-blood scene. The ground floor of another stage was used for the entrance hall of the Overlook, and for the Colorado Lounge: a spacious salon with a fireplace and tall windows that filled it with light. The first floor of this stage wasn't accessible because the actual staircase of the building served as the staircase of the hotel, making it impossible to work upstairs. Since there was no space left for the set of the large kitchen with its pantries and cold storage rooms, Stanley had to settle for building it in an old warehouse-cum-cutting room, even though it wasn't soundproofed. Torrance's apartment and room 237 were built fortuitously, too, in what was normally an office building. EMI Films was so full that Halloran the cook's apartment could only be built after the Torrance's apartment had been dismantled.

Stanley wanted the furniture, household appliances, lamps, stoves, and carpets in the hotel to be American. Murray Close had taken photos of all these things, and Stanley chose from them as if he were ordering from a catalog. All the cans of food in the kitchen and the pantries were bought from an American base in Norfolk. Stanley had sent me to the supplies manager on the base. He was of Italian origin and apparently thought it was amusing to provide a film production company with empty cornflakes packets and cans of beans. Other furniture was made ad hoc: the big wooden table in the Colorado Lounge, a huge quantity of chairs and chests of drawers, as well as the beds for the hotel and the apartments.

Nothing could stand in the way of Stanley's obsession with authenticity. Even the stones heaped in front of the hotel were extremely

carefully chosen. Stanley had sent me to pick up a huge rock in the Unimog. It was a sample that he'd had imported for inspection: the stones
had to be the same shape and color as those on the Rocky Mountains.

For all intents and purposes, the Overlook was built as if it were
an actual hotel. For example, the electrical system was designed to supply a real building. In addition to providing electricity for the lighting equipment, the electricians wired up all the household appliances,
lights and table lamps, TVs, and radios that were spread throughout
the rooms and corridors. They installed a vast double electrical system.
Behind every wall and above every ceiling, hundreds of meters of cables
supplied power not only to John Alcott's lighting rigs outside the hotel
windows, but also to the illumination of the hotel itself.

I don't know what the heads of EMI thought about having their
studios taken hostage by Stanley, but I do know what the studio staff
and workmen I met at the gates said. "Where's the governor?" they
asked me jeeringly. They were alluding to his severity. I don't know
who had saddled him with this new nickname, but it seemed appro-
priate enough to me. Like all gossip, it spread quickly, and it wasn't
long before Stanley got to know about it. When I asked him if he'd
heard what the studio workmen were saying about him, he smiled and
replied pompously, "Oh yes, I'm the governor of the state of Elstree!"

In the summer of '78, the set designers, electricians, and decora-
tors finished work on the Overlook Hotel. It was breathtaking. As you
walked around the set, you had to make a conscious effort to remember that it was precisely that: a film set. Nothing whatsoever about it
looked fake. Everything you touched was not only realistic, it was real.
Only those of us who had seen it develop day after day knew that it
was made of planks of wood, not bricks, which was the only set construction rule that Stanley had actually respected. I'd seen the photos
Murray had taken in America, and it was staggering how faithful to the
original the set was: the same carpets, the same lamps with exactly the
same number of lightbulbs in each one, even the same plants in the
same vases. That's what made it so incredible to walk up the stairs in
the Colorado Lounge only to discover that they didn't lead anywhere,

or to open a door and suddenly find yourself outside the hotel, in a corridor connecting two studios bustling with people unloading boxes and extension cables.

There was nobody left at Abbots Mead to look after Stanley's family matters, so that became my job. I would pick him up in the morning and take him to the studio. Then I would rush back to take care of his daughters, Christiane, the post, and the shopping. I bought food not only for them but also for Stanley, because even though he ate at the studio, he didn't want the meals made by the catering service. I spent all day driving the blue-and-white minibus up and down the busy roads from Abbots Mead to London, and London to Elstree. Stanley phoned me continuously with instructions to pick material from warehouses on the outskirts of the city. Sometimes it was a lamp, sometimes a table or a plant. Occasionally, I had to take back a television that wasn't working. Of course, these places were never all on the same side of town. If I had to pick up a wardrobe or a chest of drawers instead of a television, then first I had to go home, leave the minibus, and take the van.

If the twelve-hour working day had been taken less and less seriously as work on *Barry Lyndon* progressed, it lost all value during *The Shining*. That was when I realized that it had been a mistake to accept a daily rate of pay without overtime or bonuses. But it was too late. For the umpteenth time, I was caught up in that self-perpetuating mechanism, unaware of how tired I was, of my wife's complaints, and even of the laws of the space-time continuum. All I could do was keep going.

Since I was spending all my time in the car or the van, I could no longer accept to go and collect Stanley's actors from the airport for him. I had no choice but to tell Stanley that he would have to use a taxi firm like normal film production companies did. He only stopped objecting to this when I suggested he contact Mac's Minicabs and mention my name.

Jack Nicholson, one of the biggest stars in Hollywood, played the leading role in *The Shining*. I met him for the first time when I went into Stanley's office one morning to deliver some urgent documents from Warner Bros. I followed Stanley's rule about entering his rooms: "Knock and come in without waiting for an answer." When I opened the door, they were sitting in the armchairs talking.

"This is Emilio," he said to Jack. "He's my private driver. He looks after my things."

Jack got up, and when he was in front of me, smiled and bowed ever so slightly. I put out my hand, and he shook it in the vigorous way Americans do. Stanley picked up the conversation where he had left off, and Jack sat down again. I put down the letter from Warner and went to get something to drink. Stanley kept on talking and looking at Jack, but Jack was looking at me. He watched me as I moved around the office, organized documents, tidied up piles of papers, and put datebooks and notebooks back in drawers.

"You're really lucky," Jack remarked to Stanley as I silently left the room. "You should see the mess in my office."

Nicholson seemed like a calm, kind person, and the two of them appeared to be getting on extremely well. We had talked about Jack just a few days earlier when Stanley had announced to me that he would play the leading role in the film. I only knew him by name.

"What do you think? Do you like Jack?" he had asked.

"Well, I don't know . . . Isn't he a bit . . . Wasn't it better if you took that other actor, the one I like a lot . . . whatshisname."

"Who?"

"The one who does all the police movies . . . Charles Bronson!"

Stanley looked at me unperturbed. "And why Charles Bronson, exactly?"

"Because I like the parts he plays. He's good, isn't he?"

"They're not the kind of parts I need."

A few hours later he returned to the subject and tried to explain why he had chosen Nicholson: "You'll see, everything about Jack is perfect for this role: his expression, even the way he walks. He doesn't need anything extra to play this part. It's all already there inside him. He doesn't even need speech training like Ryan did for the Irish accent." And it was true: there wasn't much difference between Jack Nicholson

off the set and in the film. All he needed was the little velvet jacket that Milena had bought him, a bit of makeup, his hair quickly brushed, and, *voilà*: he was Jack Torrance. Day after day, he was faultless. He never got a line wrong and always had a professional, collaborative approach. He listened to Stanley and did what he asked. Actually, he did even more than he was asked to do: after he'd done a scene the way Stanley wanted it, he asked to do another take because he'd had a new idea. Only a few days after shooting had begun, I realized that I completely agreed with Stanley when he said that Jack was born to play that part. Jack realized this himself, too, and he enjoyed every minute of it.

Shelley Duvall, his costar, seemed to me a bit vulnerable. When I met her, she had just finished her interview in Stanley's office. She reminded me of Olive Oyl in the Popeye cartoons: she was incredibly slim and her

The famous shot of Jack Torrence as he appears through the door. It was used for the international poster of the film.

arms dangled by her sides. Vivian was in the office that day too, and I remember noticing that Vivian was the only person Shelley smiled at. It was as if, unlike the others, Vivian didn't intimidate her. Marisa Berenson had made a completely different impression on me. Even if she had been a bit worried about meeting Stanley, she was still happy to talk to me in an amenable and friendly way. Shelley had hardly even said hello. I didn't think that she and Jack seemed right for each other. Could that be the effect that Stanley was looking for?

In the days that followed, Stanley started to shoot the scenes with the two actors. It became immediately apparent that there were problems. As usual, Jack took up his position in front of the camera and delivered his lines with the determination of a charging bull. Shelley on the other hand was hesitant, and as soon as she made a mistake she stopped, afraid that she had ruined the take. When Jack made a mistake he just kept going. He improvised or tried to patch it up somehow so that he could at least finish. That way he gave Stanley the chance to think about the scene as a whole. "Don't worry. If it's not right, we'll do it again," said Stanley in an attempt to calm Shelley down, but she just became more and more insecure.

"Shelley, do the scene just as I told you, and then *after* we'll see if it's okay," Stanley insisted.

"You always say okay to Jack. Why don't you ever say that to me? Is there something wrong?" she asked, bewildered.

"Shelley, just do the scene."

I never heard Stanley treat her really unkindly, but I had no doubt that she found filming the scenes emotionally exhausting. One day, the driver who had been assigned to her by the production company took me to one side. "When I take her home in the evenings, I can hear Shelley crying on the back seat," he said. "Are there problems on the set?"

"Nothing," I answered. "Everything's just fine. Try to reassure her a bit if you can." The driver was a good person, and on the trips home he said to Shelley: "They told me that there's nothing to worry about. Stanley is very happy with you." Vivian was the only one who was able to comfort her. Whenever there was a break, Shelley went to stay with Vivian and at last a smile appeared on her face. But when Stanley appeared, Shelley left Vivian immediately and went to stay on her own again. Vivian came to me and asked: "Am I doing the right thing by talking to Shelley? As soon as Dad appears, she runs off. Has he told her not to talk to me?"

Jack's personality didn't exactly help to calm things down. He loved to rule the roost. He was always making vulgar remarks full of sexual innuendo. He made faces at anyone who turned their back on him and flirted with anything in a skirt. Basically, he invaded other people's space, and in particular, Shelley's.

To be honest, I didn't hit it off all that well with Jack myself. On the few occasions I drove him somewhere, he always had something to say about the girls we passed in the street. "Hey, slow down a bit Emilio, I want to take a look at this wonderful lady." So I had to slow down to keep him happy. "Ah ha," he smirked when we had gone past, "that one was really special."

Stanley had first heard about the Steadicam from Ed DiGiulio, the president of an American company that produced equipment for filmmaking. The Steadicam was a revolutionary stabilizing system for handheld cameras. Stanley and Ed had first worked together on *A Clockwork Orange*, but they became close friends thanks to Ed's work on *Barry Lyndon*. Ed had found a way to adapt the highly sensitive lenses used by NASA to Stanley's cameras, making it possible to film candlelit scenes.

Ed had told Stanley about this mysterious stabilizing system long before work on *The Shining* started. Stanley was so curious that he sent Jan to America to see the Steadicam in action. Jan wrote Stanley a letter saying he was amazed by the potential of the device. Stanley was so excited: every time I went to see him at Abbots Mead, he said, "I talked to Ed today!" And I nodded approvingly without really knowing what they had talked about, or who this Ed actually was.

When Ed arrived in England in 1977 for a production equipment fair, he brought Garrett Brown, the inventor of the Steadicam, with

him. They arranged a meeting with Stanley to explain how the stabi-
lizer worked. Since this new filming technique would have an important impact on set construction, Roy Walker was invited, too. The Steadicam made it possible to film tracking shots without the need for
bulky rails, boards, or camera dollies. Consequently, many of the hotel
rooms were built in such a way as to use the narrow passageways and
stairs between them as part of the set.

The following year, Garrett Brown was due to arrive on the set to
start filming. He was the only person that Stanley asked me to go and
pick up at Heathrow. Jan had already met him and told me with a
laugh that I wouldn't have any trouble finding him at the airport: "You
can't go wrong. When the tallest person you've ever seen in your life
turns up, that's Garrett!" At the arrival gate I saw a gentleman with fair
hair duck to get through the door.

That afternoon, a demonstration of the Steadicam had been
organized at the studio. We gathered around Garrett to see what he
was going to do with the harness he was putting on. I was worried
by the sight of Stanley's precious camera suspended midair. Garrett
finished getting ready without saying a word. He stood up carefully
and stretched his back. "So this is the Steadicam," he said confidently,
leaning his left hand on a vertical rod connected to his body. There
was a counterbalance weight at the bottom of the rod. The camera was
motionless at the top. Then he started to move here and there. He spun
around and pointed the lens at our faces.

"Can you lower the camera?" Stanley asked.

Garrett moved some levers, released some catches, and smoothly
lowered the camera.

"Can you rotate it completely?" Stanley continued.

"Yes," Garrett replied.

"Can you keep it focused on a fixed point'?"

"Yes."

"Can you frame that chair while you move around it?"

"Yes."

"Can you frame the top of those stairs while you're going up them?"

"Yes."

If Stanley had had his way, the demonstration would have gone on forever.

When Garrett finished by saying, "I can do whatever you want, Stanley," he was satisfied: "Good, good, perfect."

Stanley had what Garrett had filmed developed by Denham laboratories during the night, and the next day he arranged a screening to show everyone what the Steadicam was capable of. While everybody whispered in admiration, Stanley chuckled like a child who knew he had the best toy of all.

When evening came, shooting was finished and the set was empty. Only the camera department staff remained. It was their job to put away the equipment and prepare everything for the next day. I waited there with them because Stanley wanted it to be me who took the dailies to the Denham laboratories. Four hours and forty miles later, I was at home in bed at last. At five thirty in the morning, just after I'd woken up Andros and Margaret, I went back to Denham to pick up the developed film and take it to Abbots Mead. In the meantime, Andros had arrived. We threaded the reels into the projectors. Andros watched them and then went and reported to Stanley. A day's filming usually lasted about half an hour, and since fall-in on the set at Elstree sounded very early in the morning, this preview of *The Shining* at Abbots Mead rarely took place after dawn. If Andros thought the takes were good, Stanley didn't even look at them. However, if Andros thought there was a problem, for example something slightly out of focus, Stanley double-checked and decided whether or not it was necessary to shoot the scene again. If the scenes shot the previous day were particularly delicate for some reason, Stanley watched them anyway. Most of the issues concerned the acting. Stanley had the reels taken to the studio's screening room and called the actors; especially Jack and Shelley. They would all discuss each take in detail, trying to find ways to perfect how they moved during a scene, their facial expressions, or the timing and rhythm of their lines.

I had a great deal of work to do during the making of *The Shining*, but it certainly wasn't any easier for Andros. Whenever I met him at Abbots Mead, he seemed more and more exhausted. One morning, when I called to wake him up, he said: "Emilio, why don't you have a look at the dailies while you're in Denham?"

"What do you mean?"

"There's a screening room there. Before you come back, have a look and then tell Stanley whether they're okay or not."

"Andros, how should I know? I haven't even read the script!"

"Look, it's easy. You understand me when I say, 'Fuck,' don't you? Listen: 'Fuck!'" He repeated this over the phone. "I mean, you see how my lips move when I say, 'Fuck!' Watch how they talk on the screen, if it seems okay, approve it; otherwise inform Stanley."

"Andros, are you saying this because you need a hand or because you like to tell me where to get off when I wake you up?"

"No, I'm not joking. Please, can you do it? I'll be on the set soon."

Sometimes I couldn't do all the things I had to do either. Like the morning Stanley told me to stay at the lab in Denham because the dailies weren't ready. "No, no, you stay there," he said, "I'll go to the studio

Two continuity Polaroids of Danny in the corridor of the Overlook. June Randall, the continuity supervisor, took photos like these to make sure that the actors looked exactly the same from one day's shooting to the next.

on my own. The dailies are more important." That was the morning he destroyed the back of the garage with the Gold Mercedes. When he got the car back, he suggested that we swap vehicles. While I was driving around London in the Mercedes, he would go to the studio in Elstree in the Volkswagen van. "That way if I have another crash it won't cost me so much."

I met Vivian at EMI Films every day. She was in her last year at school, but she still found time to slip away and watch her father at work on the set. Even though Vivian missed a lot of classes, Stanley never told her off. He was happy, probably proud, that at least one of his daughters was showing an interest in film directing. Anya and Katharina had already become absorbed by their mother's enthusiasms: Anya was drawn to lyric opera and Katharina loved painting.

To prevent Vivian from wandering around on the set and bombarding whoever she met with questions, Stanley asked her to lend a hand in the art department. Her job was to help Milena by doing research on the costumes of the twenties needed for the dance scene. Nevertheless, she found it hard not to have her say about makeup, hairstyles, glasses . . .

Eventually, she came up with the idea of a documentary about the making of *The Shining*. "I'd like to film Dad while he's talking to the actors and technicians and explaining what they have to do," she told me.

"I think he would be happy if you learned how to make a film," I answered. This was my interpretation of what I assumed was Stanley's idea. "That way you'll be able to assist him when he needs help."

"But," she said evasively, "all that equipment is so heavy, how will I manage to handle it?"

"You could start by using a 16mm camera. They're much smaller."

When she went to present this project to Stanley, he asked her if she was really certain that she wanted to do it. He needed to make sure that she was actually going to finish the documentary. All too often, Vivian's lively personality led her to get involved in too many things at the same time. "Vivian, making a film, even a short one, takes lots of time and effort. Simply pointing a camera at something doesn't mean it will end up being projected on a screen. A film requires research and a project to work by."

"I know. I can see that from the way *you* work," answered Vivian.

Stanley advised her not to disturb the people on the set, but at the same time, to try and appreciate the most interesting aspects of their working day. "Ever present, yet invisible," he said, concisely.

The winter of 1978 was particularly harsh. The roads were covered with sheets of ice, and it was hard to get around. One day in December, paying no heed whatsoever to the dozens of police roadblocks that had been set up around Borehamwood to stop people using the roads, Stanley insisted on being taken home. He refused to spend the night in a hotel room near the studio. "You can take me in the Unimog," he said in reply to my protests.

"But it's still full of lenses," I reminded him. "It's not a good idea to move it."

"The workmen are still here. Get them to unload it. And remember the rushes to take to Denham. That way they'll be ready tomorrow morning, and we won't lose a day's work due to the bad weather."

I sat uneasily in the cabin. The Unimog could cross rivers and climb mountains, but the roads of Borehamwood were terribly narrow: all we had to do was lose our grip for a second and we would crash into the houses . . . and demolish them.

Stanley arrived wrapped up in his thick, quilted jacket. He was hugging Vivian close to him. "There isn't any room," I told her. "Where am I going to put you, in the trunk?" Stanley didn't realize I was joking and immediately said, "No, the back's airtight. She won't be able to breathe." "I'll sit in the middle," she said, contributing to the surreal conversation we were having. I tried to explain that the gear lever was in the middle, but it was impossible to contradict two Kubricks.

I took a deep breath and set off. I was nervous the whole way. This was the most precious load I had ever transported: Stanley, his daughter, and the reels of the new film. We only had to drive half a mile, but it was never-ending. Nobody said a single word. The only sound was the roar of the Unimog. When we finally saw the gate of Abbots Mead, I pulled over, and felt a huge sense of relief. Vivian ran towards the house, eager to get in out of the snow. Before he got out, Stanley looked at me and said: "You see? This is the best car in the world."

I saw how special effects worked for the first time on the set of *The Shining*. There were some violent scenes in the film, full of blood and injured actors. There were winter storms too, with snow and other weather effects. Stanley talked to the head of the special effects team before they started, and then left him to get on with it without interfering. When the work was done, he reappeared and said what he thought, which was usually either "Okay" or "Start again from scratch."

The last image from The Shining. *Jack Nicholson's face was superimposed on an original photo from the twenties. This is one of the numerous print samples that Stanley requested to evaluate the result. A slightly darker halation around Jack's head gives the trick away. Better do it again, right, Stanley?*

The latter answer had been tormenting the special effects team for weeks. They had tried and tried again to produce fake blood that convinced Stanley, but he was never satisfied with the color. They'd found the right viscosity more or less immediately. The problem was the tone of reddish-brown that he wanted. They also had to make sure that the materials they used were biodegradable and nontoxic. An enormous amount of this blood was needed on the set, and it wouldn't be easy to get rid of. If it was water-based with natural colorings, they could simply pour it down the drains. Take after take, liters and liters of the stuff were disposed of like this at EMI Films. The fake blood flowed along the gutters and reached the village of Borehamwood. The roadside ditches turned red, and there were points where this brownish liquid stagnated before it soaked into the ground. Two of the domestics at Abbots Mead lived in Borehamwood, and one day they arrived alarmed and shouting: "There's been a massacre, a massacre!"

For the scenes where the characters had to spend the winter trapped in the hotel, common salt was used to simulate snow. We bought the salt in fifty-kilo bags from factories that normally supplied it to dairies. The set designers explained to the EMI workmen how to spread the salt around the studio back lot, making sure that it was heaped up in drifts against the façade and on top of the hedges. The same thing was done on the set of the labyrinth inside the studio. The main part of the labyrinth had been built indoors just in case it rained and dissolved the salt, which would have made it necessary to start all over again.

What had been difficult about making *Barry Lyndon* was both the logistics of the production and the filming schedule fraught with uncertainty. What made things difficult on the set of *The Shining* was that Stanley wanted everything to be exactly as he had conceived it, even if that meant filming the same scene hundreds and hundreds of times. Stanley filmed a scene and when he'd finished the take, he said it was fine and that he had to do it again. Then he said that the new take was fine and that he had to do it yet again. Even if that one was fine, he still had to do a third one.

"Why are we doing the same things we did yesterday?" everyone asked. "And why did we do the same things yesterday that we did the day before?"

"I don't know," I answered simply. And it was the truth.

At the end of the day, Stanley congratulated the actors and the troupe. On the way home, I asked him how things had gone and he answered: "I am very happy with the shots of today." But if he was happy, then why do all these takes?

It doesn't take much for a question to become a complaint. "Why are we always working on the same scene? It's a waste of time," the troupe protested. "We're running late. The other productions are having to wait."

"They'll wait," I replied. "They'll start filming when Stanley has finished. He's signed a contract with the studio. It's not something you need to worry about."

Inevitably, the sarcastic remarks followed. "Oh, I get it! He's made a deal with Kodak to use up all their stock!" These remarks circulated behind Stanley's back. Hardly anybody on the set knew how close I was to him, so they talked without worrying that he would find out how dissatisfied they were.

"Stanley, the troupe is complaining," I confided.

"What are they saying?"

"Nothing serious, wisecracks, jokes. They wonder why we're filming so much."

"Everything's okay. Don't worry about them. But let me know if they say anything new."

In the end, they even started to blame themselves.

"Have I done something wrong?" a technician or an actor would ask desperately.

"No," answered Stanley, "but let's do another one."

Even the most self-confident among them started to falter.

"Is there something wrong? What do you want me to do?"

"Nothing. What you're doing's just fine, but let's do another one."

He never answered; he just kept on going. Unperturbed. He treated everyone in the same way, technicians and actors alike, regardless of their status. Not even I asked him to explain. After all, it was his job, not mine. Nevertheless, I couldn't help wondering about it all, and I realized that for Stanley time was never "wasted"; it was always "spent." Having one more day to work on a scene meant time available to improve it, not time taken away from the next scene. In addition, there were simply too many people on the set. Ignoring all their complaints was a way to avoid arguments. The lighting technicians, the special effects team, the people from EMI, and the bustling secretaries were all there to hear what he said. If Stanley had told an actor that he hadn't done a good job, then the rest of the troupe would have used him as a scapegoat, blaming him for the delays. So Stanley preferred to say nothing and place his trust in the ability of the actors he had chosen. Repeating a scene again and again helped them to achieve the intensity of expression he was looking for. Anyway, he was thick-skinned enough to handle all their restlessness and sarcasm. After all, *he was the governor.*

Despite the incredible complexity of making the film and the nerve-racking number of takes for every single scene, I never actually heard anybody raise their voice or have an out-and-out row. Stanley's set was a peaceful place. This was the paradox: enormous productions in a family atmosphere. When I arrived at the studios and walked past the stages being used by other directors, I could hear shouting, screeching, and swearing coming from behind the closed doors. On Stanley's set, I was afraid to sneeze in case it disturbed everybody.

"Can't they find a more peaceful way to communicate with each other?" asked Stanley one evening. He had overheard the voices from the other stages as we drove past in the Mercedes.

"You reprimand people too, though, don't you Stanley?"

"Yes, but never in public."

The studio technicians were devilishly good at their job, and ceaselessly followed Stanley's instructions, or nearly. Every morning and every afternoon, for about half an hour, they claimed what was unquestionably theirs: the inviolable, ever-so-British tea break. The set stopped work, and everyone got his or her cup out. Resigned to the inevitability of this ritual, Stanley spent the breaks in his office, going though his notes, making calls, and signing documents for the bookkeepers. He did all this with a cup in his hand too, but it was full of American coffee.

Stanley's sets were top secret and off-limits to everyone, but not to family and close friends. So when his parents came to visit Abbots Mead again, he took the opportunity to invite them to the set to see him film one of the scenes with Nicholson. It was the one where Jack hides behind a column in the corridor, waits for Scatman Crothers, the actor who played Halloran the cook, and buries an axe in his chest. Stanley told me to stay close to his mother and father just in case the scene shocked them. However, the only person who was actually worried was Stanley. Jack and Gertie were full of enthusiasm. They watched all the preparations for the special effects and couldn't wait to enjoy the murder.

The technicians were going to use two axes for the scene. A real, heavy one that Jack would have held before hitting Halloran, and a light fake one full of blood-like liquid that would spray all over the place on impact with Halloran's chest. Nicholson had practiced how to use the fake axe so that you couldn't see the difference in weight from the way he moved.

Stanley shouted "Action!" We watched in silence as Scatman started to trudge along the corridor. Suddenly, Jack jumped out screaming and hit him violently in the chest. Poor Scatman cried out, staggered, and fell to the ground. Jack stood next to him; the effort had left him gasping for breath. Everything had gone well, and when Stanley shouted, "Cut!" Gertie was so pleased that she almost started clapping. His father was smiling, too. I turned to look at the actors and caught Stanley's eye. He was asking silently if it had gone okay. I reassured him from a distance with a smile.

Stanley invited Janette and my children to the set, too. That day he was going to film a scene in the back lot behind the studio. When

Two stamps for *A Clockwork Orange*.

Tricorne hat for *Barry Lyndon* costume.

HAWK FILMS
BARRY LYNDON

The sign used to show the crew the road to the remote location in Ireland where Stanley was shooting.

Promotional badges for *Barry Lyndon*.

Two photographs of the concertina folder used to store pages from the *Barry Lyndon* screenplay. You can read the names of some scenes on the labels.

Two American license plates that served to conceal the English plates on some of the cars used in the exterior scenes for *The Shining*.

Key holders for the Overlook Hotel. Once the shooting was over, Stanley used some of them for the keys of his own house, Childwickbury. Naturally, too many had been made for the film. "Which one do you want?" Stanley asked me. "Number 107," I replied, "like the number of the bus I used to take every day from Edgware Lane to go to work at the Royal Orthopaedic Hospital." He gave me several more besides.

Two pieces of film from *The Shining*. These are from the early prints of the film, and Stanley screened them to check on the quality of the laboratory's work.

Some of the marines' equipment. Their uniforms were purchased in shops around London that sold secondhand military clothing, but the jackets were imported from the United States. They were new, made by a manufacturer following the original model from the sixties.

A marine's flashlight, along with personalized fabric strips and dogtags. Every jacket had a strip of fabric with the name of the Marine character. The manufacturer made a strip with "Stanley Kubrick" printed on it as a gift to Stanley, but he never used it. He preferred to be a "Mr. Nobody" and re-gifted his present to Jon, who became "the Stanley Kubrick number 3," after the original and myself. Stanley found it even less amusing to see his name on the dogtags—another unwelcome gift that went straight from his hands to mine.

Gunnery Sergeant Hartman's hat from *Full Metal Jacket*.

Eyes Wide Shut clapperboard.

The first week of shooting of *Eyes Wide Shut* in my diary. The numbers in circles are my daily working hours.

they saw the façade of the Overlook Hotel, they were speechless. It loomed out of the fog made by the smoke generators and was lit by the streetlamps and spotlights in the artificial garden. When we met Stanley, he was so busy that he only had time to wave hello from afar. He was just about to film the scene where Wendy helps Danny out of the bathroom window and then gets stuck while she is trying to escape. After he'd given his final instructions, he stopped beside one of the cameras with a megaphone in his hand. Everyone waited in silence for him to speak. Marisa and Jon leaned against my legs, fascinated by the lights and the sounds of the equipment. "They're just about to start filming. We have to keep perfectly silent," I said, hugging them close to me. Stanley raised the megaphone and told the special effects team to start the wind and snow. Then he shouted: "Roll the camera!" At the time, my children were just over ten years old. I bet they really envied Danny when Stanley gave the signal for him to slide down the mountain of salt.

Every year at Christmas, Stanley sent me to deliver gifts to the homes of his friends and assistants in London. The package for Alexander Walker was particularly large and heavy that year. When I arrived at his flat, the concierge told me that Alex was on holiday in Switzerland, so I informed Stanley that I hadn't been able to deliver the gift. When I tried again some days later, Alex was very cross.

"Do you know what Stanley did?" he said, before I could utter a word. "He looked for me while I was in Switzerland. He called around all the hotels until he found me. Then he kept me on the phone for ages to get me to do a job for *The Shining*. Did you tell him I was in Switzerland?"

"Well, Alex . . . Yes. But I didn't think—"

"On holiday. You see? He doesn't even respect the Christmas holidays!"

I didn't dare answer back that I hadn't had a Christmas holiday since 1970. Instead I made some throwaway remark along the lines of, "Well, you know, that's Stanley for you," in an attempt to calm him down. Alex took the gift and went indoors.

Anyway, Stanley's phone call to Switzerland was a success, because some weeks later Alex agreed to help Stanley by compiling a scrapbook of newspaper cuttings from Colorado. He used his skill as a journalist to put together articles that described the mysterious past of the Overlook Hotel, filled with inexplicable accidents, unexpected suicides, and escaped criminals. Stanley gave Alex 35mm microfilms containing fifty years of front pages from the *Denver Post* and the *Rocky Mountains News*. He also gave him the light box, which was as big as a fridge. Alex had no small amount of difficulty making space for it in his flat. Finally, after six weeks spent inventing headlines for imaginary news in the style of these two turn of the century newspapers, the job was done. In the end, the sequence where Jack looked through these articles was never actually used in the film. Working for Stanley could mean that, too.

One night, while we were still filming, a fire broke out on Stage 3 of the EMI studios. The security guards called the fire brigade, who managed to put out the blaze before it spread to the other stages. Another of Stanley's fears had been confirmed. In addition to the studio security, Stanley had hired additional guards to watch over his sets, and it was lucky that he had. Stanley's idea of control wasn't a person keeping an eye on something, but a controller who was controlled by another controller and so on.

The cause of the fire was never discovered, but the most credible theory was an electrical fault. The set was lit by millions of bulbs that generated an incredible amount of heat, and the wood used to make the hotel was dry and highly inflammable.

The fire destroyed everything. An entire stage reduced to ashes. Despite the general atmosphere of desolation, Stanley was the only one who didn't bat an eyelid: the damage was covered by insurance. The workmen pulled their socks up, and in less than two months, they had rebuilt all the sets from scratch. Stanley didn't want to make even the slightest change to the production schedule. All he did was add a few days' break between the last day of filming before the fire, and the first after the sets had been rebuilt. That was it: no compromises.

Nobody was in the least surprised that work on the film was well behind schedule. The troupe kept on working as they always had done, but now they were probably thinking what I had been repeating to myself for months: concentrate on today and don't think about tomorrow.

The only people who were extremely impatient about the delays were the management of EMI Films. As the days passed, they had to find new ways the keep at bay the other producers who were raring to get going on their films. These included Steven Spielberg, who had come to Elstree to make *Raiders of the Lost Ark*. His production plan included the stage where Stanley had built the Colorado Lounge. Steven walked up and down the stages wondering how long he would have to wait. In an attempt to keep on the right side of Spielberg, Stanley had offered to show him around the Overlook Hotel. They had known each other for some time. George Lucas, the creator of *Star Wars*, had introduced them. George and Stanley often talked, and coincidentally, George was filming at EMI alongside Stanley. He was using the remaining stages to make *The Empire Strikes Back*. It wasn't unusual to see little radio-controlled robots being operated by the people from Lucasfilms in the streets between the stages. More than once I came close to running one over in the Unimog. However, the studio canteen was perhaps the most surreal place of all. At any given time, you could see walk-ons in absurd hairy costumes, imperial guards in white uniforms, and clerks from some TV production in jackets and ties. They were all sitting at the same table, chatting peacefully and eating soup.

The last take of *The Shining* eventually arrived, and Stanley left the EMI studios to the sound of more than one sigh of relief. While he transferred to the offices he was using as cutting rooms, the sets of the Overlook Hotel were dismantled and demolished. The hotel furniture was put on sale: wardrobes, fridges, paintings, lamps, even the utensils from the huge kitchen: everything from can openers to ladles. So as not to waste anything, Stanley had devised a system that kept everybody happy. Whoever bought the props got good value for money: they were cheap and in good condition. At the same time, the production company recovered part of its investment and saved on the cost of having the props transferred by a removal company.

I bought two carpets from the Colorado Lounge at seventy-five pounds twenty-seven pence each for my house in Farm Road: one for the dining room and one for the living room. Stanley kept the long table where Jack Nicholson had typed his masterpiece. He also bought several dozen black padded chairs that had been used in the Gold Room for the dance scene. The others were shared among the workmen of the production team.

Finally, all the technical equipment was put in storage, including the navy black velvet curtains that had been used to improve the acoustics in the rooms of the Overlook and miles of electrical cables.

Emilio,
Please bring into the dining room all the radios and JVC video recorders from the cutting room [at Abbots Mead]. Do it now. Ray and the others are using the cut room at 11:00.

S

At the end of spring 1979, editing of *The Shining* started at EMI in the cutting room equipped with Moviolas. After over a year sitting around on the set, Ray Lovejoy could finally get down to work. It took him months just to number the reels and find his way around the vast quantity of footage. Stanley joined Ray and his assistants every morning. When he had finished working with them, he moved to the office next door where the sound engineers were mixing the audio tracks. The fact that he asked me to show up at mealtimes with gifts of cases of wine and beer for the staff confirmed what I had thought from the beginning: this was going to be a long story.

Choosing the music for *The Shining* turned out to be far more complicated than it had been for *Barry Lyndon*. Throughout the filming, Stanley had listened to absolutely all kinds of LPs and tapes: "What's this music?" he asked me one morning as I was driving him to the studios.

"It's a tape I bought." It was an orchestral piece featuring a French horn, an instrument that I had always liked a lot.

"Why did you buy it?" he asked.

"Because I liked it."

"And why did you like it?"

"I liked it, that's all!"

"I like it, too. Let me have it. You can buy yourself another copy."

Stanley ended up contacting just about anybody. The first person to arrive was Dominque Frontiere, an American composer and arranger who had written the soundtracks for a large number of TV series and Hollywood films. Then came Wendy Carlos and Rachel Elkind. Even though they had already worked with Stanley, they seemed as nervous about the interview as everybody else. "Let's hope so, let's hope so. . . ." Wendy kept whispering, as she looked out of the window lost in her thoughts while I was driving her to Abbots Mead.

When I went back to Stanley after leaving them at the hotel, he asked, "So how did it go with the girls?"

"Just fine," I answered. "They were a bit nervous and said they really want to work with you on this film. Wendy said she would have done everything she possibly could to come up with exactly the right music."

"That's good!" said Stanley.

Some days later, he sent me to get Rachel and Wendy again. I thought this was a good sign. Nevertheless, they still looked tense. They told me that Stanley had said their tracks were fine; that they were perfect. And yet he kept on mixing them together with music by other composers.

"Why does he do that?" Rachel asked me. "Does it mean he's not satisfied?"

"We've tried absolutely everything," Wendy added. "I don't know how many versions of the same track we've played him!"

"Well," I tried to reassure them, "if he's asked you back, it means he's happy. He'll ask you to change things because he knows that you can give him what he wants. Don't worry about it too much. Just keep on working."

Stanley was probably applying his usual "Let's do another one" strategy. He kept asking questions about what the girls had said because he wanted to understand what his collaborators really had in mind. He sent me to spy on them in the hope that they would reveal something to me.

When Stanley decided to hire Wendy and Rachel for *The Shining*, that was the last I saw of them. He assigned another driver to them, and I had nothing more to do with it. My mission had been accomplished.

Dear Emilio,
Thank you for being such a calm center in the midst of many storms during the past week. We shall be forever grateful.
Sincerely,
Rachel and Wendy

In the meantime, work on editing the film continued. Despite the numerous amendments that Stanley had had made to his contract with EMI, the production of *The Shining* eventually had to leave the studios. Time had run out, extensions had been conceded, Stanley's prestige had been exploited, personal favors had been granted—that was it. There was nothing or nobody left to appeal to. At the end of summer '79, Stanley packed his bags and moved to the cutting room in Childwickbury, the new house he had just bought and christened Stanley Kubrick Studios.

Editing the film took months. The film was scheduled for release at the end of May 1980, and the technicians had to work nonstop, starting in the morning and finishing late at night, in order to meet the deadline.

When spring came, Stanley had to go back to EMI Films to mix the audio because he didn't have adequate equipment at home to do the job. Stanley's reputation was enough to dispel the doubts of the studio management, and a new contract was signed. Everyone was crammed into the recording studio. Spool after spool, they listened to the music again and again to see how each particular piece would fit with a specific scene from the film.

When I went to the studio on Friday evening with the reels of film Stanley had decided to watch during the weekend, I shuddered at the thought of having to sit down in front of the Steenbecks and rewind them with that music bursting through the doors. It sounded like a siege was in progress: there were screams, bells, bangs, and whistles. Around about seven or eight, when everyone else went home for the weekend, the sound of the machines whirring in the silence was the sweetest thing I'd ever heard.

When the film was finally finished, it was taken home for the traditional family preview. I never stayed to watch. I didn't want to waste two hours watching a film that I'd already seen in the making or in the dailies for over two years.

Julian was the only one from Warner who never missed a preview. The other managers tried to go too so they could have their say, but Stanley always refused at the last minute.

The Shining was released in America on schedule at the end of May. From October onward, it was released in other countries. In England the BBC celebrated the event by broadcasting Vivian's backstage documentary about the film. Once again, Stanley had kept his word, and as usual he enjoyed his success away from the cameras in the half-light of his screening room.

Not long before this happened, when filming was finally completed, Andros and I were taking it easy in the office at the Lodge. We were both relieved that the worst was over. Stanley was busy editing the film and so Andros, Margaret, and I could get back to our usual routine, which was far more manageable and less chaotic. But there was something strange about Andros. He seemed to be forcing a smile, and most of all, he hadn't celebrated this return to normality with one of his typical colorful remarks. When I asked him if everything was okay, he said: "Emilio, I'm thinking of leaving."

That was the last thing I ever wanted to hear.

"Andros, don't you remember that you were the one who convinced me to stay?"

"I know, but . . ." He was at a loss for words. I realized that it wasn't easy for him to talk about this. And it wasn't for me, either. "I'd like to get out of here occasionally. I'm always here; I'm always on the phone. I never get to see anyone, and as soon as I get home I collapse on the bed. I haven't got the energy to do anything else, to go out with a friend, nothing."

I listened in silence. I didn't really know what to say. There was no getting away from it. "It's just that I can't go on like this," he concluded with a sigh.

"You do realize what you would be leaving behind, don't you?" Andros was lost for words again. I tried reminding him that we were a team and that if one of us left, the whole group would collapse. "Perhaps I could get a job producing films," he said, without replying to my objection. "I like production work. I'd like to try. I think I could be good at it. I'm happy here, it's been a great few years, but everything comes to an end. I think I should change, do something else, telephone different people for a different film."

"Andros, I understand what you're saying, but it's as if you were stabbing me in the back. I hate to tell you this to your face, but you're hurting me."

"I know. I'm sorry. I wanted to tell you first, before anyone else. But I need a change. I mean, I'm thirty-five years old. . . ."

There was another silence.

"Okay. If you're sure, then that's okay with me," I said. "Now go and tell Stanley."

Andros left the room and walked past Margaret's office without stopping. Thinking that this was strange, she came to the door and watched him go downstairs. Then she saw me, standing outside Andros's office looking heartbroken. "What's happened?" I told her everything.

"Don't worry, he won't leave," she said immediately. "He's knows what he would be giving up."

"No, Margaret, he really is leaving."

When Andros came back, the look on his face confirmed our fears. He had told Stanley. It was done. Andros never told us what they said to each other, but I would swear it was similar to the conversation I'd had some years earlier.

While he was standing in his room with his back to me, I asked him: "Now what am I supposed to do?"

"Margaret will help you," he answered, without turning around.

"And what about all the things you took care of?"

"You'll have to share them between you."

"And don't you think about Stanley? About how he'll manage without you?" Andros remained silent. "I think he'll really miss you," I added, "and I think you'll come back one day."

He turned to look at me but he didn't say a word. It seemed like there was no turning back. This was it—good-bye. I shook his hand. He pulled me towards him and hugged me. Then he said good-bye to Margaret and hugged her, too. Then he went towards the stairs.

The next day, at lunchtime, I called him. "How are you?"

"Great!" he replied. His voice was bright and shrill again.

"Don't you miss all this, I mean . . . us?"

"No." His reply came so quickly it hurt. "In the morning I can go out, look at the sky, and the best thing of all is that I don't have to listen to the sound of that phone ringing all the time. It's marvelous without all that pressure on my shoulders."

Stanley didn't mention Andros's leaving, and for a few days everything seemed calm while Margaret and I did our best to keep up. But it was an illusion, and it couldn't last. Every evening there were more and more things left undone. We had no choice but to put them off to the following day. Stanley must have very gradually realized that things were changing, because one evening, while I was driving him home from the studio, he started to ask me, "But, Andros . . . how come . . ." and he interrupted without finishing.

"He must have explained to you why, Stanley. We all know all too well what the problem is." I realized that I'd been too harsh. I didn't want to blame him for Andros leaving, but I was worried about what was going to happen. "I think he wanted to be a film producer, or anyway do something different," I added so as to avoid unnecessary arguments.

"But can't you try to . . ." He stopped midsentence again.

"I'm afraid not, Stanley. He's in contact with Paul McCartney about a film he's written. I speak to him on the phone every day, and he seems really happy."

"And what are we going to do?"

"We're going to do very badly, Stanley. Very badly."

The same thing happened with Margaret when *The Shining* was about to be released. She too knew perfectly well what the consequences of her decision would be, but she was tired of working at full speed every day as if there was always a new film to be made. The pace had become too much for her. "I was hired as a production secretary, but this production has neither a beginning nor an end. It was already under way when I arrived, and it will still be going on when I leave. I'm not afraid of hard work, I'm afraid of never seeing the light at the end of the tunnel, Emilio. I'm sorry."

"And don't you think about Stanley? We can't leave him alone!"

"You're here," she replied unconvincingly.

"Alone? Impossible."

"I'm sorry, Emilio," she repeated. "I've already told Stanley."

This was a terrible blow for me. How could I be the third one to go to him and say that I wanted to quit? I couldn't leave him, at least not now.

I went into the house and knocked at his office door. I wanted to see him. I wanted to know that he was okay. For the first time ever, he didn't say a word when I went in. There was an awkward silence, and then he spoke. "Why did Andros leave?" he asked yet again. "Didn't I pay him enough?"

"No, Stanley, Andros didn't have any free time, and he wanted to change jobs. He wanted to do something for himself. I think he must have thought about what his prospects were: year after year in the Lodge, always on the phone, and he can't have liked it much. He wants to change, to do something new before it's too late."

"And why's Margaret leaving?"

"For the same reason. For the workload and the pace. She needs some free time."

"I've never made demands on anyone!"

"Do you really mean that, Stanley? Do you realize what you expect of us or not? Do you realize how many hours we spend here? Or that the phone starts ringing the moment we get home?"

He looked at me bewilderedly. No, he didn't have the faintest idea. Perhaps he thought that everyone was able to work like he did: twenty hours a day, nonstop, day in, day out.

"What are we going to do?" he asked.

I didn't have any idea.

"You stay at home, in the office," he said, suddenly becoming decisive. "That way you can substitute for Margaret and Andros."

It didn't seem like a good idea at all to me. "And how will you manage to get around?" I asked.

"Minicabs."

"Stanley, have you any idea of the shambles if I don't go to London, Elstree, or Denham? Do you realize how many people you'll need to cover all that? It will end up like this: nobody will get anything done, and then in the evening, after I've finished all the office work, I'll have to go into town and clean up after everybody."

"And who's going to answer the phone?"

"Not me, Stanley! If you sit me behind a desk, you'll kill me. I'm not a secretary. I didn't study for that. Actually I didn't study anything! I'm not good at talking. I don't know how to."

"You stay here and don't go anywhere," he repeated.

"Fine!" I said, losing my temper because of his stubbornness. "Whatever you say. See you tomorrow morning."

For the first time in ten years I went home angry. Janette stopped the kids from rushing to me as I came in. She always did this when she saw that I was particularly tired. A look was enough: "Go upstairs, clean your teeth, and put on your pajamas," she told them. "Let your father relax for a moment." She gestured for me to sit down at the table. Without a word, she passed me a plate and sat next to me. After I'd eaten a couple of mouthfuls, she said: "So, how did your day go?" I loved this way she had of starting the conversation. She was perfectly aware that the day hadn't gone at all well, but she wanted me to be the first to mention it. She gave me all the time I needed; she waited for the relaxing atmosphere of home to alleviate the stress and tension of the day at work. While I was eating, I told her about Margaret and about Stanley's unreasonable proposal. She didn't let it show, but she was upset by the news. She just asked me how Stanley had taken it, but she was thinking to herself that she was increasingly worried that things were going to become even more difficult for us. Janette didn't say a word. She just sat and thought about the word "responsibility" and about everything that meant to Stanley.

I spent the next day in Margaret's office answering the phone. There was a call from America every five minutes: lawyers on line one, Warner Bros. executives on line two, another lawyer on hold on line three, English film distributors, lab technicians, the entire world was trying to get a word in. I didn't see Stanley until the evening when I took him the list of calls with the notes I'd made.

"And the shopping?" he asked.

"Precisely. And where have I been all day? On the phone, not in London."

"Why didn't you call someone and send them to do the shopping?"

"Stanley, is there anything wrong with the way I've dealt with the calls?"

"No."

"Take a look at the notes I've made. It's all there. All I've done all day for twelve hours nonstop is take notes. Everything is there on those sheets of paper. I can write down everything: who called, when, and what they said, but I would never dream of speaking on your behalf or of answering their questions. If every day I bring you twelve hours' of messages, you tell me what the point is. Tomorrow I'll spend half the day in the office and the other half in London. But you'll come up with something. If it continues like this, I'm leaving, just like Margaret and Andros."

And Stanley called Pat Penneligion—heaven-sent Pat. She did Margaret's job while Stanley looked for a full-time replacement to cover the role when she was not there. In the interim, I divided my time between London and the house, in an attempt to take on some of Andros's jobs. But it wasn't easy, and it didn't work. There was quite simply too much to do. And Stanley didn't help in the least: "What about all these people wandering around the house, why don't you make use of them when I'm away? Do you really have to call back me for the tiniest little thing?" "You were the one I needed." There was nothing to add to that.

7

390 Keys to 129 Doors

WHILE THE SET BUILDERS hired by Peregrine Films were constructing the Overlook Hotel in the EMI studios, a second team on Stanley's payroll were hard at work on another, equally imposing but less sinister building.

At an auction in 1978, Stanley had bought a property in Childwickbury in Hertfordshire.

The estate originally belonged to the English aristocracy and stretched for over a hundred acres along the left side of Harpenden Road, a few miles north of St. Albans. The estate consisted of the house, a stable block, a large park with woods, rose gardens, greenhouses, gardens, two ponds, a few small cottages for the servants of the previous owners, and Childwick Green, a little village with a country church. The main residence was an old, redbrick manor house, which had been extended over the years to include a rooftop terrace.

Childwickbury was the perfect place for Stanley. It had taken a long time to find, but at last there would be enough space for all his equipment and enough peace and quiet for his family.

When Stanley arrived in London in the sixties, he rented a flat in Kensington where he lived while he was making *Dr. Strangelove*. Then he relocated to a house in St. John's Wood. He didn't stay long there either, and towards the end of the decade he moved farther out of town to Abbots Mead. He was getting away from the chaos, and as soon as the city expanded and it caught up with him, he moved further away, seeking out the peace that he had lost.

Childwickbury.

The previous owners of Childwickbury hadn't taken very good care of the property. The second floor was totally abandoned, and despite a few pieces of period furniture on the ground floor, most of the house was empty and looked as though nobody had lived there for years.

For over a year, teams of builders, carpenters, electricians, and plumbers restored floors, consolidated walls, and rewired the building. The property was fenced off, and Stanley had two gates built: one at the main entrance and the other at the side, near the stables and greenhouses. A private road ran through the grounds, so Stanley made sure that passersby couldn't see the house and its annexes. He did this by increasing the double hedging along the road and repairing the wire fence behind it.

Everything had to be approved by the National Trust, the organization that protects cultural and environmental treasures in England. No drastic changes were authorized. The aim was to conserve what was already there. "I really like this place," said Stanley, as he surveyed the endless space surrounding the house, and dreamed of building warehouses and studios on it, "and it's cheaper than Abbots Mead, but all these conservation laws have thrown a wrench in the works!"

Stanley never once went to Childwickbury to see how the renovation work was going. He was too busy filming and editing *The Shining.* Christiane didn't go to check up on the builders either, but as soon as one of the outbuildings was ready, she started to spend all day painting in the park. She couldn't wait to live in the country. What's more, for an artist, an empty house was a tantalizing prospect, rather like a blank canvas to paint on.

In the meantime, Stanley had asked me to take care of moving his belongings from Abbots Mead. I was about to call a removal company when he told me he wanted me to do everything myself.

"It's easy: start with the small things; start with the library. Mark each box. Get help from the studio, take a few of the workmen from the set. Roy's nearly finished, and they've got nothing to do all day. Choose who you think best. Get the Unimog out, load everything in the back, and move it all a little at a time."

"But Stanley—"

"Nobody gets to touch my stuff."

So I started with the books as he had suggested. Then I moved the bulkier things. I carefully put them in numbered trunks so that it would be easier to unpack them and put them in the various rooms in Childwickbury. Records, videotapes, televisions, radios, all the ornaments, chairs. . . . I regularly made photocopies of the inventory and kept them in various places, just to be on the safe side. For the very first time, I went into Stanley's private room on the first floor. I'd never seen anyone else go in there. He gave me the keys and told me to carefully pack everything on the shelves and in the

One of the stickers I used to put on the boxes of Stanley's private documents. They were simple and effective and kept nosy people away.

drawers. I found mostly cameras. I put them in a couple of cardboard boxes that I labeled CAMERAS, SK PRIVATE.

Then I dismantled the furniture and loaded it along with some shelves and cupboards into the Unimog. The most difficult thing was getting the filing cabinets down the stairs. These tall, narrow steel lockable objects accounted for most of the furniture in the second-floor offices.

While I was packing and moving, Stanley and Christiane were deciding how to allocate the rooms. There was enough space in Childwickbury to give them both the chance to work undisturbed. Stanley mapped out routes between the rooms based on their activities: his phone calls, the guests who came to talk about the films, and Christiane's studio, space for her paintings, and the friends who came to visit her. He devised a plan to allocate all of the rooms. However, letting him do this wasn't exactly a good idea.

Childwickbury Manor wasn't so much a big house as a collection of rooms randomly added onto a narrow Georgian building. When you opened a door, you never found quite what you expected. Stanley's idea didn't help to improve the logic of the layout, especially on the ground floor. There were two entrances. The main one was on the north side and opened into a large hall. The secondary entrance was set between two semicircular colonnades. Stanley thought this was an atrocious waste of space. What was the point of an entrance hall for receiving guests anyway? He immediately decreed that it be used as an office, so that anyone who entered by that door had to weave their way through the people working there. Stanley decided to use the right-hand side of the ground floor. This part of the house had previously been reserved for socializing and consisted of a long line of rooms that could be accessed only from the outside or by a few doors that connected the area to the rest of the house. Once these doors were closed, nobody would have been able to disturb him.

They were the finest rooms in the manor. In keeping with the tradition of aristocratic residences, each one had a name. And the names of the rooms were the only things that survived Stanley's restructuring work. The Green Room had precious velvet green wallpaper; the Red

Room was filled with red furniture; the Dome Room had a glass cupola in the ceiling. They were all emptied out to make room for Stanley's things. Even the billiard table disappeared from the Billiard Room at the end of the west wing, to make room for the meetings Stanley held with the people who worked for him. The ballroom was in the center of the building; it too was emptied out, painted dark blue, and renamed the Projection Room. It had taken a couple of months for Stanley and Christiane to agree on where to put the projectors and armchairs. She didn't want any of the bright airy rooms to be condemned to the darkness required by the Zeiss projectors. The projectors were the only things I didn't handle while he was moving. Stanley called some specialized technicians to load them onto a lorry and reinstall them in Childwickbury. The screens were put on two walls at right angles; one for the 16mm films and the other for 35mm. All you had to do was turn your chair around and the cinema was ready.

Christiane occupied the left-hand side of the ground floor. She had a view of the park with the plants and animals that were a constant inspiration for her painting. Next to her studio was the Pine Room, thus called because of the pinewood finishing on the walls. It was an elegant lounge, which led to the large kitchen that took up most of the southern side of the building. The brown tiles, red hobs, wooden furniture, and freshly cut flowers that Christiane chose herself made this room cozy and friendly—perfect for family get-togethers and meals with friends.

At the end of 1979 I'd finished moving. I'd been quicker than Stanley, who still hadn't finished work on *The Shining*. "You know what?" I said, reflecting on how moving house for him had made me something of an expert. "I might even try my hand at the removal business."

"You're joking, aren't you?" he asked seriously.

"No, no, I mean it," I insisted. "If you give me the Unimog, I'll start my own business!"

I'd packed up Stanley's precious books, put his cameras in boxes, dismantled and reassembled furniture, loaded chairs and tables, and traveled with canvases and easels; but none of this helped in any way to deal with the most difficult task of all: the cats.

Christiane and the girls had been living at Childwickbury for some weeks; Teddy, Lola, and Phoebe were there, too. Even the film editors who were working on *The Shining* had set up camp in one of the outbuildings. And yet Stanley wouldn't make up his mind to leave. Abbots Mead was empty. All that was left was him, his bed, and the cats. Christiane started to get impatient: "Emilio, for heaven's sake, convince him to come away from there!" But every time I tried, Stanley became evasive. When I insisted, he poured out all his anxiety. "What if they don't like it there? What if they want to come back home? And what if the cars there run them over? And what if we can't catch them?"

Theoretically, everything was ready. He had decided to give the cats the Green Room, the room in the center of the west side looking out on the back garden. He didn't want them to wander freely in the park, even though Childwickbury was a long way from the busy roads. "Absolutely not outside," he had answered. By that time I had fully realized how intransigent and irrational Stanley was when it came to his animals.

Eventually, I managed to convince him: "Okay, I know what we can do. You take the Gold Mercedes with Freddie, Jessica, Polly, Priscilla, and Pandora in their boxes, and I'll take Leo on the passenger seat with me in the Unimog, because if they smell each other in the car it will be a killing. I'll lead the way. I have my car phone on and also a two-way transmitter if you need help."

"No, you follow me. That way, if one of the cats jumps out of the car—"

"Stanley," I said exasperatedly, "just don't open the windows, and you'll be fine!"

It was only twelve miles from Abbots Mead to Childwickbury, but Stanley drove slowly and it took ages. Leo gave me a confused look from the seat beside me, disturbed by the roar of the Unimog. As soon as we went through the gates and stopped in front of the colonnades,

Stanley braked suddenly and ran towards me. "Freddie is out of the box! What do I do?"

"Do nothing," I ordered. "Stay away from the car. Go into the house, or better still, in your office and wait for me to come around! I'll take the Mercedes around the back entrance and use the French doors of the Red Room." I said it again. "Please go there and wait for me. Starting from now."

"No! The dogs are out. They could scare them!"

"Well, you shut the dogs in one part of the house while I take care of the cats. Go, Stanley, go! See you in the Red Room."

I found Freddie under the driver's seat, and it was no easy job to get him out. I drove the car full of cats around to the back of the house, where Stanley helped me to take all the cages indoors.

"And Leo? Where have you left Leo?" he asked in as state of panic.

"He's still in the Unimog. And don't you dare say that he can't stay there for another five minutes!"

When the cages were opened, the cats peeked out, but their hind legs were still inside. "Look at them. They don't fucking know where to go or sleep! Emilio, I don't see any of their things here. It's getting too late for you to make another trip now."

"Stanley, please calm down. This is the Red Room, your office. Where did you want to put the cats? The Green Room, over there. Now, if you take a look in there, you'll see everything where you wanted. In fact, why don't you walk in there now, and with some luck, they'll follow you in, and you'll just close the door behind you."

Stanley opened the door of the Green Room, had a look inside, and turned around with a smile. Everything I'd said was there, and it was all arranged the way he wanted it. The worried expression vanished from his face. He entered the room and called the cats. I tried to push them, and when they were in, I closed the door. I went to get Leo and locked him in the Dome Room. Stanley had made some notices to warn Christiane and the builders who were still working in the house—DO NOT OPEN THIS DOOR, PLEASE—and I stuck them on every door. I found Stanley in the Green Room, sitting on the sofa surrounded by his cats: a king on his throne.

"Emilio, please can you clean it at least twice a week? That way I can sit down here with them when I want to."

I had the feeling that the drastic increase in space and the number of rooms in the new house would have meant a proportionate increase in the number of things to do. We all have the gift of second sight sometimes.

"Make sure each of those keys works," said Stanley, handing me the keys to Childwickbury.

"Better still," I answered, "why don't you come with me? That way you can check for yourself."

We went around the ground floor and wrote the name of each room on the labels hanging from the keys. The rooms without names were given a number.

"How many keys are there?" he asked, as we went upstairs. The girls' rooms and the guest rooms were on the second floor.

"I haven't counted them. There'll be one for each door."

"That won't be enough. We need one for me, one for you, one for Christiane, and a spare copy, just in case all three of us lose the same key."

"You're saying that you want three copies of each key?"

"Yes."

As we were going upstairs to the third floor, where Stanley and Christiane's private apartment was, I started counting the keys.

"Anyway, in answer to your question," I said, while we were fumbling with a door at the end of the corridor in his apartment, "there are a hundred and twenty-nine keys. So who's the idiot who's going to spend an entire week having four hundred copies made?" Stanley looked at me and changed the subject: "Where do we keep all the keys?"

He decided to convert a small storeroom opposite his bedroom into the Key Room. I screwed a couple of wooden panels with hooks

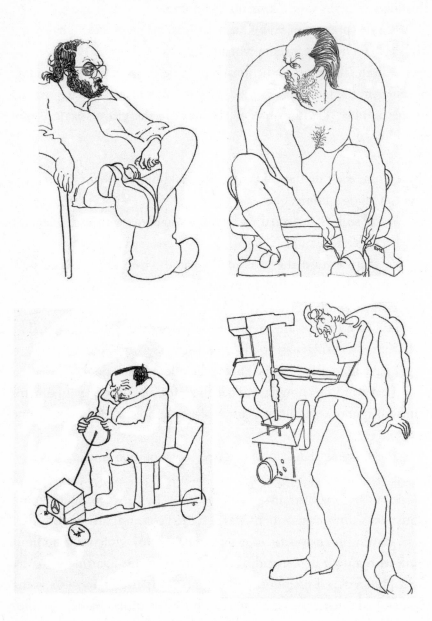

Tom Smith's caricatures. Try to guess who's who.

to two of the walls. Then I put a label with the name or number of the room above each hook, like in a hotel. There was a large padlock on the door of the Key Room, with three identical keys: "This one's for me, this one's for you, and hide this other one somewhere. Don't let anyone see where you put it."

The next thing to do was to put Stanley's stuff somewhere. Since the Green Room had been reserved for the cats, there wasn't much room for anything else. However, I did manage to put some of the books and Stanley's collection of *Look* magazine, which he'd worked for as a photographer when he was an adolescent in New York, in an old bookcase with glass doors. On another shelf I put the caricatures that Tom Smith, who had been in charge of special effects makeup for *The Shining*, had drawn of everyone who had worked on the set. This didn't turn out to be a good idea because one day Stanley forgot to close the bookcase and the cats decided to use the album as a litter box. I managed to save a few of the pictures by photocopying them.

The long table from the Colorado Lounge in the Overlook Hotel that Jack Nicholson had used as a desk went in the Green Room, too. The cats had a great time using it as a slide. They took a run up, jumped onto the table, and slid from one end to the other.

The other private rooms on the ground floor were filled with more than thirty filing cabinets. They stood in long parallel rows like in the police stations in American movies. I lined Stanley's typewriters up on the shelves in what had been the hall of the main entrance. It became a sort of typewriter cemetery.

Stanley often said that books are precious. They were what he was most concerned about while relocating. He asked me straightaway which boxes they were in among those on the ground floor waiting to be unpacked. He had decided to move the bookcase that had been in Abbots Mead to his apartment on the third floor, but while I was putting his books away, Anya noticed some cracks in her bedroom ceiling. Stanley told me to stop putting books on the shelves and immediately called Roy Walker for an opinion. The diagnosis was simple: the third floor of Childwickbury Manor hadn't been built to bear the weight of Stanley Kubrick's library. We had to put all the books back in boxes again, make note of the exact order in which they were packed, and take them back downstairs. The only place that could be sacrificed was the Concert Room. In this long space we had found a period harpsichord, and it was now being used for Vivian's guitars and the drum kit Stanley used to play when he was young in New York. "Get rid of everything!" said Stanley before letting the boxes of books inundate the room.

The Stable Block was a square building with an internal courtyard. It turned out to be a good place to store Christiane's artist's materials that couldn't fit into the house. Stanley used the large room on the right to hold the trunks where he stored everything he'd kept since he had started making films. There were hundreds of them, a pyramid of trunks made of wood or steel. They were green, black, big, even bigger, and enormous. The sight of them heaped up in the courtyard of Childwickbury was, to say the least, impressive. Most of them contained the things Stanley had brought with him by ship when he moved from the United States to England, and they hadn't been opened since then. There were various objects, books and other odds and ends he'd had in his apartment in New York, as well as all the production material from the films he'd made in America. Some of them were still sealed with the string and labels of the Cunard Line, the transatlantic shipping company Stanley had traveled with in the sixties. All Stanley's American life was in there.

Before Stanley decided to move them all to the new house, they had been stored in two rented warehouses in Bullens and Bushey. They had been there for at least ten years, in no particular order, with just a number to identify them. The inventory had long since been lost, so every time we had to look for something it was a disaster.

Andros and I would pick up a trunk, remove the shipping company label, and open it up to see if what Stanley was looking for was inside. More often than not it wasn't. So we had to open another one. Stanley usually asked us to find books or magazines. The instructions he gave were sometimes rather vague: "Look for a big black trunk with metal edging."

Fortunately, at times he was more specific: "Trunk number 150." All this was fine until we discovered that either there were at least twenty big black trunks with metal edging or that trunk number 150 didn't actually exist.

Together with Andros, during these visits I started making a list of the contents of every trunk we opened in an attempt to gradually reconstruct the lost inventory. There were old issues of *Look*, old issues of other American magazines, newspaper cuttings, contracts with United Artists, data sheets of the personnel on the set of some old film, Stanley's high school diploma, letters from lawyers, letters from assistants, letters from admirers, other letters, books, big books, small books, and various other stuff.

When we got back, we would show Stanley the list. He would look at it and decided what to keep and what to throw away: "Get rid of it! But keep the trunk. We'll use it for something else."

After what had happened in the past, this time, since there was plenty of space, I asked Stanley to store the trunks more methodically. He asked me what was making it difficult to find the right trunk. "Finding it!" I answered. I suggested we put them in rows and give a letter to each row. "The trunks are already numbered, so it will be a bit like Battleship. We'll be able to find them easily like that." "Right," agreed Stanley, "and what's the second problem?" "Getting to the ones at the bottom of the pile." I suggested that instead of putting the trunks on top of each other, we put each one on a shelf.

"Emilio, let's do an inventory. What do you think?"

"Sorry, Stanley. No way."

"Perhaps I could get someone else to do it."

"Whatever you want. But I don't even want to hear his name mentioned, okay?"

There were plenty of dogs to keep us company at Abbots Mead: Phoebe, Lola, and Teddy, and Vivian's dog, Fanny, a small, energetic hunting hound. Not long after we moved to Childwickbury, there was a new litter of golden retrievers: Jezebel, Barnaby, Lilly, and Possum. Then, over the years, there were the strays found by Christiane or the girls, and those that Stanley was given by the studio workers: George,

Wesley, Alf, and Harvey. The increase in the canine population seemed never-ending.

It wasn't at all easy to look after and train such a large number of animals. Teddy was so big that when we were at Abbots Mead, my son Jon used to ride him like a pony. Teddy ran through the ground floor corridors of Childwickbury, crashing into doors and knocking over chairs, plants, and everything in his way. The other golden retrievers sniffed and breathed all over the kitchenware. In the past, this habit had caused much consternation among the dinner guests. Harvey was the worst of all. He enjoyed peeing on the vases of flowers that Christiane used to decorate the dining table.

In the end, we gathered together all their food and bowls in a room that came to be known as the Pet Kitchen. Gradually, they learned to behave themselves at least there. Training the cats, however, was impossible. For the first few months they were restless and nervous, and as a result, so was Stanley. One morning he came to me shouting, "She's gone, she's gone!" Pandora, the female Siamese cat had disappeared. Stanley kept on looking under the sofa and under the table from *The Shining*. He continued to call her. "Where are you? Where are you?" He even started to look in unlikely places like the drawers in the bookcase.

"Why are you looking there? Try to think like a cat!" I said, as I went towards the fireplace where I had caught a glimpse of a furry tail hanging in the dark. I don't know whether Pandora was in search of adventure, or whether she just wanted to get out of

A well-deserved rest after the move to Childwickbury.

the room. Either way, she had tried to climb up there and had got stuck.

"Gee! What are we going to do now?!" Stanley exclaimed, rushing closer to see what had happened.

"Call the gardener and tell him to come here with a metal bar. We can try to widen the gap so that she can get out."

"No! No! She'll get hurt! This is a job for the fire brigade! Call them! Call the RSPCA! Call the vet!"

All this sounded familiar. Andros, where are you?

"Stanley, calm down. Calling all those people won't help. The more Pandora gets nervous, the more she'll move, and the more she'll hurt herself. Trust me. Do as I said and call the gardener."

"And what do I have to do?"

"Nothing. Just go. Leave the room. I'll call you when it's over."

"God bless you."

With a bit of patience, the gardener and I managed to free Pandora's head. The cat slipped out and fell on the ground in a cloud of soot. She didn't move. She was curled up, frightened and stunned. I picked her up and cleaned her with a damp cloth. She was so covered in soot you couldn't even see her eyes. Then I put her down again and called Stanley. When he saw her, he shouted, "Christiane! Come in here! The cat's all right!" And went towards her to pick her up.

"Stanley, she's been hanging by her neck all night. Leave her alone for a minute!"

"You're right, you're right," he said, and stopped. Christiane stood behind him, smiling. "I'll go to the office then. Call a vet to make sure she's okay."

"First, we'll see how she is. Then, if necessary, we'll call the vet."

I stayed on the sofa in the Green Room to keep an eye on Pandora. Gradually, the cat calmed down, and then she came close to my feet and looked up at me, motionless. She had always been mistrustful. She never let anybody pick her up and scratched anyone who tried to stroke her. She was the one who had destroyed most of the upholstery of the sofa I was sitting on. Suddenly, she jumped up beside me and, tilting her head, observed me. After a couple of minutes she came even closer and jumped into my arms, then she climbed onto my shoulders and wrapped herself around me like a stole. I got up very carefully and went towards the Red Room to show Stanley. When I popped my head out of the door, he saw me standing there with this fur collar and said, "Is she dead?"

"I suppose it must be her way of saying thank you!"

He called Christiane to come and look, and they moved closer. Suddenly, Pandora jumped down and went back to the middle of the room. "Just a moment," I said, and sat back on the sofa. Pandora saw me and climbed up onto my shoulders again.

"I can't believe it!" said Stanley. "It's a miracle!"

"Of course, it's not a miracle," I answered. "She knows who saved her, that's all!"

Two women answered the ad in the local paper for domestics. They both seemed willing and discreet. But Stanley found it hard to trust anybody, especially now that Andros had left. At Abbots Mead, he had authorized the domestics to clean both his bedroom and the office on the ground floor, but not the office on the second floor: only he was allowed in there. When he moved to Childwickbury, he made a rather drastic decision. Nobody was to be allowed into his apartment on the third floor or to the rooms on the ground floor where he worked on his films. The domestics could look after the public areas on the ground and second floors. I had to take care of everything else. "Will you, Emilio?" said Stanley, much as expected.

"The ground floor is too big. I can't clean it on my own. It would take me all morning just to sweep the Billiard Room!"

"Let's buy a floor washer."

"It wouldn't solve the problem. What we need here is a cleaning company!"

"I don't like having strangers rummaging through my things."

I was just about to give in, but I tried to salvage what I could. "I could be there when the domestics do the cleaning," I proposed.

"All right then, let's do it your way. Get them to help you on the ground floor, but only in the Billiard Room and the Green Room. I don't want anyone going into my offices, and you take care of my apartment, please."

And so I became Stanley's personal cleaner. I cleaned his rooms, made the bed, did the washing up, and cleaned the windows. And if I didn't have time, he waited. Everything was left exactly as it was until I could find a couple of hours to spend tidying up. I was gradually turning into a plumber, electrician, technician, and all-around handyman too. "There's no water in the bathroom. Have a look, will you?" "The light in the library doesn't work. Have a look." "The television in the bedroom isn't working. Have a look before sending it to be repaired. It might just be a fuse, and they'll cheat us by saying it needs something complicated to be done to it!"

"But I don't know how to do these things, Stanley!"

"Last time you fixed it."

"That was just luck!"

"Try anyway."

The trouble was that one way or another I managed, and so all these little jobs gradually took up most of my time. I dusted his books every week. I cut the grass, being careful not to disturb the cats. I was responsible for making sure there was food in the pantry. I took the videotapes off the shelves in the corridor to make room for new ones and put the old in numbered boxes downstairs, then added them to the inventory. I made two or three photocopies of the inventory to make sure it didn't get lost. I planned to have all the cars serviced in rotation. I took them to specialized mechanics and renewed the insurance. I renewed Stanley's personal documents, too. He delegated me to go to the American embassy, and I took checks on his behalf to the National Westminster Bank. I went to law firms, the offices of the major film companies, and to the homes of writers and consultants to deliver documents. "Be extremely polite," he urged, and I understood that I was the only ambassador of Stanley Kubrick in the world. "Since you're going to Hampstead, go to Maxwell and get me some hamburgers."

And then the pita in Camden Town and the bagels from the baker at Marble Arch that he was convinced were identical to the ones he ate in New York when he was little; the casual shirts at Lillywhites in Piccadilly and the French collar ones at Aquascutum in Regent Street: he wanted twelve, all the same. I gave the shop assistant a note where Stanley had written the color, sleeve length, and collar size. I went to the baker in St. Albans, whom I had convinced to leave me a sack of fresh bread outside the back door. I came to a stop and, without getting out, hauled the bag into the car. It was a bit like the toll barrier on the motorway. Then I went to the post office for the usual sacks of letters, and then back to London, to Harrods, Fortnum & Masons, Selfridges, and Marks & Spencer: "The salami you bought last time was better. Did you go to the same shop? Ask them where the salami comes from." Then I had to stop at the fruit farm, where I only ever bought seasonal fruit, or the ethnic restaurants in the center of town, where I picked up takeout meals that had been ordered over the phone. I was exhausted, but when I finally finished everything and went home, Stanley was so happy that his smile compensated for all my hard work.

With a bit of luck and no small amount of goodwill, I managed to keep up with Stanley's requests without disappointing him. Then one day in that unexpected way that the obvious sometimes happens, he asked: "Why don't you come and live here with us?"

"What . . . sorry . . . Stanley?"

"Yes. Choose one of the outbuildings, whichever one you want, the one you like best."

"But I already have a house of my own," I replied, confused.

"Here is better than London, isn't it? And when I call you, you'll be nearby so you'll get here immediately."

Now I get it. Great idea! "No, Stanley, no," I answered, and dropped the subject. I was already working on average sixteen hours a day, and I lived a long way away. If I had moved to Childwickbury, I wouldn't have had a minute to myself. Even if I knew I was going to go back to him, the distance helped me to clear my head and go on. I didn't even tell Janette. I wanted to avoid another argument.

The Kubrick family settled in well at Childwickbury. The new house was spacious, peaceful, and gave all of them the chance to use their time as they wished.

Stanley passed the whole day in his office on the second floor. He liked spending time with his books so much that doing anything else seemed to him like a waste of time. During the night, while the others slept, he came downstairs to work in his rooms, pamper his cats, and have a late-night snack with them.

Christiane, on the other hand, loved the outdoor life. She would take her paints and canvases to some distant corner of the park and spend the whole day painting there. Stanley had bought her a new Mercedes ORV to move around Childwickbury. We'd had the roof rack enlarged and reinforced so that Christiane could sit on top of the car with her wooden chair and easel and paint from a higher point of view. When the weather was bad, she painted and listened to music in her studio on the ground floor. Stanley had a stereo in his office on the second floor, too. Vivian had chosen it for him. Anya still took opera singing lessons and practiced in the Pine Room, where Katharina and Christiane also went to play the piano. Sometimes Stanley picked up his drumsticks and played the kit in the Billiard Room. I always thought it strange that a whole family with such good ears for music didn't play more together, but they never lasted more than a few minutes at the Christmas party.

Even though Stanley wasn't Catholic, they always celebrated Christmas. There was always a huge tree with hundreds of tiny lights in the Pine Room, and Christiane put up garlands of holly around the house.

Stanley wasn't particularly interested in religion, nor did he really understand religious fanaticism. The Lodge at Abbots Mead had been a perfect example of religious tolerance: Stanley was Jewish, I was Catholic, Andros was Greek Orthodox, and Margaret was Protestant. Not long after I met Stanley, I remember telling him a story that made him laugh out loud. It was about Claude, a French friend I'd met when I worked at the hosiery factory. Claude was Jewish, and his wife was a strict Orthodox Jew. Claude had trouble respecting some of the limitations imposed by their faith, especially when it came to eating, because he loved bacon, sausages, and other forbidden foods. Every Saturday morning, when his wife went to the synagogue for Shabbat, he invented an excuse, usually involving his car, and snuck around to my house: "Emilio's going to fix the carburetor," "Emilio's going to change the oil," or even "Emilio wants to have a look at some hosiery samples." When he arrived, he stuffed himself with food. That sinful breakfast seemed to be the best thing he had ever eaten.

"Wasn't that a problem for you, Emilio? The fact that he was sinning?"

"No. Why should it have been? Jesus said, 'You shall love your neighbor as yourself.' Mine was an act of Christian charity. If anyone got angry, it was his God!"

Suddenly, an earthquake shook the peace of Childwickbury. Katharina announced that she wanted to go and live on her own. She was thirty, and it was understandable. But Stanley couldn't understand it. He tormented himself for days on end, trying to find a reason for why his daughter should want to leave them. At last, downheartedly, he agreed to let her look for an apartment. When Katharina found a place she liked, Stanley asked me to go and view it. Barnes was an excellent area in the southwest of the city. It was enclosed by a hook in the Thames and so was spared much of the city traffic. I couldn't see anything wrong with it and gave my approval. "You take care of moving her things, Emilio, like you did with mine."

Some time later, Anya wanted to follow in Katharina's footsteps.

"Why are they doing this to me?" protested Stanley uneasily.

"They're not doing something bad to you," I explained. "It's normal, Stanley. They grow up and want to be independent. They want to learn from their own mistakes. That's how it works."

"Why?"

"There isn't a reason why, or at least I don't know of one. That's how it is. It's always been like that. So I'd say you've got nothing to worry about."

And Stanley gave up. Anya moved into a house in West Hampstead, another peaceful area of London. Stanley asked me to check this house out, too. He wanted to know what the neighbors were like, if there was a burglar alarm, if there was a risk of fire. . . .

Katharina had worked as an assistant in the art department on both *Barry Lyndon* and *The Shining* and discovered that she had a flair for set design. She found a job at Pinewood, where Oliver, one of Christiane's nephews, joined her. I got to know him well because Vivian often invited him to Farm Road for meals. "They

Stanley asked me to take care of the cake for Anya's twenty-first birthday.

always cook strange stuff at home," she said. "Mum eats things I don't like, and Dad has meals at totally impossible times. . . . Can we go to lunch with Marisa and Jon?"

In the meantime, Anya had started work, too, mostly in theaters, where she sang in operas. Gradually, as she became more experienced, she started to take an active role in production. Just as with Stanley's work, Anya's involved the entire Kubrick family: Katharine helped design the sets, and Christiane gave her daughters advice and commented on their work. The Kubricks simply weren't able to stay away from each other.

8

STANLEY

"EMILIO, COME HOME IMMEDIATELY! It's a disaster!"

I rushed from the center of London to Childwickbury, where I found Stanley staring at the drain in the middle of the kitchen floor. Right beneath his eyes, thousands of ants were swarming out of it and heading towards the food cupboards.

"The gardener wants to use insecticide, but you can't in the kitchen. The dogs' bowls are just over there. I don't want to kill the ants; I just want to get rid of them. What can we do?"

"Let them get on with it, Stanley."

"But they'll go all over the place!"

"That stands to reason."

"And so?"

"We use boiling water. We pour it down the drain and they'll go away. You'll see."

"But they'll die!"

"Obviously. But it's less risky than using insecticide."

"You deal with it. I'm going to my office. I don't even want to watch."

Stanley's love for animals was limitless, bordering on the preposterous, and was extended unconditionally to all living creatures. He would even have taken a bee that had hit his head against the window to the vet.

The vets had been chosen extremely carefully while he was at Abbots Mead. Andros had been given the task of finding the best

possible clinic and had come up with
the Department of Veterinary Science
at the University of Cambridge. Over
the years, I'd got to know the veteri-
narians all rather well, because Stanley wanted me to be present at every
medical examination. In Cambridge, I
even had to stay with the animals in the
operating room. "That way, they'll see
you and they'll calm down."

*Me in John Wayne mode, trying
to get Puff onto the trailer.*

He was just as considerate at
home: the dog food was bought only
in Stokenchurch, and in addition to
their canned food the cats ate the same
steak that I bought for his family, as
well as frozen coley fish that I had to
cook in the microwave on the ground floor. According to Stanley, I
should have served all this on Chinese porcelain plates: "It's the same
dinner service that Christiane uses," he explained simply, and when
he saw my look of dismay, he insisted: "I don't see why we should eat
off expensive plates and they shouldn't." Without getting caught up
in the logic of what he was saying, I replied with the only thing that
could have convinced him: "Have you by any chance seen them use
Chinese porcelain in Cambridge?"

When we found mice in the basement of the house, I suggested putting
down traps. "Yes, but not the ones that kill," he ordered. A few days
later I caught him taking the mice from the cages and setting them free
in the garden.

"What are you doing, Stanley?"

"I'm setting this mouse free. Why?"

"Because it'll come back! Let me do it, I'll take it to the gardener."

"No! He'll kill them!" he exclaimed worriedly.

I gave him a nasty look.

"Take it to Julian's birds," he said. Julian had a birdcage in his garden with a variety of birds of prey. Every day he gave them dead mice to eat.

"What difference will it make? It will die anyway!"

"Nature is the difference."

What with all the cats, dogs, birds, and various wild animals or strays, Childwickbury had been turned into a zoo. It wasn't long before the donkeys arrived too. First there was Puff, a present Christiane had received from one of her painter friends, then came Rupert, Mabel, Fern, and Daisy, who were in care from the International Donkey Protection Trust. "Stanley," I said, "the stables are full. As long as the animals are healthy that's fine, but if they start to fall ill . . ." I could already see myself driving a Unimog full of donkeys back and forth to Cambridge.

Victoria at the vet's.

When Victoria fell ill in '96, the vets suggested that she stay in the clinic for a few days for some intensive therapy. Before I left for Cambridge to entrust their feline specialist with looking after Victoria, Stanley gave me a camera. "Go and take some photos of Victoria. I want to see if she's happy. Take a photo of the plate when they feed her, and one when she's eating, and another when she's finished. Keep taking photos for about twenty minutes, and don't use the flash because it startles her. Keep one at the end for the vet. I want to have a good look at her face."

And not only his requests concerning the animals were on the verge of the absurd. When we had to buy a towel for the bathroom, Stanley specified what color it should be, the type of material he wanted, and at least four types he didn't want, as well as the exact size of the towel in inches, where to buy it and where not to buy it. When I had put some toilet paper in the flat used by the actors in *The Shining*, he wanted to know what type of toilet rolls I'd chosen (normal or maxi), what color they were (white or patterned), the quality of the paper (soft or rough), and where I'd put them (one roll in the dispenser and the others in the cupboard).

> Friday
> Emilio,
> 1) Food tonight and every night until further notice. Check with me every day for the food order of the day.
> 2) Go to some hardware store and get me some samples of cheap room temperature thermometers—1 of each type. Nothing fancy. I want to check the room temperature in every room over the weekend in the main house and I want to see how much thermometers cost to see how many of them it makes sense to buy.
> > Thanks.
> > S

Everything had to be personally approved by him. It was hardly surprising that he still couldn't trust the new staff and kept sending me to the Stable Block to supervise the new assistants and secretaries. In the meantime he asked me to perform tasks that should have been dealt with by the staff at Childwickbury.

"Emilio, can you have a look at the hedges? Go around and see if you can find any holes in the fence."

"The gardeners do that kind of thing, Stanley."

"Please, Emilio."

"But it's as long as the maze in *The Shining*!"

"Do what you can today and then do a bit more tomorrow."

"What if I miss a hole on the way around?"

"When you've been around once, go around again."

With Stanley, every job had to be done twice. There was a draft and a fair copy of everything. "Stanley, you have to learn to trust people. I can't do everything myself." I'd already said this to him time and time again, but his answer was always the same: "They're all fucking idiots!"

It's true that things had changed when Margaret and Andros left. The heads of the other film distributors, laboratories, and production companies didn't hide their disappointment when I went to their offices. The stationers who used to make sure that Stanley received all the latest catalogs simply disappeared. Even the secretary at Warner wouldn't let me through the door, saying that Mr. Senior was busy. I was treated as if I were a nuisance.

"I'm Emilio D'Alessandro," I explained patiently. "I'm here on behalf of Stanley Kubrick, not that name you've got written there in your datebook."

"Just a moment please," she said, and called Julian on the intercom. Then I heard Julian shout from down the corridor: "Send him in!"

One of the staff boasted in the bars in St. Albans that he worked closely with Stanley Kubrick and then lost his wallet, containing private addresses and telephone numbers, on the underground. Another person was caught looking at private notes and documents that had been left open on a desk. Yet another was caught cheating on expenses to earn a few pounds off that "moneybags he worked for." Then there was the electrician's father-in-law, who tried to steal the fireplace from Abbots Mead while we were moving, and the gardener who left the diesel generator unattended: it caught fire and nearly burned Childwickbury to the ground. Stanley couldn't stand superficiality, ineptitude, and opportunism, and putting up with all this was becoming increasingly difficult: "Emilio, come upstairs for a cup of Nescafé," said the voice on the intercom. It meant I had to expect an awkward conversation. I went upstairs to his flat and found him in the office sitting behind his desk with a gloomy expression on his face; nothing like the relaxed and happy way he'd always looked with Margaret and Andros. Under his breath he told me about the umpteenth disaster that someone or other had caused and about all the calls he'd had to make to fix it; and the delays, and the need to tell people off for the same things again and again. Sometimes he was so angry that he smashed the telephone on the floor; other times he talked to me for nearly an hour.

"Stanley, can I go back downstairs?" I said, when he'd finished venting his anger. "I've got some work to do for you."

"You're working for me now, too!"

Once at the end of our chat he asked me, "Emilio, what do you think about bringing your parents to live here?"

"To do what?"

"What you do. What Andros did."

I didn't think it was a good idea. My father wasn't getting any younger, and I tried to explain this to Stanley as tactfully as I possibly could. My father liked working far more than I did. When he was a child he pulled cartloads of stones up the hills of Sant'Angelo for the builders who were working on the houses there. There isn't a single house in Sant'Angelo that wasn't built on my father's stones. If he came to Childwickbury, with its park, its grounds, the house with all those rooms, he'd work himself to death. My father would be out there digging even now.

Since he couldn't change reality, Stanley wanted to keep it under control as much as possible. This made the ground floor of Childwickbury hard enough, but Stanley's private rooms became sacred and inviolable. Apart from Christiane, I was the only one to have keys to the offices in the north wing and to his flat on the second floor. When he was shooting on location, I was the only one allowed into his trailer, one of those enormous vehicles that served as a production office. "Stanley, you've got so many assistants. There must be one you can trust. Someone who can have access to your office." No. "At least Jan can come in, can't he?" No. Jan had to give the documents to me, and I took them into the trailer, but only when Stanley said it was okay to come in.

This secrecy at work corresponded to a search for anonymity and tranquility in his private life. Stanley sent me to deal with most of his personal matters. I was always answering, "Here! That's me!" when they called "Stanley Kubrick," in the post office, the bank, or the vet's surgery. Inevitably, people started to mistake me for him, or to think I was some relative looking after the house while he was away. Stanley hadn't managed to keep the purchase of Childwickbury secret, but once he was there, the strategy of red herrings and wild-goose chases he put in place was remarkably successful. Nobody in the area really knew who lived in the house, and yet Stanley went in and out of the shops in St. Albans undisturbed. Especially WH Smith and Ryman, the stationery chain. When he had to buy something, book rooms in a hotel or seats at the theater, he used his wife's name or Jan's, or even mine. Everyone thought he lived in the United States and only came back to Childwickbury when had had to make films in studios in England. "When is Stanley coming back?" the inhabitants of St. Albans asked me. "I don't know. When he's ready, I suppose," I replied. And yet he was right there beside me, with his back turned, praying that nobody would recognize him.

Nobody recognized him because hardly anyone knew what he looked like. The rare photographs published in cinema magazines were the only clues that could "blow his cover." But it happened only a couple of times. The worst one was when we were walking together with Christiane in Covent Garden market. Someone in the crowd pointed at us and shouted: "That man is Stanley Kubrick!" Stanley froze. "What do we do now?" "Nothing," I answered quickly. "Pretend nothing has happened and keep walking with Christiane." I walked straight towards the man in the crowd and in a loud voice, so that everyone could hear, told him, "No, you're wrong. That man's name is Jan Harlan." "Oh, I'm sorry," he said, and went on his way.

Stanley's tastes in clothes also helped to keep people off his back. His standard outfit was as far as you can get from that of a film director or, for that matter, a respectable middle-aged man. He owned lots of clothes, mostly casual trousers and shirts, but he always ended up wearing the same two or three things he was most comfortable in. At his best, he could have been mistaken for a factory worker or a gardener. At his worst, he looked more like a tramp: threadbare baggy trousers; frayed, faded shirts; worn jackets with ink-stained pockets; and tattered tennis shoes.

At the beginning Christiane despaired, but then she accepted it. Where clothes were concerned, Stanley only ever gave her the right of veto on those rare occasions when they went out together to visit friends or to an exhibition. And for Katharina's wedding. That was the first time I ever saw him wear a tie. It was also the last: when Anya got married, he wore a black, polo neck sweater.

If anything, Stanley's reticence and discretion made the press more curious than ever. Newspapers relentlessly published articles full of hearsay. He had already had a taste of this while he was filming *Barry Lyndon*, and now, years later, the press hounded him again. Whenever I drove someone to see Stanley, they asked me how I could "work with a person like that."

When I took Charles Aznavour from Heathrow to Abbots Mead, the first thing he asked unashamedly was whether Stanley was "a bad person." "No, not at all," I answered, surprised at his bluntness. He was so nervous that his voice was trembling.

Nino Rota was even more anxious. As soon as I saw him, he rushed up to me and, reassured by the fact that we could speak Italian, poured it all out: "How am I going to deal with this? Help me!" He was stammering and trembling. I tried to reassure him, but it was no good. He moaned and gasped for the entire journey.

Ten years later, Matthew Modine found himself in the same predicament. He reacted in the opposite way, by not saying a single word. Stanley had told me how much he was looking forward to talking to a kind, calm person like Matthew. "He's got James Stewart's tone of voice," he said. But I didn't hear Matthew utter a single word. He was petrified.

I was also driving Candia McWilliam, the writer Stanley had called on for the adaptation of *Traumnovelle* by Arthur Schnitzler (*Dream Story*, in English). Candia did a good job of hiding her anxiety. Since she knew Italian, she tried to relax by asking me to tell her about life in the countryside around Cassino.

"How much further is it?" Matthew finally spoke when we were already halfway to Childwickbury.

"Not far now," I replied. "I'll let you know when we're nearly there."

"But honestly, what's Stanley really like?" Candia asked, giving herself away.

"See this car?" I told her. "Stanley wants me to use this Mercedes, his Mercedes, when I travel with my family, when I go away with my wife. I've always refused because my Datsun is perfectly good enough, but he insists and tries to convince me every time. You'll see for yourself soon enough that it's not at all easy to talk Stanley out of something."

"But what people say about him . . ." continued Nino, his tattered nerves having loosened his tongue.

"A load of nonsense!" I answered, watering down Andros's version of the phrase.

"But it says in the papers that—"

"And so what the papers say about you is all true then, is it?" I laughingly replied.

"Do you like working for him?"

"Yes, a lot."

"Does he ever criticize you?"

"Never. Not even once."

Once more the Mercedes was filled with silence. He's not going to bite your heads off!

In the rearview mirror Candia looked more disorientated than reassured: she clearly wasn't prepared to see the myth of this solitary tyrant suddenly debunked. I suppose it was like a knight who, ready to fight a dragon, finds himself faced with a lizard.

"How much further is it?" Matthew repeated as we turned into Harpenden Road.

"Just a few minutes now."

The countdown had begun. The nervousness increased.

"He'll ask for the impossible!" complained Aznavour.

"If he has called for you, it means that you are able to do what he is going to ask you to do," I said. It was more reassurance than contradiction.

"Not necessarily, not necessarily," they all muttered before falling silent again.

"Is Stanley's house here?" Matthew ventured, deceived by the road crossing Childwick Green.

"No, still half a mile to go."

After I'd opened the first gate with the remote control, Matthew tried again: "Is this it?"

"No, that's the Stable Block," I corrected him again, "Stanley lives down here, after the next gate." Matthew didn't say another word, nor did he move a muscle until I'd switched off the engine of the Mercedes.

Stanley always received new guests in his office, and it was my job to show them in. They always found him sitting behind his desk. Then he got up, came towards them, and held out his hand. Sometimes he even phoned me in the Mercedes to make sure that he could take up position among his papers in time. However, when visitors came again, he waited for them at the front door and showed them in himself.

"I'd rather you stayed with me during my meeting with Kubrick," Nino asked, lingering at the front door.

"I can't. It's a private meeting. Just the two of you." His eyes were begging me. "I know what we can do," I suggested. "I'll stay in the office until you nod to let me know everything's okay. I won't leave until you do that."

I noticed Candia straighten her dress nervously before following me inside.

I knocked on the door of the Dome Room and went in, introducing Matthew to Stanley. Matthew shook his hand, so did Nino, and Candia, and Monsieur Aznavour. I said to all four of them, "I'll be back in half an hour with some coffee." I'd said this to those who had come before them; I would say it to others who came after. It's what I always said. Nino turned around, and for the first time I saw a smile of relief in his little eyes. I closed the door behind me and left them alone.

None of them knew that I'd told a little lie. Only Stanley could decide when to take a break for coffee. It was always at least an hour before he called me on my pager. When I went back and opened the door again, Nino, Matthew, and Candia, like dozens of others in various rooms over the years, had that unmistakable thrilled look on their faces.

"You'll tell me on the way out!" I said to them all. And there they were: shaking Stanley's hand without the slightest inclination to take their leave of him.

"What an incredible person!" Matthew exclaimed before he had even got in the car. He started to ask me a load of questions about how I'd met him, how long I'd been working for him, and whether I was satisfied with my job. There was no stopping him talking now.

"I couldn't believe he was how you'd described him," admitted Nino. "Stanley Kubrick is exactly the opposite of how people say he is."

In the collective imagination, Stanley Kubrick was a kind of ogre. A misanthrope, who lived alone in his castle, isolated from the world. Stanley was quite the opposite: he was an altruistic man, capable of generosity without the need for recognition, an artist who valued his privacy because it allowed him to devote himself to what he cared about most of all: his family, his animals, and the cinema.

"'Congratulations on buying' . . . 'Introduction' . . . There it is: 'How to play cassettes'—do you follow me, Emilio?"

"Yes, Stanley, I'm listening."

We were lying side by side on the floor of the Pine Room in front of the instruction manual of this new, extremely complicated VHS recorder. Stanley read out the instructions full of technical terms I'd never even heard of and told me to press buttons, turn knobs, and raise or lower tiny switches.

"Perfect! It works! See?" he concluded, after having tried out all the machine's different functions.

"If you say so . . ."

Stanley was mad about mechanics and electronics. He wanted to know the secret behind every object, every production process. As the years passed, his vast collection of technological curiosities grew relentlessly. Every new gadget was welcome, especially if it claimed to increase efficiency and order at work. In the mid-seventies, he had radiotelephones installed in all the cars so he could use all that time wasted on the road to call lawyers, writers, and technicians before getting out of the car, going into the studio, and concentrating completely on the film. Having a phone in the car meant he could sort out all the organizational aspects of his work, and kept this separate from the time and space reserved for delicate, creative decisions. Stanley's brain was compartmentalized, and when technology came to his aid, he became extremely efficient.

Around about that time, pagers appeared on the scene. Stanley gave one each to me, Margaret, Andros, Jan, Christiane, Katharina, Anya, and Vivian. At last he had the means to track us down, at any time of day, wherever we were: "Whenever you take a new battery, remember to put the old one on charge." There were three batteries in all. One in use, a reserve battery (fully charged), and one at home connected to the power supply.

When satellite TV kits first became available, he had one installed in his flat so that he could tune into TV channels from all over the world, including the Italian ones. "Emilio, come up and see. I've found Rai Uno." He made me stay in his room for half an hour to translate the news for him.

Above all, Stanley watched news programs. In his flat there was always a TV tuned to CNN so that he could keep up with the latest from America. Sky TV was also very popular at Childwickbury. Sports were high on Stanley's list, too, especially American football: "Emilio! Come upstairs, there's the Super Bowl."

"I won't come up until you watch the Grand Prix!"

He rarely watched TV series or films on TV. He was more interested in the commercials, though he did sometimes go and check out his own films when he knew they were being shown. As far as all other films were concerned, he only ever watched them on the big screen: in the dark, alone or with friends. When Stanley wasn't working on a film, he would send me to rent as many as six films every weekend. That way he could catch up after his period of reclusion.

In the early eighties, personal computers were added to the list of electronic gadgets that Stanley collected. His first experience with them came just after he'd finished work on *The Shining*. But the noise they made was remarkably different from his beloved typewriters, and this dismayed him. It was only when Jan gave him the computer printout of the address book that his face lit up; the layout was perfect, the addresses and phone numbers were perfectly aligned. There were no smudges of ink and no "Xs" to cross out mistakes. It wasn't only a question of speed; the overall result was better. It was tidier, with no mistakes, and even smaller and more compact than the version Margaret had laboriously typed out manually. "It works!" said Stanley. He immediately overwhelmed Jan with questions about what tasks the computer could carry out and how he could learn to use it. Then he wanted all his friends to buy the same model. It was fundamental for Stanley to share his enthusiasms with others. The people who were closest to him all had something in common with him: curiosity about new technologies; love of art, music, and especially literature; an interest in current affairs and international politics; hobbies like photography and chess. From this point of view, I was a total disappointment. He enthusiastically told me about the latest tough game of chess played against Garry Kasparov, but I barely knew what the names of the pieces on the board were. I never went to the cinema; I never even saw his films from beginning to end. I didn't read any of the books he recommended to me. I listened to music on the radio instead of the cassettes he left for me in the car. I found conversations about politics boring and point-less. I wasn't in the least bit interested in military history; the subject actually rather irritated me. I shunned his beloved fountain pens, pre-ferring to use far cheaper ballpoints. And yet I didn't feel at all guilty. Stanley didn't love racing cars.

Despite the fact that Childwickbury was equipped with greenhouses and plots of land for growing fruit and vegetables, Stanley ate only products bought at the supermarket. There was lots of space, and any-one with even only slightly green fingers would have been delighted by it. But it wasn't for Stanley. He preferred industrial, carefully controlled products with the expiration date and the address of the factory clearly printed on the package. That way he knew who to contact if he had to lodge a complaint. The same satisfied look my father had when he picked a head of lettuce could be seen on Stanley's face when he took a can down from a supermarket shelf.

Sometimes Stanley asked me to take him to St. Albans to buy food. "Shall we take the Unimog?" he asked smiling, and off we went to awake the beast sleeping peacefully under the arch of the Stable Block. We always bought the same things: porridge, muesli, and breakfast cereal, orange and pineapple juice, Nescafé, beef sirloin, cherry jam, Coca-Cola, and hot dogs. Tons of salmon, swordfish, and other kinds of fish were added to this list when mad cow disease broke out.

When he bought a new type of food, it was almost certainly so that he could try cooking it in the microwave, the household appliance he loved most of all. Then there was frozen food: he liked to walk up and down the aisles of freezers, picking up boxes and reading the labels. He went back and forth saying, "This one's good. . . . This one isn't good." If he liked the product, the next day he had cut the label out and it was on his desk along with a note: "Buy six of these, thanks."

Before starting work on his new film, Stanley decided to lose weight. Months spent in the EMI studios without moving to other locations had made him a bit plump, so he changed his diet: more fish and vegetables, less meat and fewer desserts. The first thing he did when he got home from a day around London with me was to eat a bowl of strawberries or a couple of melons.

"Have you tried them?" he asked as he scooped out the melon with a spoon. I shook my head, and Stanley commented: "Oh, they're so lovely. How do you know they're good if you haven't tasted them?" "From the smell." "But how can you be sure?" "Stanley, are they good or aren't they?" "Yes." "Then just eat them!"

I chose cherries without tasting them either. I checked the stem to see if they were fresh. If it was green, they'd just been picked; if it was brown, they hadn't ripened on the tree. There was an enormous cherry tree in my grandfather's garden. When I was little, they let me climb up it to pick the fruit at the top. I used to sit astride the branches and put the cherries in a basket that I then lowered to the ground. My grandfather had the biggest cherry tree in the entire valley. It was so important to him that at night he kept watch over it and even slept in it.

In these comparatively quiet periods, without the constant pressures of the set, Stanley amused himself by playing around with our routine.

One day, he called me on the intercom: "Emilio, I've got some documents to send you."

"Fine, I'll come up and get them."

"No, it'll take too long. I'll throw them to you from the window. Go out into the garden under my office," and with that he switched off the intercom.

Stanley was waiting for me at the second floor window. His hands were full of sheets of paper.

"It's windy, Stanley; it won't work: the papers will get blown away," I said skeptically.

"Let's try anyway."

He dropped a sheet of paper. It started to sway here and there, carried by the wind. We silently watched it spiral downwards. When it finally reached the ground, I looked up at Stanley.

"See? It doesn't work."

"You're right. Just a second."

When he came back, as well as the papers, he had a box of colorful plastic paperclips. He folded a sheet of paper in half and fixed it with a paperclip. Then he threw it out of the window. It fell straight down and landed at my feet.

"Ah!" he exclaimed, "That's the best way of communication!"

Stanley was fond of paradox. His typical remarks wavered between the plausible and the absurd. He would comment on something in a dry, neutral tone of voice to see how you reacted. He liked to put his listeners in a difficult position, to see if they ended up really believing the unlikely things he was saying. Now I come to think of it, a lot of what he said to me in a serious tone of voice might just have been a joke. But how can you be sure? For example, when he saw me talking to one of the workers at the gas factory in Beckton, which was one of the locations for *Full Metal Jacket*, he called me over and said: "Find out who that man is."

"Why? Are you thinking of hiring him as a builder?"

"No, as an actor. He's got a look in his eyes just like Marlon Brando," he replied impassively.

Was he serious? Was he joking? Since I wasn't sure, I did what he had asked. I turned around and went back to the man. "Excuse me, I'm Emilio, Stanley Kubrick's assistant. . . . Would you by any chance be interested in acting?"

One of the paradoxical things about Stanley was that he was an untidy perfectionist. I had already noticed this at Abbots Mead where there were piles of books on the floor of his office and heaps of paper all over the place. Magazines, screenplays, production reports, newspaper cuttings, and all kinds of printouts: everything had been abandoned, left there on the floor.

What's more, Stanley did too many things at the same time and as a result, he was easily distracted. This led to an impressive list of little disasters. What went on in the kitchen was particularly spectacular. While he was waiting for dinner to cook, he would go back to his office to read or make some calls. He invariably forgot that there was a saucepan on the burner. When Vivian gave him a brand-new model of microwave oven, he wanted to unveil it by cooking some hard-boiled eggs. He'd started the microwave, and, as usual, he'd gone back to his office to work until a terrible explosion distracted him from what he was reading. "Emilio, come upstairs, it's a disaster!" When I went into his flat, I found the oven swathed in a cloud of gray smoke. Stanley was just standing

Well done, Stanley!

there, petrified. The oven door was five meters away and there were bits of egg everywhere. "I put the eggs in the microwave and it all blew up. Sorry." If he'd read the instructions, he would have found out that you can't cook eggs in their shells because they explode. This was good coming from the man who told everyone: "Don't touch anything until you've read the instructions!"

Stanley was forgetful, too. It was difficult for him to remember dates and anniversaries, and he was always losing things. I even had to keep two or three spare sets of keys to Childwickbury with me; otherwise sooner or later we would get locked out. I kept getting copies made at the hardware store in St. Albans. "But what do you do with all these keys? Do you sell them?" the shop assistant asked.

One evening, it must have been at least eleven, I'd just got home when the phone rang. "Yes, Stanley . . ." It could only have been him at that time of night.

"My wedding ring is missing," he said.

This was how he constructed sentences when he did something wrong: not, "I've lost my wedding ring," but "My wedding ring has disappeared."

"Can you come and empty out the vacuum cleaner to see if it's in there?"

"Stanley, I've only just got home. It can't be in the vacuum cleaner. I put the Hoover away around three days ago, and you've only just noticed that the ring is missing. Have you got your jacket on?"

"Yes."

He was wearing one of the military jackets from *Full Metal Jacket*. It had lots of pockets and he filled these with notes on bits of paper, notebooks, pens, recorders, and goodness knows what else.

"Put your hands in your pockets," I suggested, "and tell me what's there."

After a few seconds he said, "There are only notes."

"Have a better look. Make sure you've checked all the seams and folds in the cloth."

"I'll try that," he said and searched silently. Then he implored me, "For God's sake, don't tell Christiane!"

"Don't worry. Look for the ring."

There was a pause that seemed to last for ever. I could already see myself putting my jacket back on, getting back in the car, and going back to Stanley's house.

"Well, fuck, I got it!" he exclaimed at last. "It was in the bottom of my pocket! Thanks, Emilio. . . . Sorry I disturbed you. Good night." Then he added, "Don't tell Christiane anyway, okay?" I didn't then, nor did I when it happened again, and again, and again.

I'd been hired as a driver, but in fifteen years I'd become an electrician, plumber, vet, gardener, carpenter, and builder. Every day there was something new. I spent less and less of my life away from Stanley. At home the phone rang day and night. For some years Janette had stopped complaining, but after the move to Childwickbury she ran out of patience. "I can't stand it anymore," she said one day in an angry voice. "I start to do something and the phone rings! I stop and answer, then I go back to what I was doing and it rings again. Everyone who comes to visit me complains that the phone is always busy. Tell Stanley to stop it!" Stanley had a second phone line put in, with a phone on my bedside table. "And so that's his idea of a solution?"

Occasionally, Stanley gave me three weeks off, but he kept calling me. It was almost always about the animals. Luckily, I had organized everything beforehand. I'd hidden cans of food in every room, and I could guide him to them over the phone. Actually, I was pleased to get these calls. I felt I was helping him, that I was keeping him company even when I wasn't there.

Now that my children were old enough to stay at home on their own, I asked Janette to come with me on my occasional trips to Germany. It was a way to spend a few days quietly together. I've always had the impression that the driving seat is the best place of all to talk: the passing scenery, the sound of the engine, a little music, it's all conducive to a pleasant and intimate conversation. If the journey was particularly long, we stopped somewhere on the way. Otherwise we went straight to our hotel in the town. Now and then, we had time before we left to eat in a nice little restaurant that Janette had chosen. With just a little imagination, these trips seemed like holidays on the road, or even the secret adventures of two sweethearts.

Every time we said good-bye, Stanley smiled at me. He didn't say anything, but I knew that he meant, "Thank you." But then he was always so kind to me that I couldn't say no to him. With all his strengths and weaknesses, his eccentricity and his admirable integrity, Stanley had won my respect. I loved him. Working for him was tiring but extremely gratifying. Even when I was exhausted, I knew that he had only ever really asked for what was necessary. The mechanism of our relationship worked perfectly. We didn't even have to talk anymore. I went into the house, and I already knew what to do or where to find the instructions he'd left for me. When I wasn't sure about a solution I'd come up with, he'd interrupt me before I could explain: "Use your head. Don't bother me with details. Do what you would if the problem was yours." My job was to see to it that he didn't have to waste time. I was there to spare him the small, and sometimes not so small, burdens of life, so that every day he could quite simply be Stanley Kubrick.

9

DEMOLITION MAN:
FULL METAL JACKET

"I HAVE A LETTER from Stanley Kubrick," I said into the intercom.

"Emilio! Come on up!" replied a deep voice. I was surprised to be called by name and in such a friendly way. I was sure I had never met Michael Herr. That was the name in Stanley's handwriting on the front of the sealed envelope I was holding. "Come on, let me offer you something to drink," the voice continued, interrupting my thoughts. I turned around and glanced at the car parked in front of the terraced house in Gledhow Gardens.

"I'll be pleased to come up and give you the letter," I answered, "but I can't promise to stay."

The door opened, and I went upstairs to the second floor where a corpulent, kind-looking man offered to shake my hand. "How are you?" he asked, as he literally pulled me inside without introducing himself, as if we'd known each other for ages. He took the letter, invited me to sit down, and asked me if he could offer me something to drink.

"I'd better not stay," I answered. "I've only put an hour on the parking meter, and I've got other things to do for Stanley in the neighborhood. Besides, he's bound to call me with something else that needs sorting out."

"What? No! Sit down," said Michael, going towards the kitchen. "So, tell me a bit about yourself."

Before I could say a word, my pager started to beep. Michael was coming back with two glasses. He stopped and looked at me disappointedly. "Oh, dammit, he's really calling you."

It only took him a couple of days to appreciate how I felt. Stanley started to hound him, too.

In February 1984, when Michael was finally invited to Childwick-bury, I went to pick him up in the brand-new metallic dark-gray Mercedes 500 SEL. He jumped in beside me without even giving me time to open the rear door for him. Michael was the writer Stanley had chosen to adapt Gustav Hasford's novel *The Short-Timers*. Hasford was an ex-marine who had firsthand experience of the Vietnam War. Michael had been there, too, as a war correspondent. Stanley thought he was just the right person to work on the new film. After that first visit to Stanley's house, Michael worked at Childwickbury every day, from morning to evening for at least six months. We only ever talked during the short car journey to and from his house, but during those months we got to know each other quite well. We didn't talk shop, preferring to tell each other about our families, London, and Italy.

Stanley and Michael got on swimmingly. "How come he never gets angry?" asked Stanley. "Why doesn't he ever tell me off?" asked Michael. I'm convinced that along with Diane Johnson, Michael was the writer Stanley worked most productively with. Their meetings were prolific, and they freely exchanged ideas. They rarely disagreed and never to the point of spoiling the pleasant atmosphere, enjoyable lunches, and relaxing walks in the grounds of the house.

One day, Diane arrived with Michael and Alexander Walker, and I met Gustav Hasford, the author of the book that *Full Metal Jacket* was based on. Stanley liked to organize group gatherings at the start of a new project. He invited all the people involved to the Dome Room for a series of meetings

The M-16 rifle that Matthew Modine used in Full Metal Jacket.

where they could express their opinions and comment on the each other's ideas. About every two weeks, they arranged to be free at the same time, and I went to pick everyone up in the Volkswagen minibus. They were rather like students on the school bus on their way to be tested by the strictest teacher of all.

Stanley wanted Margaret to work with him on the production of *Full Metal Jacket*, especially after seeing how disorganized the Stable Block offices were without her.

After leaving the Lodge, Margaret had worked for other production companies and had managed to get from them what she couldn't get from Stanley. She had also found time to get married to one of the cooks from the catering service. Even though we hadn't seen each other for a couple of years, we spoke on the phone every Saturday morning. She told me how things were going on the set, but most of all she asked about Stanley. And Stanley always asked about her: "When did you last speak to Margaret?" he began, and each time he asked for more details about the other directors' productions she was working on.

When Margaret arrived at the Stable Block and I showed her the production offices, her face lit up. All of a sudden, Stanley popped around the corner. "How nice to see you back together," he said, and put his hands on our shoulders. We were all a little bit tearful. All that's missing now is Andros, I thought; but he hadn't yet finished his time off from Stanley's world.

Margaret moved into one of the rooms on the first floor of the central building of the Stable Block. She sat at her desk, opened and closed a datebook, glanced at the phones, the fax, the photocopier, and smiled at the mountain of notepads and registers in front of her; then she took a deep breath and said, "Right. Let's get started again."

Stanley already had the preparatory work for the film well under way. Though not quite like *Barry Lyndon*, *Full Metal Jacket* was still a historical film. It was necessary to reconstruct a distant time and place: Vietnam in the sixties. With the help of historians and members of the armed forces, he had learned about the technical aspects of combat, the vehicles used during the conflict, and the weapons and ammunition that the marines and Vietnamese guerrillas had at their disposal. He had requested thousands of photographs taken by war correspondents at the time, as well as other pictures of Vietnamese towns, the countryside, and forests.

The most important decision of all was to shoot the film without leaving home. If Ken Adam had been there, he would have laughed hard and breathed a sigh of relief at not having to struggle again with Stanley's stubbornness. There wasn't even a second unit for outdoor shots in Asia. Stanley had seen on TV that the industrial area of Beckton was going to be demolished, and he immediately thought that it would make the perfect location: the industrial architecture of the forties was similar to the buildings he had seen in photos of Vietnam. In addition, he was enthusiastic about the idea of destroying the buildings as if bombs really had hit them. He made a few calls, got in touch with the owners of the factories, and arranged to rent the entire area. Then he sent Martin Hunter and me to photograph every inch of the place.

Martin, a photographer, had rescued me at Childwickbury. Without Andros, and faced with thousands of problems to solve, I desperately needed help. One morning, Martin roared up in front of the Stable Block on his motorbike. He took off his helmet, said hello to me, and went into the offices. We had just been evicted from EMI Films. I remember seeing that shy expression on his face in the sound editing room. If I remember well, we might have spent a few evenings together packing up the props to be loaded into the vans.

"Sorry, could you remind me of your name?"

"Martin Hunter. I'm Wyn Ryder the sound technician's assistant. I've got something from him to give to the editors."

"Have you got anything planned for when work on *The Shining* is finished?"

Martin looked at me a bit surprised. "Don't know . . . I'll go on working with Wyn, I suppose."

"What do you do, exactly?"

"Well, a bit of everything. I work with sound, but I know how to use editing machines, too."

"No, I meant apart from film. I saw you at EMI while you were moving furniture, and I asked myself—"

"I can cut wood, paint, I'm a bricklayer, stuff like that," said Martin, shrugging his shoulders.

"You might be just the person I need."

With Martin's help, we finished restructuring the Stable Block. We repainted all the walls and even built some walls with a bit of cement and a few stones. Martin was so good at this that I asked him how he'd ended up as a sound engineer instead of a builder. I liked working with him so much that I often invited him for Sunday lunch at Farm Road. Jon was fascinated by his motorbike and kept on asking Martin to take him for a ride. I was pleased to see that all the mechanical parts of the bike were clean as a whistle.

Stanley had also noticed how thorough Martin was, and had entrusted him with the maintenance of his Zeiss projectors and all the camera lenses. Gradually, Martin became to me what I used to be to Andros.

Like Andros, Martin had his personal mantra, but instead of "Fuck!" he said, "*Con calma,*" in Italian. He had picked this up during the frenzied mixing of *The Shining* from Wyn Ryder, who had learned it from Dino De Laurentiis a couple of years earlier.

So it was "*con calma*" that we went on our way to Beckton with Stanley's instructions still ringing in our ears: "Whatever you need, take it. Just bring back some good work." We soon discovered what we needed: two heavier coats. The area around the factory was freezing. It was far colder than Childwickbury, probably because it was outside town and near a hook in the river Thames. The partially demolished buildings were exposed to the wind, which whistled through the cracks and holes in the cement, and the ground was covered with frozen snow that cracked under the weight of our boots. After five minutes, Martin's fingers were so numb that he couldn't adjust the focus of the camera. Our ears and noses were starting to

Martin took this photo while we were inspecting Beckton during the winter of 1983–84. I was using this abandoned wreck in the factory to make fun of his passion for motorcycles.

freeze too, so we took refuge in the van and tried to warm up a bit. While we were silently eating our sandwiches, we thought about what we needed to buy to get the job done. During the following days at Beckton, we wore heavy, padded jackets with fur-lined hoods, woolen gloves, scarves, and hats. Wrapped up like that, we looked like two fat Eskimos.

The wind whipped up the toxic, foul-smelling detritus from the old factory. The sulfurous dust stuck to our clothes and made our eyes water. Stanley had told us to be careful. He insisted that we wear white overalls under our jackets and that for no reason were we to remove our protective masks. However, the foul, chemical stink that rose from the ground was the only warning we needed.

For nearly a month we went to Beckton every morning, loaded with camera film, sandwiches, and padded jackets. Sometimes there were a couple of days of sunshine, the snow started to melt, and the temperature became more bearable. Then, other times, we stayed at home for a day because of the wind and rain, torn between the relief of not having to go to Beckton and worrying about the severe conditions we would find there. In fact, when we returned the next day, the temperature was so low that we couldn't stay outside for more than an hour and had to take refuge in the nearby café.

Martin had to photograph absolutely everything, from buildings to walls, from the off-white rocks to bars of rusting metal that protruded from the ground. He told me where to stand in the picture while I held a two-meter ruler, which was to make it possible to calculate the heights of the buildings from the photos. He took pictures of the surrounding area too, so that Stanley could see what was beyond it as well as the modern buildings in the outskirts of London that appeared on the horizon here and there. I walked from one building to another, trailing a tape measure behind me to measure the distances. Then I shouted these to Martin, and he wrote them down in a notebook. He had to draw the entire ground plan of the site because Stanley hadn't managed to get one from the company.

When Stanley went to inspect the factory for the first time, he wanted to protect himself from the toxic dust, but he refused to wear one of the white suits we'd been using because they didn't have any pockets. So he turned up dressed as usual in his thick dark quilted jacket to keep out the cold and looked at me questioningly, expecting me to find a way to solve the problem of the dust. I cut up two trash bags, wrapped them around his legs, and fixed them in place with adhesive tape.

The bulldozers from the demolition firm had stopped work and were waiting for instructions from Stanley as to exactly what to demolish. Three brick towers that dominated the skyline at one end of the factory had been condemned. They were the smokestacks of the blast furnaces. The demolition squad had placed small charges of dynamite at the base. Stanley looked on baffled as they prepared the wires and detonators. "Are we sure they won't fall sideways?" he said, saying what we were all thinking. "Emilio," he whispered, "where did you park the Mercedes?"

The set at Beckton during demolition and reconstruction. Harrier Production *on the Jeeps was the name Stanley chose for the production company of the film.*

"Ready when you are, mister," said the head of the demolition squad to Stanley, who after a moment's hesitation gave his okay. We heard a small bang, followed by the crackle of small explosions, then for a moment, everything stood still. Next, the top of one of the towers started to collapse; the others followed a few seconds later. They fell vertically, as if somebody had suddenly dug an enormous hole beneath them and the earth had silently swallowed them up. "Amazing!" exclaimed Stanley, as the dust started to clear.

From then on, the set design department took control. The demolition squad used the bulldozers and wrecking ball to move the rubble and demolish parts of the buildings that were still standing. They used small explosive charges to simulate bullet holes in some of the walls. The photos that Martin had taken of the façades of the buildings clearly showed the positions of the doors and windows. They were used to plan the transformation of Beckton into an Asiatic town. The set designer covered the photos with transparent tape so that he could use black and white pencils to draw in the shapes and decorations for each building. Photographs were much better than sketches: it was quicker, more immediate and accurate. It was a brilliant solution.

For weeks on end, the workmen constructed the set, paradoxically by demolishing it. What with the dust from the factory and the dust from the demolition work, the air had become so unbreathable that Stanley decided to leave the Mercedes at home for fear of contaminating it. So we used the ORV to go to Beckton, and we still left it a long way from the entrance gates. Stanley had rented a Land Rover to get around inside the area, and we left it there when we weren't using it.

In true Kubrick style, a disused warehouse had been chosen for the set of the Marine Corps base. The warehouse was in Brimsdown, the industrial zone in Enfield about sixteen miles south west of Child-wickbury. Another location, this time for the outdoor training scenes, had been found in Epping Forest, less than half an hour's drive east. Nevertheless, most of the outdoor scenes set in the Parris Island camp were filmed at Bassingbourn, a real military base in Royston, half an hour to the north of Childwickbury. It was a vast area with a number of small buildings and tree-lined avenues. The security check was a problem: Stanley wasn't at all happy to let the guards rummage around in the Mercedes or ask him questions about what he had in his pockets, so he asked Margaret to contact the person in charge at the base to see if it was possible to simplify the procedure. Thanks to a case of whis-key delivered direct to the commanding officer's house, it then became enough to show a pass from the car window to get into the base.

Stanley was always happy to see how work was going at Bassing-bourn. He adored military history and found even just walking around the barracks gratifying. "Look over there," he said once, pointing at one of the buildings and reading the writing outside. "It says 'Cassino'!" I exclaimed. "The barracks have all been named after famous battles from the Second World War," he explained with a smile.

A few weeks later, after one of our pre-shooting reconnaissance trips, Stanley showed his pass to the soldier at the gate and said, "We're going to keep this." The soldier tried to object: "That's not possible, sir. That's a numbered pass and has to be returned to the base on leaving. We can't have a number missing." "Emilio," said Stanley, looking away from the soldier, "call Margaret and see if she can't come up with another case of whiskey."

The clock tower, a large space on the first floor of the south side of Childwickbury, was chosen as the nerve center of the operation. It was equipped with all kinds of chairs and tables, a huge, brand-new word processor, a stereo with turntable and tape deck, a photocopier, and a TV with video recorder. The walls were covered with blackboards and cork panels, each at least two meters square. Christiane simply hadn't been quick enough to stop Stanley Kubrick the producer from sneaking through the back door and setting everything up at home.

The marines' training scenes and the mission in Vietnam in *Full Metal Jacket* called for a large number of supporting actors. Stanley adopted a practical approach to the problem. In February 1984 he started to advertise on the leading radio stations and in the most important daily papers in America. The ad asked prospective actors to send a video demo to the producer care of Warner Bros., London. This time, the actors would reach Stanley directly by airmail.

Filming started in Beckton at the end of August 1985. Two years had already passed since preparations began, and filming was already six months late. Work on the set usually started at nine in the morning. Stanley had had three Winnebagos taken to the set. These huge, long, rectangular motor homes were fully furnished and had a bathroom and kitchen. One was Stanley's office, another was for Matthew Modine and the other leading actors, while the third was for the remaining members of the cast. The secretaries and the production offices used caravans. There were also a number of buses with the seats taken out. These served as wardrobes and changing rooms. This system turned out to be very convenient. We could move the production unit quickly from one location to another without having to set up a base in a building. If we'd had these facilities during the filming of *Barry Lyndon*, we would have saved ourselves a lot of trouble in Ireland and the South of England. Stanley was constantly improving.

Every morning, half an hour before the actors were called, I took him to the set. He went into his Winnebago, made himself some coffee, and had a look at the day's schedule: which scenes he was going to film, which actors had been called, what equipment needed to be ready. He stayed holed up in there for a while, trying to concentrate. Sometimes he gave me letters to deliver to his assistants, and while I was walking around the set, I would hear the assistant director receive a call on his walkie-talkie: "Is everything ready? Are the cameras all in place? Is the cameraman in position?" Only when he had received three positive replies did Stanley open the door of his Winnebago and head towards the set.

When Stanley first introduced me to the guys he'd chosen from the videotapes, he was rather brusque. There were more than seventy of them, and they were all about twenty years old. He told me to not to get too friendly with them because he was afraid of news about the film leaking out. However, some weeks later he seemed more relaxed. One evening, while I was driving him home, he commented with satisfaction: "They're not professional actors, mind you . . . I didn't expect them to be so attentive or to act with such precision. They really are a bunch of good guys."

In the morning I would find them sitting on the ground under the pagoda, waiting for the director to arrive. "Good morning!" they said, and waved. "How's the governor today? Is he in a good mood?" I nodded and went back to Stanley's motor home to tell him what I'd seen.

"Are they all there?" he asked. "Are they happy?"

"They're all smiling."

And Stanley smiled, too: "Okay, today we're gonna do it right."

Two sad things happened in Stanley's life during the filming of *Full Metal Jacket.* At the end of April 1985, his mother Gertie died at the age of eighty-two. Stanley's sister, Barbara, went to the funeral in New York, and so did Vivian, who flew out to say good-bye to her grandmother.

Stanley decided not to go. Partly because he was worried about the flight, but also because he preferred not to appear in public and risk being pestered by photographers during his mother's funeral.

A few years earlier, I had taken Stanley to Peter Sellers's funeral at Golders Green Crematorium in London, and I noticed how only a few of the people there behaved appropriately for the occasion. Stanley and I had stayed in the background to avoid the photographers.

Around about the same time, Stanley's father Jack became seriously ill. Stanley asked him to come to England so they could spend some time together, and we prepared Anya's room for him. During the weeks he stayed, I never left Childwickbury. When Jack decided to go back to California, father and son embraced each other for a long time. As Jack got in the car, Stanley said to me, "Give him another kiss from me when you say good-bye at the terminal, and don't, I repeat don't, leave the airport until the plane door is closed and they have taken off. Actually, would you like to take a camera with you so you can take some photos?"

Emilio,
My father has arrived home, he's well. Everyone is grateful to you for what you did. Thank you on behalf of my father and again from me.

S

Not long afterwards, Jack's health worsened dramatically and he passed away in October at the age of eighty-three. Stanley decided to do the same thing he had done a few months earlier when his mother had died, and sent Vivian to the funeral.

Needless to say, the fact that Stanley hadn't gone to either of the funerals caused something of a scandal. The press wrote that Kubrick had preferred to keep working on his film rather than go to his parents' funerals. All I know is that Stanley stayed in his apartment for two days and told me that he was not to be disturbed for any reason whatsoever. Mourning was an extremely private matter for him. When he finally came downstairs, I looked at him but couldn't say a word. He put a hand on my shoulder and nodded.

That night I dreamed of Jack Kubrick. I met him as he was slowly coming up the large staircase in Childwickbury. He looked smart in the dark trousers and pullover he often wore, and he had a peaceful expression on his face. He turned towards me and said with a radiant smile, "Tell Stanley that I'm just fine now, and that I'm happy here. Promise me you'll tell him that." As soon as I said yes, Jack continued going up the stairs. I moved towards him to take a closer look, but he was gone. When I saw Stanley, I didn't tell him anything. I didn't want to upset him, but a couple of days later, Jack came back to see me again. This time he was leaning over the banister. "Emilio, tell my son that I'm okay. Otherwise, he'll worry. Write this message on that notepad you always keep in your shirt pocket, that way you won't forget." "I don't need to, Jack. I'll remember," I told him. He smiled, moved away from the bannister and disappeared. The next day, when I saw Stanley, I decided to tell him. "Stanley, something has happened," and I told him about my dream. "I didn't want to upset you, but I've dreamed of him twice now, and I can't keep it to myself anymore." "I'm moved, Emilio," said Stanley when I had finished telling him about it. "Thanks for letting me know."

When filming at Beckton was over, work started on the first part of the movie: the training of the recruits at Parris Island military base. The first thing the actors had to do was have a buzz cut. In disciplined silence, Stanley's soldiers lined up for the barber in the warehouse at Brimsdown. The cameras filmed their dismayed expressions. To get the quick, radical haircut that Stanley wanted, the barber used the electric razor that Stanley had asked me to buy to trim the dogs' fur instead of using scissors. It had been left untouched in a drawer for months because we thought it seemed too powerful and dangerous, but for the recruits it turned out to be just perfect.

The sergeant whose job it was to transform these average American guys into marines was Lee Ermey. Lee was a retired soldier who had been in Vietnam during the war, and Stanley had hired him as a consultant. One of the first things Lee had to do was teach the right posture to the actor who was going to play the sergeant in the film. It gradually became clear that Lee was actually the right man for the part. Why teach someone to play the part of a drill instructor when you have a real drill instructor at your disposal?

Lee did an audition, learned his lines, put on a costume and was stood in front of a soldier to see what he was capable of. When Stanley said, "Action!" an endless stream of orders and vulgarities poured forth from Lee's mouth. Lee exploded. He seemed to want to bite the head off the man he had in front of him. It was all so real. And frightening. Suddenly I was looking at the sergeant I had met during my five days in a barracks in Rome when I was eighteen. He had yelled his head off, too. We had to stand up straight in line. He made us march up and down all day. After letting us sleep for four hours, he came back and made us do push-ups in the freezing cold. He didn't let us stop until we were racked with pain, and even then he made us stand there holding our rifles and staring into space, trembling with cold until dawn broke. It was hell, and it went on for days. I had joined up as a volunteer, choosing to train as a mechanic so that I wouldn't have to handle weapons. I was terrified of guns after what I experienced as a child in Cassino. The ads I'd seen made the army sound like a civilian or military training school, but it wasn't true. I requested leave to go and visit a relative and ran away from the barracks and from Italy.

Lee had finished. The seemingly endless stream of insults had dried up. We were all astounded, especially the actor playing the soldier who had been on the receiving end. Lee looked at us as if he were expecting a round of applause. Once I had got over the initial shock, I saw that there was something ridiculously surreal about Lee's performance, but it still made me uneasy. "Perfect! Let's start shooting; no need to waste time," said Stanley.

When I met Lee in the morning, he always seemed to be in a good mood.

"You're looking good, today," I said.

"Ah! This is the life!"

He really was having a great time. It was fascinating to see how kind and helpful he was when he stepped out of his role. On and off: on the set he yelled obscenities; off it he was a peaceful person who never used bad or offensive language. Sometimes he improvised and used expressions that were far more indecent than the ones Stanley had written with Michael Herr. They were unrepeatable, and Stanley went into raptures about it.

Shooting the training scenes wasn't any easier than the filming at Beckton had been. For weeks on end we were at the same place in the screenplay: endless marching and exhausting obstacle course sessions at dawn. Despite all this, I'd never seen Stanley so happy on his way home from the set. During the other films, it had always been up to me to ask him how things were going. This time he told me all about it as soon as he saw me. And he kept on praising his soldiers: "What do you think of these boys?" he asked, and then added without giving me time to answer: "They seem kind and nice, and hard workers."

Nothing could dampen his enthusiasm for *Full Metal Jacket*. He kept on calling me to enthuse about it while I was trying to deal with millions of things at the same time. At the end of every day, when I was just about to go home, I got yet another call about yet another job to start on. "Can't we do it tomorrow, Stanley?" I begged him, and wondered if there was anything or anyone in the world capable of tiring him out.

As usual, we were running well behind schedule, but everyone had accepted the fact that *Full Metal Jacket* would go ahead regardless of what happened. All we could do was go with the "flow" and do our best to get to the end of the project, and in the end we did: in autumn 1986. We'd been filming for over eleven months. *The Shining* had taken ten. Every time, Stanley managed to beat his own record.

When the set was dismantled, Stanley's animals were treated to a new dinner service: he kept all the marines' metal mess tins to use as bowls. Even after the spades and flashlights had been shared out among all the technicians who had worked on the film, there were still plenty left, so we took them to Childwickbury for the gardeners to use. All the military vehicles had been rented, so these were simply returned.

The film's main legacy was a significant number of green jackets with lots of pockets. These ended up in Stanley's wardrobe. He used them all the time. He kept twelve: six green ones and six that had been dyed dark blue. He gave me a couple, so that I would have somewhere to keep my planner and all the notepads I gradually received from him.

When all the takes had been developed and catalogued by Martin, it was time to start editing the film. Stanley had been impressed by some of the music that Vivian had written, and he decided to entrust her with the soundtrack without even taking other composers into consideration.

Vivian had been a constant presence on the set. With her father's blessing, she had started to make another backstage documentary, but her passion for music had drawn her away from the cameras. She spent all her time with her synthesizer. Like her father, she loved to collect technological devices.

Vivian recorded the tracks at the De Lane Music Center in the studios in Wembley right next to the old football stadium. The area was quiet and practically deserted: just right for the job. The only noise that could be heard through the soundproofed walls was the roar of the jets that took off and landed at Heathrow Airport. Fortunately, there were hardly any flights after midnight, so it was enough to postpone the start of the recording session until ten in the evening. The only people around at that time were the night security guards, firemen stationed at the facility, and the odd technician.

"How's it going at the studio, Viv?" asked Stanley.

"Just fine. It's a great way to work: alone, at night."

"Alone?" he asked, apprehensively.

"Yes, there's nobody there. Just the occasional technician now and then."

"Emilio, what are you doing?" asked Stanley's voice on the phone, after midnight.

"What do you think I'm doing? Sleeping."

"Go and sleep at Wembley, at Vivian's."

When I got to the recording studio, I found Vivian and her pestiferous hound, Fanny. Stanley must have thought that one guard dog wasn't enough. There was a sofa-bed made up in the next room, so I lay down and continued sleeping. I slept there for two weeks while Vivian recorded the soundtrack.

"Why does Daddy make you do that?" she asked. She was clearly confused and sorry for me.

"Vivian, there's nothing you can do. Actually, if you do want to help, try to finish recording as soon as you can."

The many battles that constituted *Full Metal Jacket* weren't over yet. Shortly before the film was released worldwide in December 1986, and just as Stanley was preparing to launch his advertising campaign, Oliver Stone premiered *Platoon*, a film about the exploits of a group of American soldiers in Vietnam. Stanley knew that other films were being made about the subject, but he hadn't expected there to be problems of timing.

A few weeks earlier, there had been a meeting in the Stable Block. Jan was there, and so was Phil Hobbs, Katharina's husband and co-producer of the film. After they had watched a preview copy of *Platoon* that Julian had managed to get hold of, there was very awkward meeting. Stanley tried to stay calm, but he was clearly very worried. For a couple of days he was unable to decide what to do. Some of the helicopter flight sequences in Stone's film were terribly similar to Stanley's. The best thing to do was to wait, let *Platoon* come out, give it time to find an audience, and then release *Full Metal Jacket* some months later. Otherwise: "What are we doing, a fucking sequel?"

At the end of June 1987, after a further period of editing, *Full Metal Jacket* finally made it to the projection room. In the meantime, at the beginning of May, Francis Ford Coppola had released a film about Vietnam, too: *Gardens of Stone*. Stanley's film found itself surrounded by competitors who were all contending for the same territory. At the end of the summer, yet another film appeared: *Hamburger Hill* by John Irwin. In less than a year, four films about the Vietnam conflict had been released. Evidently, Stanley had had the right idea at the right time. In the mid-eighties, the public was ready for a film about America's war in Asia, but seen from a different, more detached perspective compared to the films about the conflict made in the mid- to late seventies. He had perfectly understood the collective feeling of the time, but he hadn't arrived first, even though he had been the first to start work. His dedication and perfectionism had meant taking more time than he had planned to finish the film, and there was no doubt that *Full Metal Jacket* had suffered at the box office because of the competition. Nevertheless, I don't think he would have changed even the slightest thing about the movie.

A week before *Full Metal Jacket* was released, Stanley went to Pinewood for a series of interviews to promote the film. I was just about to leave for Italy on holiday, so I had explained to him how to get to the studios. When I came back, one of the sound engineers who worked there called me and said with a laugh, "Have you heard what Stanley did? He reversed his Porsche into the wall behind his private parking space. He destroyed everything, even the sign with his name on it!" He couldn't be left on his own, not even for a moment.

10

TOUGH DECISIONS

JON WAS WAITING FOR the bus in front of the garden at Waitrose in Brent Cross, where he worked in the warehouse. It was a freezing cold evening at the beginning of February, and he paced up and down beneath the dim streetlights in an attempt to keep warm. The sound of an engine coming in his direction made him look up. Then he saw two headlights coming towards him.

After his kart-racing debut, Jon had continued racing. He always managed to start at the front of the grid and was among the first to pass the finish line. Like me at the beginning of my career, he opted for a fast but safe style that pays off in the long run. Year after year, he continued to be among the first in the driver rankings and had an excellent racing record with no accidents or infractions, which would have been a perfect introduction to the next categories. He became more and more interested in mechanics and decided to study aeronautical engineering the Hendon College of Engineering and joined the 20th squadron of the Air Training Corps, a group of Royal Air Force cadets. I liked to think that my past as a driver and apprentice mechanic had influenced his decision. Jon had met a girl at college, too. Her name was Sally-Anne Salter and she was studying to be a secretary. She was very pretty, and Jon seemed to be really in love with her.

It would soon be his nineteenth birthday, and I knew exactly what to give him: I had called Brian Jones and booked a single-seater car for him in the first Formula Ford race at Brands Hatch in March. Nineteen was just the right age: he would have had plenty of time to practice, race, and become a champion.

"Why hasn't he arrived yet?" asked Janette, clearing away after dinner.

"He went by bus. The Mini's at the mechanic," I answered distractedly.

"Yes, but even so, it's late."

The doorbell rang. Janette went to open the door and found herself face to face with a policeman in uniform. He took off his hat and hesitated for a second before speaking.

"Good evening, madam. Are you Jon-Pierre D'Alessandro's mother?"

"Yes, but . . . what's happened?"

"I'm afraid your son has been involved in an accident, madam."

"No . . . that's not possible," said my wife, refusing to believe it. "Jon . . . Jon went by bus today."

The officer explained that a car had hit Jon while he was waiting at the bus stop. "You'd better go straight to the hospital," he added, "your son has been seriously injured."

When we arrived at the accident and emergency department of Edgware General Hospital, there were policemen everywhere. One of them took us by the arm and led us to a small room with white walls and nothing inside except four white wooden chairs. He showed us in and closed the door. There was no ceiling. The room was nothing more than panels used to close off part of the larger area, which hummed with the presence of dozens of people. Another policeman came in and asked us to sit down. "Your son has been taken to the radiology department," he told us. "What happened?" asked Janette, terrified. But the policeman shook his head and said that we would have to wait for one of the nurses. We stayed closed in the room for several, long minutes. I was standing; Janette was sitting down. We stared into space unable to utter a word.

Then the door opened and in came a nurse. She sat next to my wife and said, after a hesitation, "Madam, your son is in a coma." The word seemed incomprehensible and was left suspended midair. We looked at the nurse with tears in our eyes. The nurse put a hand on Janette's shoulder, then stood up and turned towards the door. "But what happened!" yelled my wife, no longer able to control herself. "I'm not in a position to say," replied the nurse. "As soon as one of the doctors has finished examining your son, he'll explain everything to you." And we were alone again.

Another policeman showed Marisa into the room. She ran forward, hugged us, and we all cried for a long time. The white walls of that cubicle were all we had. There was nothing to look at, nothing to cling to.

The nurse came back in and showed us to the emergency room, where at last we saw Jon. His legs were tightly wrapped in wide, white bandages with small, dark red bloodstains here and there. His neck was immobilized by an orthopedic collar. There were other bandages around his head, and two tubes came out of his nostrils. "What happened?" repeated Janette, without taking her eyes off Jon. Neither Marisa nor I managed to say a word. The nurse said that Jon had sustained a traumatic brain injury and that there was a problem with his legs. However, she couldn't be more specific until the surgeons had examined him.

We were taken back to the white room, where we asked ourselves what kind of operation Jon would have to have. Another nurse came in: "Are you Anglicans?" she asked. "No, Catholics," I answered distractedly. The nurse paused for a moment, took a deep breath, and said that if we wanted, we could call the hospital priest, who would administer the last rites to Jon. It took me a few seconds to grasp the meaning of those words. I looked at Janette. She was staring passively at the nurse. "Yes, all right," I replied, and I heard Marisa start sobbing again.

Later the charge nurse came in and asked us to sit on the wooden chairs again. The surgical team had arrived: Doctor Fox, the vascular surgeon, was going to try and solve the most urgent problems. "They need to try and reduce the hemorrhaging," said the charge nurse, "but it's not easy. We haven't managed to do it yet. Only when we do, can Doctor Angel, the orthopedic surgeon, operate to reconstruct the

thighbone." The nurse suggested that we go home and rest. The operation would take a long time, and we weren't allowed to stay in the
hospital overnight. When the three of us left the room, the accident
and emergency department was completely empty. The lights had been
dimmed, and in the shadows, the gray of the deserted corridor seemed
even more subdued. The charge nurse took us to the exit and closed
the door after we left.

It was eleven thirty. The streetlights lit the few cars left in the
parking lot. They seem blurred by the humidity of the night air. For
a moment, we stood between the hospital entrance and our Datsun
without knowing what to do. Nothing seemed to make sense. The
thighbone, the charge nurse had said. They had to reconstruct the
bone in his leg. My son's legs: the legs he had used to walk and run and
dash upstairs to his room. He had wrapped them around my neck as
he sat on my shoulders near the starting line at Brands Hatch. He used
them to drive his kart, the most important thing in his life, his future,
the dream we both shared.

I don't remember exactly how we got through the night. At six
in the morning I called Stanley and woke him up. "I can't come to
work this morning. It's my son Jon . . . my son Jon . . ." I tried to tell
him, but I couldn't. Stanley listened to me sobbing on the phone,
tried to comfort me and asked me to keep him constantly informed.
The charge nurse had said, "Call this number tomorrow morning at
eight thirty." So as soon as the first rays of sunlight came through the
windows, we got ready to call the hospital. The nurse who answered
told my wife that Jon had just come out of the operating theater.
The operation had taken all night. We wanted to go straight there,
but they advised us to stay at home. Jon was in the ICU and nobody
would be allowed to see him.

Waiting now was even worse than it had been during the night.
At least then we had our hopes to cling to, our faith in the skill of the
surgeons. But now there was nothing. Our minds were empty, vulnerable, overwhelmed with despair. We arrived at the hospital at midday
completely exhausted. I parked the Datsun, and as I got out and closed

the door, I suddenly felt the oppressive weight of the place, so much so that I found it hard to make my way to the entrance.

Janette insisted on being told about the accident, so one of the policemen in the corridor agreed to explain exactly what had happened. While Jon was waiting at the bus stop opposite Waitrose, a car accelerated towards him and ran over him. The impact was so violent that Jon was thrown into the garden of a nearby house. The car crashed into the house itself. One of Jon's classmates was driving. He knew how much Jon loved motor sports, so when he saw Jon at the bus stop, he thought it would be fun to drive straight at him and then brake suddenly, a bit like a pit stop during a race, but he lost control of the car. Jon was fighting for his life because of some stupid joke. When the policeman finished telling us all this, I was feeling physically sick. Janette reached to steady herself against the wall and slid down onto a chair in the corridor.

A few minutes later, one of the doctors came out of the theater. It was Doctor Fogg. He was the assistant to the surgeon, Doctor Angel. Doctor Fogg looked straight into our eyes as he explained what had happened during the night. His face was tired, but his voice was calm and reassuring. The impact had been so violent that the car had destroyed the bones in Jon's left leg; his right leg had been damaged too, but to a lesser extent. Jon's left thighbone had been shattered and had severed an artery, causing what seemed to be an uncontrollable hemorrhage. Fortunately, the ambulance crew managed to reduce the bleeding by applying emergency tourniquets to Jon's legs. Otherwise he would never have arrived in hospital alive. I realized that this was the first time someone here had called our son by name. When Doctor Fogg saw that Marisa had put her hands in front of her face, he started talking again in an attempt to distract us and stop us from imagining the worst. "During the night, Doctor Fox reconstructed Jon's severed artery. He managed to stop the bleeding . . . but the prognosis is uncertain. He's keeping Jon under constant observation. He lost a lot of blood last night. To be honest, I don't know how on earth he survived: we gave him fifty-five bags of blood before we managed to stop the hemorrhaging." He said that number slowly. "When his condition was a bit more stable, around dawn, Doctor Angel and I tried to take care of his legs. We managed to reconstruct his right thighbone and knee; it was an extremely complicated operation."

Doctor Fogg stopped talking, but I had the impression that there was more to be said. He kept looking at me, Janette, and Marisa in turn. Then he looked down at the floor and said: "The left leg is very badly damaged. We couldn't . . ." He hesitated, as if he were looking for the right choice of words. "We couldn't solve the problem, and there is a chance that it might be necessary to amputate the limb." I felt as if an old rusty knife had been driven right through me. Doctor Fogg broke the silence by explaining that the impact with the bus shelter, the asphalt, and the hedge had lacerated Jon's skin and muscles so badly that there was a serious risk of infection. "If his condition doesn't improve soon," he finally said in a low voice, "the only way to save him will be by amputating his leg." Marisa and Janette were speechless. Their faces were pallid, and tears trickled down their cheeks. I felt as if I were underwater. There was a strange buzzing in my ears.

"Jon's a racing driver," I suddenly said out loud, clinging on to a feeble hope. "Can't you do something so that he can keep on racing?" Up until that moment I'd been trying not to think about the single-seater I had booked for my son. It was just sitting there, abandoned in the pits at Brands Hatch, with nobody able to drive it, nobody to put his foot on that damned pedal. "Don't you understand?" I said, raising my voice. "Jon was supposed to make his debut in Formula Ford in less than a month! Can't you do something? Can't any of you do something? Anything!" The doctor put a hand on my shoulder and allowed me to let it all out. I cried all the tears I'd been holding back until then. When I calmed down, I felt totally lifeless: a sad corpse abandoned on a wooden chair in the unreal silence of a hospital corridor.

That afternoon they let us see Jon again. The nurses had picked the glass out of his hair and tended to the wounds on his face and arms. There was a metal pin in his right knee to keep his thighbone in traction. His left leg was still covered with bandages, so it was impossible to see what, if anything, the doctors had done to it. I looked back at my son's knee. I couldn't bear the sight of that metal pin; I closed my eyes and left the room.

When we got home, we phoned a few close relatives; his girlfriend, Sally; and Stanley. Having to go through explaining what had happened, even briefly, destroyed me all over again. By actually saying it, I made it real. It was hideous. I don't remember anything anyone said to me on the phone, and after all the calls were finished I was exhausted. The most difficult thing was calling Brian Jones to tell him to cancel the booking I'd made in Jon's name. There would be no debut in Formula Ford. It was going to be a surprise, and I'd done a good job of keeping it a secret. Now all that effort, care, and attention had been useless.

I decided to go out. I took the car and started driving aimlessly. I went through Edgware, Mill Hill, Stanmore, and Kingsbury. I ended up in front of the Brent Cross shopping center. I parked the car some distance away and walked to the bus stop behind the Waitrose garden. The bus shelter was destroyed. It looked as if had imploded; there were shards of broken glass all over the road. The car was still in the garden next door, cordoned off by police barriers. All that was left of the desperate attempt to brake was a couple of black skid marks on the road. He must have been going incredibly fast.

When we went back to the hospital that evening, the charge nurse told us that Jon had been rushed back to the operating theater. The blood in his left leg was not circulating and his foot was turning blue. Doctor Fox had tried to improve things by lowering Jon's blood pressure. It was a relatively short operation, but Jon's leg was in such a bad state that his blood was not flowing properly, and worse still, an infection was stopping the transplanted veins from working. For the second time we heard that horrible word that the doctor insisted on referring to as a solution and I interpreted as the end of everything.

Janette told the doctor that she would never be able to make such a decision for Jon. Doctor Angel tried to get us to understand that the more time passed, the worse the risk would become that the infection would spread to the other leg, but my wife insisted: "I know Jon. I can't do this to him, I just can't." Doctor Angel nodded and took us to the ICU. When we went in, all the other patients fell silent. Janette went to Jon and stroked his hair and forehead. I couldn't even manage to look him in the face.

The nurses advised us to talk to him constantly, so that he could feel that we were there. Janette sat down beside him and started to tell him all about our house, about Ginger and Rosie, about the Mini being at the mechanic, about college and Sally. She talked about absolutely everything and nothing in particular. She was strong and determined in a way that I never could have been.

Nothing happened for a whole week. The doctors took Jon to the operating theater twice a day to disinfect his leg. All that Doctor Fox said every evening was that his condition was stable, even though "stable," since there was an infection, actually meant that things were getting worse.

Sally came to visit Jon with her father, James. It was the first time we had met him. My wife and I were both struck by the fact that, despite the tragic situation, they behaved so affectionately and decently.

Eight days after the accident, John came out the coma. "It really is a miracle," the charge nurse whispered in my wife's ear. Marisa hugged me tight, and I couldn't let her go. It was if he had just woken up normally: he simply opened his eyes and asked where he was. In tears, Janette explained that he had had an accident, but Jon said he didn't remember anything about it. He needed to rest, so all we did was kiss him and sit beside his bed.

Doctor Angel told Jon he would almost certainly lose his leg from the knee down. "Absolutely not," replied my son with determination. Doctor Angel got up and calmly left the room. He didn't talk to Jon for the rest of the day.

That evening, Jon asked us to tell him about the accident. "I want to know what happened to my leg." His resolve was disarming. This was the boy I knew and loved, and I was proud of him. I told him what had happened: I told him that eight days ago, he had been run over by a car traveling at high speed. When he heard this, he interrupted me immediately and said he remembered being blinded by the two headlights coming towards him. After that, it had all gone blank. He couldn't recall anything else, so he wanted me to tell him.

We wrongly thought that because Jon had woken up, he would soon recover. Doctor Angel took us to one side and explained that Jon's leg had turned gangrenous. If we didn't decide to do something about it quickly, his entire body would be at risk. Jon refused to change his mind. His answer was still no. Even the priest, who came to see him every day, and the nurses who looked after him, were unable to make him think differently.

One afternoon, a well-dressed young man carrying a case came to visit. He was twenty-six, a policeman, and had been invited by the hospital to come and see us. He said that some years earlier he had been involved in a road accident. His leg had been crushed between his motorbike and a car, and it had been necessary to amputate it. He rolled up his trouser leg to let us see his artificial limb and show us how it was possible for him to walk normally even after the operation. "Can I talk to your son alone?" he asked. We agreed. He stayed with Jon for nearly an hour, and when he asked us to come in, he was putting the variety of prostheses that he had laid out on the bed back in his case. "I've explained to your son that losing a leg isn't the end of anything. It's just the beginning of something different," he said as he closed his case. He shook our hands with a smile and in a low voice suggested that we not say anything about the leg until Jon mentioned it.

Despite all this, Jon kept on saying no to everyone. One evening, while we were leaving the room, Doctor Angel took us to one side again. "We've come to the end of the road. The gangrene is spreading. If Jon doesn't let us amputate his leg within the next couple of days, we won't be able to save him. He's already lost too much weight, and the results of his blood tests aren't at all good."

Janette went back into the room, sat next to Jon, and said to him with determination: "Do you want to come home with us?"

"Yes," replied Jon in a frail voice.

"You can't come back like this. You just can't. It will all end here." She looked Jon in the eye, trying to hide how much this was hurting her, and said: "Either you agree to have the operation, or that's it. They can't disinfect your wound anymore. The infection has spread too far. Agree to the operation and have an artificial leg fitted like that policeman." In the meantime, Doctor Angel and the charge nurse had joined Janette at Jon's bedside. He looked up at them, and they nodded. Janette left the room, closed the door behind her, and as soon as she was out of Jon's sight, burst into tears.

The first thing Jon said when he saw her the next morning was that he had decided to have the operation. Six weeks had passed since he had come out of the coma. Janette kissed Jon before he went back into the operating theater the following Friday. We waited in the corridor outside, staring at the floor. The only thing I remember about that day was that I kept trying to understand whether the doctors had already cut off his leg or whether they were about to do so.

The operation was a success, and Jon was no longer in danger. When they brought him back to the ward, I couldn't muster up the courage to go into the room. I was terrified. If Janette hadn't taken me by the hand and led me in, I would have stayed outside the door forever. We stood at the sides of his bed, and when I finally managed to stop looking at the floor, I was surprised to see that nothing had changed: it was Jon. When he realized we were there, he smiled, first just with his eyes and then with his mouth, just as he had always done, ever since he was a baby. He was exhausted and sedated, but he was still my son. He closed his eyes again and went back to sleep. "It's worked," I said in tears to my wife, "you see? His face has changed color."

Time seemed to pass more and more quickly as Jon got well again. A few days later we took him home for a visit, and one Sunday we went to Childwickbury. We walked him around the gardens in his wheelchair and stopped at the lake to look at the wild ducks. When Stanley arrived, he hugged Jon with tears in his eyes. "I cannot believe it!" he kept on saying, amazed at how well Jon was looking. We had called Stanley or pushed notes under the door of his office every day so that he knew how things were going in hospital. As usual he had done everything he possibly could for Jon, Janette, and me.

"What do you need at home?" he said, now that he could once again take control of the situation.

"Nothing," I said with a smile. "Jon is still in the hospital. He can only come out for a walk on Sundays."

"And when he comes home, will you need anything?"

"The healthcare people have taken care of everything. They have given us this wheelchair, fitted ramps to the steps, and handles in the bathroom so he can pull himself up. They've brought us a special bed as well. They've got everything under control, and it's all paid for, too," I added, having understood what he was thinking of doing.

"Is there really nothing I can do?" he said, sadly.

"Stanley," said Jon, to help me out of this embarrassing situation, "when I had the accident, I was wearing the watch you gave me for my confirmation. Somehow it got lost. I'd really like to have another watch of yours to wear."

Stanley smiled with satisfaction and patted Jon on the shoulder.

The following autumn we took Jon to Italy for a couple of weeks in an attempt to take his mind off things. My parents had phoned every day while Jon was in the hospital and couldn't wait to see him again. While we were in Italy, my mother cooked for everybody so that Janette could have a rest, and the warm September sun helped to ease our suffering.

When we came back to England, Jon decided to go back to college. "Isn't that what you have always taught me?" he said, when I suggested that it might be better to wait until he had completely finished his period of rehabilitation. Some months later, when he had to come to terms with the prosthesis, he acted in exactly the same way. He didn't

Three generations of D'Alessandros. Marisa took this photo. It is one of my very favorite pictures.

seem to be at all in difficulty. He even said, "About time, too!" when the doctors told him that he could start to try and use his artificial limb. As a boy, Jon had always kept to himself, especially when compared to Marisa, who had an outgoing and self-confident personality like her mother. Nevertheless, his shyness had never stopped him from saying what he thought or behaving decisively.

Jon had every intention of going back to work, too. He could no longer be a warehouseman at Waitrose, and his dream of joining the Royal Air Force was gone forever, so he started looking through ads and found a vacancy at the Biomedic Center at the Royal National Orthopaedic Hospital in Stanmore. He was determined to go for an interview, even though he didn't have the necessary qualifications for the job. Two weeks later, we received a phone call. Professor Audear, who was in charge of the center, had been impressed by Jon's courage and resourcefulness and had decided to offer him a job as an apprentice under his personal guidance. It was wonderful news.

There was just one thing missing. A piece of the puzzle still had to be put back in place if Jon were to rebuild his life. One afternoon, he asked me to take him to the circuit at Rye House, where he used to go kart racing. We stood at the side of the track, and while his erstwhile opponents hurtled around the bends, Jon told me that he wanted to try to race again. His right foot hadn't been injured and he felt sure that, even with the prosthesis, he would be able to brake just as well as he had done before. I didn't have the courage to tell him that it was too dangerous, especially so soon after the operation.

"You have to tell me if it feels the same when you brake as it did before the accident," I said, after I'd helped him into the kart.

"Everything's okay, Dad," he said reassuringly. "I think I can brake just fine."

"'I think' isn't good enough. You need to be one hundred percent sure." The way this slipped out was rather abrupt, and clearly revealed how worried I was.

Jon smiled, waited for me to step back, accelerated and set off around the circuit. I held my breath. Everything seemed to be going just fine as usual. Then I saw him accelerate into a curve and swerve off the track.

"I put my foot on the pedal, or at least I thought I did," he explained when I reached him, "but the car didn't stop. So I took my eyes off the track to look for the brake and then—"

"That's no good. You know you must never take your eyes off the track," I said. "Wait until you get used to the prosthesis. We can try again next week."

But the same thing happened. He wasn't able to brake accurately enough. He would have been fine driving around town, but he no longer had the reflexes necessary to drive at high speed. "Let's try again next week," said Jon, optimistically. I knew how he felt, and I knew that he realized it was hopeless. That evening I called the guys at the circuit and asked them to talk to Jon and convince him to change his mind about racing competitively. For the next few weekends, Jon went to the circuit, but only to watch from the stand. One day a few weeks later, he came close to me and said quietly, "Dad, I think I'll sell the

Like me, Jon was destined to watch the races from the pits. While I worked as a scrutineer, he talked to the drivers and took photos of their cars. This is me with Bette, Damon Hill's mother. It was on the day of her son's debut at Brands Hatch.

kart." "That's what I was hoping you would say," I answered, and gave him a big hug.

Vivian was the only one of the girls still living at Childwickbury, and she took advantage of the sheer size of the manor to organize parties on weekends. "Safety, safety," said Stanley. He was always worried when he knew that Vivian's friends were about to arrive. "Close everything, lock everything away, don't let them bring too much alcohol, and if they need someone with a firm hand, please take care of it yourself, like Andros did. I'm simply not able to."

It wasn't easy to understand what Vivian had in mind. She had a difficult relationship with Stanley and interpreted any kind of advice he might give as an invasion of her privacy. I was more like an uncle to her, and sometimes I tried to find out for Stanley what she was getting up to when she wasn't at home. It wasn't easy, because Vivian was always doing too many things at the same time, and the trouble was that she did them all well.

During the filming of *Full Metal Jacket*, Vivian had spent nearly every day on the set, wandering among the actors and technicians, pointing her video camera at anybody and interrupting any conversation. A few years had passed since *The Shining*, and now she felt more confident as a director. What she was doing wasn't just an experiment anymore: it was a real film. Her film. And like her father, she wanted to have complete control over it. Everything would have gone just fine if the actors and technicians at Beckton had been working for her. Unfortunately, they were there for somebody else's film. "Vivian, get out of the way, move, stand back, don't talk to Martin, and don't disturb the actors." Stanley kept on telling her what not to do, but it wasn't much use.

On the way home from the set, the atmosphere in the Mercedes was always strained. It usually started with something trivial, a technical consideration, a question asked by Stanley, such as, "Why were you using that lens today?" Followed by Vivian's sharp reply: "Because it was the one I wanted to use." Stanley asked her why she hadn't used the light meter to calculate the right aperture, and she answered that she made a rough estimate without the meter and she hadn't got it wrong so far. Stanley grumbled that it was "No good," and Vivian answered resentfully that if he needed to rely on what the instruments said he was free to do just that, but she was perfectly able to manage on her own. The further we drove, the worse it got. When we arrived home, they raised their voices and started arguing in the corridor, went into a room, told each other where to get off, and disappeared in opposite directions after slamming the doors and leaving me alone in the middle of the battlefield.

Sometimes they wouldn't speak to each other for days. They would come to me separately in secret to ask if the other one was okay.

"Why does my father treat me like that?" Vivian asked me.

"Because he's trying to teach you something," I explained, "and you shouldn't answer him back like that. He is your father, after all."

Only after I'd told her all the things Stanley told me to do to make certain she was okay, and about all the times he had asked me to keep an eye on her, only then did Vivian calm down and smile at how exaggerated yet affectionate her father was.

Dear Emilio,
When you give Vivian the money in the a.m., please make SURE she gives you the airline, time of departure, destination in Canada, and flight number for her trip to Canada on Monday. She will probably say she hasn't got it, or she will tell you or me later, but try not to let her get away without telling you. Say I asked you especially to get this information.
Don't let her see this note.
Do the best you can.

S

In the end, Vivian always went back to Stanley and gave him a kiss. He hugged her tight and ruffled her hair, but the truce never lasted long. In less than two weeks, they would be back where they had started again.

When Vivian decided to leave Childwickbury and go to live on her own, it became obvious that Stanley hadn't learned anything when Katharina and Anya had gone. "You've got to call her every day," he said gruffly, and when I objected and told him that he wouldn't have to worry because Vivian was going to live near Andros, he replied, irritated, "He doesn't care about my daughter! He doesn't care about me!"

Jessica, one of the first cats I'd met at Abbots Mead, had grown old. During the editing of *Full Metal Jacket*, her health had got considerably worse. She wouldn't eat, continued to lose weight, and found it increasing difficult to get around.

Stanley tried everything but without much success. Without warning, he asked me not to leave Childwickbury. If the cat suddenly became very ill, there would be no time to waste if we hoped to save her.

I wasn't the only one who had to change routine because of Jessica's illness. All of Childwickbury was involved. The volume of all the phones was turned down, because Stanley was afraid that a sudden, loud ringing sound might give her a heart attack. The domestics were quieter than usual. They would ask me in a whisper for the latest news about Jessica. Every evening, when he'd finished his shift in Cambridge, the vet came to Stanley's house to give her medicine and vitamins. I hadn't set foot outside Childwickbury for ten days. I ate the meals that Christiane cooked and kept in touch with Janette by phone.

"Stanley, I need to go home and get a change of clothes."

"You can borrow some of mine."

"No, Stanley! I want to go home. You stay with Jessica for a couple of hours. I'll be as quick as I can. I'll go home, have a shower, and get changed. In the meantime, Janette will pack my things, and I'll be right back."

But it was useless. That evening he made me come back to Childwickbury four times because he was afraid the cat was suffocating. In the end I gave up. When I finally saw Janette for the first time in two weeks, I said: "Pack me a large suitcase and put all the underpants and socks I have in it."

Stanley wanted the vet to sleep at Childwickbury, too. Given Jessica's condition, if there was an emergency, the hour's drive from Cambridge could be fatal. At regular intervals throughout the night, the vet gave Jessica some little white pills. He also gave her a series of hypodermic injections, but Jessica didn't get better. We took her to the Fax Room so that Stanley could keep an eye on her while he finished editing *Full Metal Jacket*. When Martin went home late in the evening, I started the night shift and watched over the cat while Stanley continued working in his offices. We had put Jessica on a soft cushion on the floor, but after a few days she decided to go back to the Dome Room, where she snuggled up under the radiator behind the door. It was the last thing she did.

A few months earlier, illness and old age had been too much for Teddy. It had been a terrible blow for Stanley. "There's nothing more we can do for Jessica," I told him, as gently as I possibly could. "Instead of easing her pain—"

"I've made a decision," he said, interrupting me abruptly as if he already knew what I was going to tell him. "Call me when it's all over."

"Let's proceed," I said to the doctor. "How long will this take?"

"Only a couple of minutes. She won't realize what's happening," he answered, as he prepared a syringe. I stroked Jessica on the head for the last time, and he put her to sleep forever.

I opened the door and walked out onto the green, fresh-smelling grass in the garden. The spring air felt warm, and drizzling rain fell like thick mist from the sky. I was wearing a T-shirt, and I stood with my arms outstretched and my palms turned upwards. I looked up to let the clean drops of rain wash the stagnant air of the Dome Room from my skin. I hadn't been home for two months.

I went to tell Stanley. "It's all over." "Have you got the box ready?" I answered that I had, and I took him into a little room to the right of the colonnade, where he saw Jessica in a little wooden coffin. She was lying on her blanket with her toys next to her. When Teddy was ill, I had built two wooden boxes the right size for the body of a cat or dog. I didn't tell Stanley I was doing this so as not to upset him, but with so many animals around the house, I thought it better to be pre- pared. I always had two ready just in case. "It's good wood," I added, as I showed him the little coffin. "It's what Martin and I used for the furniture in the Stable Block."

I dug a hole in the garden behind the house, near the donkeys' enclosure and next to Teddy's grave. We put the coffin on the trolley the gardeners used for pots and tools and took Jessica to her last resting place. Stanley and I pulled the trolley and Christiane followed behind. For a whole day Childwickbury stood still. There were no phone calls, no faxes, no visits, the gates were closed, and all three floors were silent.

Two years later, Polly passed away, too. She was Stanley's favorite cat. He liked to have her around when he was working, and she always showed how fond she was of him by jumping up onto his lap when- ever he sat down. Polly had decided to live in Stanley's apartment, and thanks to the loving care she had received, she reached the ripe old age of twenty-two. When she died, Stanley spent hours in the room at the

Dear Emilio,
Thank you again what you
did for Polly and for me.
I miss her terribly.

S

Farewell to our beloved Polly.

end of the colonnade. He just sat there on the director's chair made of wood and green cloth that he'd brought from America, and looked at Polly in the little wooden coffin.

Apr. '89
Emilio,
I couldn't find Freddy's thyroid tablets. And your beeper + phone were off. But just give him 1 when you come in.
Thanks again for what you've done. No one could have done more. I couldn't have gotten through it without you!

Stanley

As soon as *Full Metal Jacket* was finished, Christiane evicted Stanley from the first floor of the house, regained possession of the room in the clock tower, and asked me to take all of her painting materials there. While I was carrying easels, canvasses, and frames upstairs, Stanley looked on and scratched his beard. "Emilio, go and get Martin. I have something to tell you."

He took us to Anya's bedroom. It had been empty since she had left home.

"I want to turn this into a photographic studio, for tests on costumes and props."

"We'll have to replace the floor before we can put down the rails," said Martin.

"Fine," said Stanley, and went downstairs.

We decided to make a wooden grid with different sized planks to level off the floor. Then we nailed solid plywood boards to it; they were one-and-a-half meters by two and three centimeters thick. That way we made sure that the new floor was sturdy and perfectly horizontal.

We bolted the rails for the dolly to the floor. Stanley had also said he needed a long ruler showing both inches and centimeters to make it possible to exactly calibrate the position of the photos, so we nailed that down, too. The dolly rolled smoothly along the rails. "Well done," said Stanley, when he came into the room. Then he added: "And what about the brakes? Come up with an idea for that." And he left me alone again. I found two wedge-shaped pieces of wood, and I screwed them together. When you lifted a lever, the two wedges went down between the rail and one of the wheels and blocked the dolly. I called Stanley: "Are you satisfied with this brake?" I said, showing him how it worked. "Perfect. Call Martin. Let's see how it all works."

I spent the rest of the afternoon motionless, leaning against the wall at the end of the room, while Martin rolled the dolly back and forth along the rails and took photos of me.

Martin developed the photos and showed them to Stanley, who was pleased with the dolly and the measurements but said that the camera we had used wasn't any good. "Martin, while you're about it, find a new fashion model, too."

Stanley thought the right camera for the job was an old-fashioned view camera. It folded up into a case, and when in use, stood on a wooden tripod. Stanley had seen one in a catalog and sent us to London to collect it. I thought you could only find cameras like that in museums. It was cumbersome, with three dark wooden legs and a huge viewfinder where the image appeared upside down. To see it properly you had to put your head under a thick black cover that kept out all the light. It was difficult to focus, too. You had to gradually turn some little wheels that aligned the front part where the lens was with the back that held the plate. There was a little gold nameplate nailed to the wood; it said WISTA CAMERAS. "Perfect," decreed Stanley. "Martin, try it out." And so I spent another afternoon in the garden modeling for poor Martin, who fiddled with the camera from beneath the thick, black cover.

The home photography studio was inaugurated later, at the end of the eighties, when there was an opportunity to publish a book about Christiane's paintings. Some of her pictures had been sold, but many were hanging in the house or stored in the Stable Block. The time had come to produce a complete catalog of her works.

Stanley had reached an agreement with Warner for the publication and distribution of the book. Christiane was working with the *Sunday Times* art critic to decide which works to choose and what to write in the introduction. Martin had just left Childwickbury to go back to America to work, so there was no longer an official photographer at the Kubrick home.

"Emilio, do you think your daughter might be interested?"

Thanks to a course organized after school by one of her teachers, Marisa had been enthusiastic about photography since she was a teenager. When she was eighteen, she went to study at the Ealing Technical College & School of Art, but she left the course because it wasn't creative enough for her. She didn't want to know all about the history of photography; she wanted to understand the creative process that lies behind a perfectly taken photograph. At the beginning of 1984, she got a job as an apprentice at Charles Green's studio in Edgware. There she improved her ability to "paint a portrait by illuminating the subject," as she once described it to me enthusiastically. Green also taught her a lot about developer baths and post-production in general. Getting her hands dirty and being involved in every step of the process is what Marisa had always wanted to do. When we were talking in his office, Stanley often asked me how Marisa was getting on. I told him that she had decided to start work as a freelance photographer and was getting plenty of assignments from Cameo Photography and Hills & Saunders, two of the best portrait photography studios in London. During the three years that she worked for them, Marisa had the chance to photograph members of the Royal Family and pupils at Eton College as well as lords and ambassadors at their country homes. In 1989, she became an associate member of the British Institute of Professional Photography. She was the youngest girl ever to have achieved that status in the portrait photography classification.

"I don't know. Give her a ring," I had answered Stanley.

"What do you mean, 'Why are you worried?' Dad," she said when she called me that evening to tell me about the offer, "he asked me to take photos of his wife's paintings! That's not my field! I'm specialized in portrait photography. I don't know if I can do it. And what's more . . . you've seen the photography in *Barry Lyndon*, haven't you? How can I live up to that?" Marisa had always regretted that she had never had the chance to watch Stanley and John Alcott at work on that film. She was only ten at the time. *Barry Lyndon* was the only one of Stanley's films that she mentioned continuously. John's ability to work with light and composition, as well as his sense of history, had moved her deeply. Light and composition were the fundamental elements of all photography, and she always said, "Every single frame of that film is a unique, perfect photograph."

"Marisa, if you don't feel up to it, say no. It's not a problem," I said, in an attempt to calm her down.

"But I want to take those photos!"

"Good. Then you're ready."

Marisa went to Childwickbury. Stanley briefed her about the job, he showed her the Wista, and took her upstairs to the new photographic studio. Christiane's works were oil paintings, etchings, and charcoal drawings, so different photographic techniques would be needed to reproduce the colors accurately.

In the end, Marisa braced herself and decided to accept the job. She asked me to help her move the paintings, while her boyfriend gave her a hand with the Wista from a technical point of view. They spent a couple of days trying out different types of film, exposures, and lighting with the Lowel rigs that Stanley kept heaped up in the cellar at Childwickbury. Once she was satisfied with the test photos she had developed, she finished the job in less than a week. Stanley

Marisa photographing Christiane's paintings.

and Christiane were impressed, and sent the pictures to Warner to be published.

In 1990, *Christiane Kubrick Paintings* reached the bookshops. "Emilio, go to London and make sure the book is displayed properly on the shelves." When I went to Foyles or Dillons, I only found a few copies of the catalog, and they were hardly ever on display. If I asked the shop assistants why this was, they told me that the book had quickly sold out. When I went back to Childwickbury and told Stanley about the excellent sales, he didn't comment. He picked up the phone immediately and called Julian: "Call Warner and tell them to print more copies of the book. They've already run out in London." Sometimes he only seemed happy when he had managed to solve a problem.

11

KUBRICK

STANLEY STARTED FILMING WITH the actors only after he had spent more than a year learning about his subject, about the historical period the film was set in, and about any particular technical requirements the film might have. He worked more like an essayist than a director. First he studied and read everything the others had said, and then he expressed himself.

At Abbots Mead, one of the first things I had to do every morning was pick up the papers and magazines he subscribed to: the *Times*, *Guardian*, *Wall Street Journal*, and *Spectator*, as well as any movie magazines that were available. Andros and I had to prepare a sort of press review. We went through all the papers and magazines and photocopied all the articles we thought were of interest. I remember how Andros had explained to me what to do when I first arrived: "It's easy. If the article mentions a movie camera or a lens or an important film on release or a famous director or actor or a new piece of equipment, or if it is about someone you've heard Stanley mention, or if . . ." As he went on, the smile that was forming beneath his mustache got wider and wider, so I interrupted him and grumbled: "Okay, Andros, okay, it's all perfectly clear!" When we'd finished choosing the articles, we bound the photocopies together and took them to Stanley's office. The actual magazines were filed away.

Stanley also had subscriptions to magazines that had nothing to do with movies. His favorites were about animals, but there were also less obvious choices, such as *Country Life*, which was full of photos of luxurious English country houses, or *The Lady*, which was an exclusive women's magazine about culture, fashion, and current events. So much printed material arrived at the house that we could barely manage to sift through it all.

When one of his films was released, it started all over again: "Buy all the national and international papers. I want to know what they are saying."

As well as the magazines, there were the books that Stanley borrowed from the London Library. In the period before work started on a film, I went to the library as many as two or three times a week. The young man at the desk invariably said: "You still have to bring back this book, it was borrowed over five months ago." Stanley shrugged his shoulders, and I tried to find it somewhere in his office. When I finally did, Stanley said, and he said this every single time: "I haven't even opened that one yet. Could you photocopy it for me, please?"

I had to photocopy books he'd read, too. There was always an important part of the text that Stanley wanted to keep. When we moved to Childwickbury, Stanley put together a team of readers. They included newly hired staff members and Katharina, Anya, and Vivian's boyfriends. Their job was to read novels, short stories, and essays and write a half-page summary for Stanley. That way he could save a lot of time by immediately discarding books he knew he wouldn't be interested in reading. He took on other people too, even in America, but he didn't tell them who they were working for.

Once Stanley got his hands on the screenplay, and sometimes even beforehand, he started to choose the actors.

Even though he was a demanding director, Stanley had no trouble finding actors who wanted to be in his films. Actually, it was the contrary.

During the filming of *The Shining*, Anne Jackson, the pediatrician who comes to examine young Danny at the beginning of the film, asked me if there was a part for her husband, Eli Wallach, who had been in the western *The Good, the Bad, and the Ugly*. She was rather insistent, but Stanley turned her down: "I like him as an actor," he said, "but I just wouldn't know what part to give him." Jack Palance wasn't any luckier: he was in London when Stanley was editing the film, and he had asked Wendy Carlos, who was a good friend of his, to help him find a part. Wendy had put Jack in touch with me, but we'd already finished shooting and there was nothing I could do for him. The most bizarre episode of all had happened a few months earlier when George Lucas was making *The Empire Strikes Back* at the EMI studios. A walk-on actress from Lucas's film had found out who the Unimog belonged to, and when she saw me coming, she threw herself in front of me. I had just enough time to slam on the brakes and narrowly missed her.

"Are you crazy? Are you trying to kill yourself?" I shouted at her.

"I thought it was Stanley Kubrick. Why are you driving it?" she said, still lying on the road.

"If he drove it, I wouldn't have a job. Get out of the way!"

What this resourceful actress hadn't realized was that to get something from Stanley, a favor, some help, or an opportunity, all you had to do was ask. During the filming of *Full Metal Jacket*, one of the marines came shyly up to me to ask if I could put in a good word for him. He wanted to know if he could stand closer to the camera, at least in a couple of scenes, so that he would stand out from the group of actors. "He's a student," I told Stanley. "He's finishing an acting course in New York." Actually, he always really had been too far from the camera. "Okay, for the next scenes, point him out to me and we'll put him nearer the front." *It was as simple as that.* A few days later, Stanley handed me an envelope and asked me to give it to the young man. It contained a short letter of introduction, praising the young actor for his meticulousness and skill, signed Stanley Kubrick. It was a passport to success for any cinema school.

Sometimes I asked him how things had gone with the actors in his American films, but all I ever got out of him were brief comments about Tony Curtis ("A great friend"), Sterling Hayden ("A true professional") and Kirk Douglas. I liked Kirk Douglas a lot as an actor, and since I knew they had made two films together, *Paths of Glory* and *Spartacus*, I asked Stanley what it had been like on the set. Stanley told me that they had argued a lot, and that Kirk had made him lose his temper more than once. Everything had worked out well in the end, though, because, as Stanley put it, Kirk was a great artist and was able to understand by himself whether an idea was good or not.

As a general rule, Stanley preferred to choose actors he had already worked with. For example, many of the costars who had acted in *A Clockwork Orange* also appeared in *Barry Lyndon* and *The Shining*. He used a similar strategy for the technical department, often "promoting" his staff from one film to the next. Douglas Milsome was focus puller for *Barry Lyndon*, director of photography of the second unit for the *Shining*, and director of photography for *Full Metal Jacket*. Martin Hunter went from being assistant sound editor for *The Shining* to editor for *Full Metal Jacket*. Stanley agreed to hire new personnel only when members of his usual team were busy working on other productions, and even then he asked them to provide a list of people they themselves had worked with in the past or whom they had heard good reports about. What Stanley was interested in was technical and artistic excellence, but he also sought out realistic people he could get along with. Stanley saw the team he worked with first as a group of friends and then as a group of colleagues.

However, things were a bit different with the editors: Bill Butler had worked on *A Clockwork Orange* but didn't come back for *Barry Lyndon*, which was edited by Tony Lawson. Ray Lovejoy had done a great job on *The Shining* but wasn't contacted for *Full Metal Jacket*. I think this was mostly for technical reasons. During the years that Stanley wasn't working on a film, new editing machines appeared on the market. He bought them all and got in touch with the people who knew how to make them work. He was always in favor of technological progress, so long as he could control it. The interview he put Martin Hunter through before entrusting him with the editing of *Full Metal Jacket* would have worn out just about anyone. "Are you sure it's like that?" was the question he asked every time

Martin finished saying something. To work with Stanley, you not only needed to be very good at your job and sure of yourself, but also very, very patient.

Stanley was totally uncompromising about many things, but he was still able to accept suggestions from others. He thought his ideas were good. Actually, he thought they were the best, but he wasn't proud. Having said that, it was not a good idea to decide things on your own when you were working with him.

Stanley moved to England in the sixties and never expressed a desire to go back to the United States. The British film studios could provide him with everything he needed. Apart from the tea breaks, he was more than satisfied with the competence and commitment of the English technicians. He tried them all: from MGM in Borehamwood to EMI in Elstree; from Shepperton Studios to Pinewood Studios. Stanley tried to use them in rotation to make sure they didn't close down. Since the beginning of the seventies, the English film industry had been making major cutbacks, and a large number of studios had been abandoned. The vast MGM studios where Stanley had filmed *2001: A Space Odyssey* had been closed and demolished. This had deeply upset him. From the middle of the eighties, EMI suffered the same fate. A number of the stages he had used were sold off, and the back lot, where the façade of the Overlook Hotel had been built, was bought by Tesco, which built a supermarket on the site. I think Stanley chose to mix the sound for *Full Metal Jacket* at Shepperton Studios because business there wasn't good and he wanted to give the technicians some work.

While he continued to use the English studio facilities, Stanley nevertheless forged ahead in his quest for independence. He was trying to find an area where he could build stages, warehouses, and offices; where he could make a film completely independently, without any restrictions in terms of time, space, resources, or personnel. Stanley came close to achieving this goal in the mid-nineties when a large property in Leavesden near Watford became available.

The area covered nearly three hundred acres and used to be a small airport. The hangars were still in good condition and could be easily transformed into warehouses and workshops just as we had done at Radlett. The runway was perfect for the small planes carrying American actors and technicians, and the surrounding space was large enough to ensure silence and secrecy, not to mention freedom from the strict limitations imposed by the National Trust. What's more, Leavesden was only twenty minutes from home by car, a factor of which Stanley never underestimated the importance. Basically, it was perfect.

But then George Lucas beat Stanley to it. While Stanley was still negotiating, George bought the property.

"How could he have done that to me!" protested Stanley, hitting the desk with his fist.

"I'm sure he didn't know that you were the other bidder!" I said. "What name did you use when you made the offer? It wasn't Stanley Kubrick, was it?"

Stanley grumbled crossly. In the meantime, at Leavesden, Lucas and his set designers were building the sets for *The Phantom Menace*, the new episode in the *Star Wars* saga.

Stanley had yet to find the film laboratory that completely satisfied him. While he was happy with the labs he'd worked with in the past, whenever he started a new film, he chose not to use the same lab as last time again.

Before he actually started shooting a film, and sometimes while he was in the process of doing so, Stanley would ask me to have reels of film developed at a number of different labs, including Rank Laboratories in Denham, Technicolor in London, and Humphries Laboratories in Whitfield Street. He was cross-checking: by having different parts of the same reel developed by different labs, and the same negatives printed by different machines, he could get a clear idea of the results each lab was capable of. This is how he decided who was going to develop the dailies and subsequently print the final copies of the edited film. But just because a lab was chosen to develop the reels didn't mean it would be asked to print the copies of the film for release.

15 Feb 1975
Emilio,
1) Go to Denham dispatch, ask for dispatch manager, Alf Thompson, he has one can of reel 8, Paths of Glory, finegrain. Make sure this is the reel he gives you.
2) Treat it very, very carefully.
3) Bring it to Humphries lab reception and tell whoever is there that this is for Bob Ellis's immediate attention.
4) Get a written receipt from Humphries reception and give it to me.

Thanks,
SK

However, Stanley was never really happy. During filming, he often complained that the quality of the developed dailies was deteriorating and would invite the manager of the lab in question to Childwickbury to see for himself. Halfway through the filming of *Barry Lyndon*, for example, Stanley noticed something seriously wrong with how Humphries Laboratories were developing the dailies. I think that's why he immediately stopped working with them altogether and started using Rank Labs in Denham. But even this wasn't enough to placate his suspicions. He asked me to follow the person from Ardmore Studios who picked up the rushes. I used to sit a few seats behind him on the plane. I tailed him at a distance, waited for the lab technicians to give him the developed negatives, and then followed him all the way back. I don't know what Stanley was afraid of. There was nothing at all suspicious about this guy. He was punctual and never in a hurry, so much so that it was easy for me to keep an eye on him. When I asked Stanley what the point of all this was, he answered rather vaguely, "I just want to make sure that everything's all right." But that wasn't the end of it. When he received a definitive copy of the edited film, Stanley insisted on random checks: as soon as they left the printing machines, the reels of film were scrutinized for gradation and overall quality. *Either you care, or you don't.* I'm not sure whether Stanley had been in the habit of doing this before I started working for him, but I do know that from *Barry Lyndon* onwards, he applied this strategy for the rest of his career.

Stanley's attitude to his films was applied to his private life, too. He never trusted journalists and tried to stay as far away from them as he possibly could. In his opinion, some sort of unredeemable, original sin blemished the category. "If they find out what I'm doing, they'll write about it in the press, and then in a couple of months someone will make a film about the same thing and they'll beat me to it." He was clearly worried when he said this, because he knew all too well that he took a long time to finish a project.

Generally speaking, his precautions were successful. From *Barry Lyndon* onwards, little or nothing ever leaked out. Of course, Alexander Walker was a risk. Every time a film was about to come out, he transformed, to a certain extent intentionally, into a scoop-hungry reporter. When he published an exclusive in the *Evening Standard* about what was happening on the set, he was severely reprimanded. "It's all free advertising, Stanley!"

"I'll be the one to decide when to promote my film!"

Stanley even tried to defend himself against the people financing his films. He wasn't happy about sending drafts of the script to Los Angeles to have the budget approved, so he had the two managers from Warner Bros. come to London especially and instructed me to personally deliver the envelope with the script. They weren't allowed to leave the hotel until they'd finished reading it, and only when they had returned it to me were they free to go back to California.

Photographs of locations or film stock tests were another cause for concern. Up until the making of *The Shining*, the location photographs had been handled by a lab in Bushey, but as the number of fashion photographers, advertising agencies, and illustrated magazines using the lab increased, so did the risk of news leaking out. Stanley asked Martin Hunter and me to set up a darkroom in the Stable Block, where we could safely work on the photos of the factory at Beckton. The considerable space available at Childwickbury made it possible for Stanley to solve many of these problems himself.

The name used for all the *Full Metal Jacket* production documents was "Timberland." It brought to mind Canadian forests or a brand of clothing and so was hardly related to the actual content of the film. Stanley wanted to throw everyone off the scent. This meant not only outsiders but also the people at the lab where I took the dailies to be developed. Stanley had already chosen the name of the film, but he never used it to label the rushes.

Entrusting the labs with the day's filming was one of the conditions laid down by the insurance companies. Stanley accepted it reluctantly. He would have preferred to do all the developing in the darkroom at the Stable Block. In any case, when I checked the dailies, everyone else had to leave the screening room. They were all invited to stop viewing their work and leave me alone in front of the screen.

"Who was at Rank Labs today?" Stanley would ask me.

"The usual people, Bob Monkhouse and Des O'Connor from TV and someone from 007."

"Did they see anything?"

"No. Behind closed doors as usual!"

"Good, good," he said, chuckling approvingly.

I was always alone in the screening room, and everybody else had to wait. People were starting to talk. Bob Monkhouse and Des O'Connor tried to find out what was going on, and someone from Rank Labs told them that everything else got postponed because Stanley Kubrick had to develop and view the dailies of his latest film. One day, as I was leaving the screening room carrying the reels of film, I found them right there in front of me waiting to say hello. "Good morning, Mr. Kubrick," they said with a huge smile. I was so taken by surprise and worried about this breach in security, that all I did was shake hands quickly and reply: "Good morning to you, too. See you tomorrow," hoping that they wouldn't have the courage to try to engage me in conversation. "How did they find out that my work was at the lab?"

asked Stanley immediately, and without even waiting for me to answer, he called Chester Eyre, his contact at Rank Labs, and bombarded him with the sort of trick questions you would expect to hear in an interrogation room at Scotland Yard.

Years later, when Tom Cruise and Nicole Kidman arrived in England to film *Eyes Wide Shut*, nobody had the faintest idea who had called them or why they were here. For months, all the local papers could find out was the address of the cottage they had rented.

Stanley made this effort to throw the press off the scent because he wanted to surprise people. He loved to catch his audience unawares. It was up to him to present a new film. He would use a few carefully chosen words to introduce the plot and cast. Nobody could know anything beforehand. The public had to be full of anticipation. After all, Stanley's films were all different; he certainly wasn't making James Bond movies.

The way Stanley introduced the public to one of his films was inviolable. He considered it part of his job as a director, and once shooting had started, choosing the designer for the poster, as well as gadgets and promotional stickers, kept him busy and ruined most of Julian's attempts to have a quiet dinner at home.

Stanley had placed his trust in Chapman Beauvais Ltd., a graphic design studio located between Islington and the City. He often went there to talk to the managers Frank and Tom and to look through artists' portfolios. He had the distributors send him films to watch in his private screening room at home, and Julian sent him all the promotional material that had been made for other films so that he could get ideas from it and discover new artists.

When I met Stanley in 1971, Philip Castle was the designer who had been chosen to work on the *A Clockwork Orange* logo. Philip was an airbrush specialist with a flair for technological or mechanical subjects. His works depicted planes, cars, details of chrome work, and beautiful, half-naked women. Philip's poster for the film showed a close up of Malcolm McDowell emerging from a triangular opening and clutching a knife. It was a striking image that caught and kept the attention of passersby. It was used for the promotional campaign and printed on cards that were widely distributed in the shops and newsstands around London. I remember seeing Malcolm's sardonic expression all over the place.

There was also an idea for a metal badge using the same shape, but Stanley didn't approve it. Badges, though, were at the heart of the campaign for *Barry Lyndon*. They were round with the film logo, a white pistol and a red rose, on a black background. Jouineau Bourduge, an amiable French artist I met several times at Abbots Mead, had designed this elegant logo, and as soon as the badges arrived, Vivian, Anya, and Katharina put them on. Stanley gave me a bag full to take home to Jon and Marisa so they could give them to their friends.

When shooting was over, an important task still remained: choosing the most expressive individual frames to be used for posters in the cinemas or to illustrate magazine articles. At Abbots Mead, this was Andros's job. Stanley narrowed down Andros's selection and then called Julian to discuss his choices.

Gadgets and other paraphernalia came back into fashion at the time of *The Shining*. There was a yellow, short-sleeved T-shirt with the image from the film poster printed on it in black. This time, Stanley's daughters and my children ended up wearing the terrified face of little Danny Lloyd.

The press campaign for *Full Metal Jacket* was reworked several times due to the release of *Platoon*. For the logo, Stanley had originally chosen a silhouette of four marines jumping from a helicopter in flight, but when he found out that there were a lot of helicopter scenes in Oliver Stone's film, he opted for something more minimalistic: a soldier's helmet on a white background, once again designed by Philip Castle. Stanley also worked personally with the Warner Bros. creative department to come up with memorable slogans to launch the film, such as: "In Vietnam, the wind doesn't blow, it sucks!"

Even when the promotional campaign and the release of the film were scheduled, Stanley still had work to do. He made sure that everything went according to plan. First, he wanted to be certain that the posters were displayed exactly where, when, and how he had agreed with Warner Bros.

The reconnaissance team consisted of Andros, Julian, and me. Julian took care of the posters printed in the papers, while Andros and I checked those in the cinemas. Other people were doing the same job in America, elsewhere in England, and all around Europe. On reporting back to Abbots Mead in the evening, I found photos from all over the world.

When I first went around town to take pictures for Stanley, there were problems: "How come they're all out of focus?" he said, fiddling with my first, unsatisfactory attempts at photography. "And yet it's easy. Listen: center your subject in the viewfinder, hold the camera still, estimate the distance between you and the subject so that you can calculate—" "Stanley, I can't keep up with you! It's too complicated." "No, no, it's really easy." "For you maybe it is. I'm not interested in photography."

Not long afterwards he gave me a compact camera. "You can't go wrong with this," he said. "It's completely automatic. The photos will come out fine, and you might even start to enjoy it. I started with a little camera myself, you know?" I tried taking a few pictures of Jon and Marisa at home in Farm Road, and they weren't bad at all. At least they were all in focus and I managed to get what I wanted in the picture. If nothing else, it was a start. "See?" said Stanley. "Now go and take pictures of the books in Foyles."

We had to make sure that the books he'd based his films on were prominently displayed in the leading London bookstores: *A Clockwork Orange* by Anthony Burgess, *Barry Lyndon* by William Makepeace Thackeray, *The Shining* by Stephen King, and *The Short-Timers* by Gustav Hasford. They all had to take pride of place on the shelves or the displays at the entrance, so that anyone who came into the shop simply couldn't miss them. With the Olympus, I could take photos quickly without being seen. Neither the bookshop managers nor the staff at Warner realized we were running these checks. All they knew was that calls and letters arrived with instructions to change the positions of the books on the shelves. The only one who knew was Julian, and, faithful as always, he kept the secret.

When I checked the newsstands, I occasionally found military magazines that mentioned the battle of Monte Cassino, so while I was about it, I made sure these were on show, too.

At the beginning of the eighties, videotapes began to appear on the scene. Obviously, Stanley was interested, but he wanted to have his films restored before they were transferred to VHS. It wasn't easy to find the ideal lab for the job. He investigated labs in England but also in France, Germany, and Spain. In the end, he entrusted the task to an Italian, Ettore De Cinque from Technospes. Stanley had come across him thanks to Riccardo Aragno and Mario Maldesi. Stanley sent Ettore the reels of film and was literally astonished by the result: "This is beyond my expectations," he said, praising the skill of the Italian lab technician. "Italy always creates masterpieces," he added, hoping to please me, "but it's strange. What with all the problems they have . . ." When I asked him what he meant by that, he answered: "Ettore De Cinque told me that the town where he lives is full of delinquents. He sleeps with a pistol under his pillow because it makes him feel safe. He told me that it's the same in other places there, too. It's total chaos." I didn't know what to say. I hadn't lived in Italy for twenty years. I only ever went back to spend a few days with my parents in Sant'Angelo, where nothing ever changed.

Julian took care of how the videotapes were promoted in the shops. He negotiated agreements with the large sales and rental chains and then told Stanley which of them would have his films on display in the way he wanted. Obviously, Julian couldn't personally make sure that all these agreements were respected, but Stanley insisted on it: "Emilio, since you're going to London, pop into Blockbuster and let me know how they are displaying my films. And take some photos, that way we'll have proof." So just as I had done for the books, I went to London to take pictures in newsstands, video rental shops, bookstores, and anywhere else that sold videotapes. I even became a member of the well-stocked rental places, but just so that I could get in quickly and take all the pictures I needed.

A Clockwork Orange needed special attention. The 1974 ban was still in effect, so Stanley hadn't authorized distribution of the film on videotape in England. The tapes were legally manufactured and sold in America, Italy, and everywhere in the world except the country he lived in. After the film had been withdrawn from circulation, theoretically, no English person had been able to see it. But then there was the illegal home video market to be dealt with. Some newspapers had revealed that pirated copies of *A Clockwork Orange* were being smuggled in from Holland and sold on the market in Camden Town, so Stanley sent me on a reconnaissance mission. I followed the trail described in the papers, and found myself among groups of youngsters with their hands full of CDs and videotapes, but I never did come across a copy of that tape to take to Stanley.

While Stanley paid such careful attention to the ideas and reactions of the public that they became instrumental in deciding how to promote a new film, he showed no interest whatsoever in critical acclaim. He was indifferent to film awards, and whenever a new one was delivered to the Warner Bros. office, he sent me to pick it up and told me to "Stick it in a cabinet somewhere, wherever you find the space." He didn't even want to know where. The framed certificates and diplomas that arrived were relegated to some forgotten wall at the back of the house. I threw a lot of them away because they had become illegible. When we moved from Abbots Mead to Childwickbury, I gathered the awards together from all over the house and stored them in one chest, which I put in Stanley's apartment on the second floor. He never opened it.

He was far more interested in the books that critics wrote about his films, even though this often meant that he wasn't happy with what they had written. When he heard that a new writer had produced an essay about Stanley Kubrick, he called Julian and the usual outpouring of questions began.

The book that satisfied him the most was written by Michel Ciment. There were boxes and boxes full of copies at home. Stanley used to sign them and give them as gifts to his friends and collaborators. He was also quite pleased with the massive biography Vincent LoBrutto wrote in the mid-nineties. Stanley thought that the author had done his research well. I had the same impression when I saw the imposing set of proofs for the book, which Stanley had managed to get his hands on from the publisher. "Not bad," said Stanley, "but it's a bit superficial here and there."

However, the biography John Baxter wrote was a problem. I heard Stanley say: "I told his people what to do, but it wasn't written the way we agreed!" He received lots of faxes about the book, but in the end he gave up: "How am I supposed to behave when I'm dealing with someone who doesn't understand what I mean and insists on doing whatever he wants?" He adopted the attitude he always took with newspaper articles that repeated the same old nonsense: "As they say, there's no such thing as bad publicity." What matters are the facts, and if the others say things that are inaccurate, well, never mind.

Warner Bros. distributed the films Stanley directed. Despite his exclusive contract with them, he kept in touch with all the other film production companies. From the very first day I worked for him, he made it clear that good relationships with the studios were fundamental. It was the only way that Stanley could preview films by other directors or have access to promotional material and contacts with technicians and artists. It was also an easy way to get other directors' phone numbers. If he liked one of their films, he would call them just to congratulate them, though it often ended up in hours of conversation about every technical aspect, problem, and solution of the film.

One of the directors he contacted most often was George Lucas. Stanley had held George in high esteem ever since they had met at EMI Films, in particular for his use of special effects. It all had begun on the back lot when the head of the special effects team was trying to create the blizzard that was supposed to rage against the façade of the Outlook Hotel. Stanley was worried about the results, and couldn't calm down because he was afraid that the technician was too young and lacking in experience to do a good job. The truth was that Stanley had never worked with weather effects, so he didn't know if what the technicians were doing was right or not. "How powerful are the wind machines? How many did you get? Have we got at least two spare ones?" And so on. After hours and hours of tension, Stanley decided to call George, who assured him that everything was fine. Only then did Stanley manage to calm down.

George was a regular consultant when Stanley started work on a new science fiction project called *A.I., Artificial Intelligence. 2001: A Space Odyssey* was proof that Stanley had brilliantly mastered the mechanical and optical techniques needed to realistically simulate outer space, but the arrival of the computer had revolutionized everything, and George was just the right person to bring him up to speed. James Cameron helped, too. He became one of those lunch guests that Stanley showered with requests.

Needless to say, Steven Spielberg was also part of the group. They could spend four hours on the phone without getting tired. That is to say, *Stanley* didn't get tired. Steven was probably fairly exhausted. One of the things they talked about was production. The success of Steven's films had allowed him to become relatively autonomous and fairly independent of Hollywood. Like George Lucas, he seemed to share Stanley's belief that it was better to work alone, to stay in the background, and to keep away from the offices of the major film companies. George had actually taken this even further than Steven. The home he had built, called Skywalker Ranch, had a lot in common with Childwickbury. Stanley had encouraged Steven to do the same thing. During the filming of *Eyes Wide Shut* he heard that Luton Hoo was about to be put up for sale. Stanley had used it as a location and said to Spielberg, "Why don't you buy it, Steven? It's like my house. Very spacious and near the film studios." Stanley sent me to see how long it took by car from Luton Hoo to London, and to the airports and studios, so that he could call Steven and tell him. As it happened, another bidder beat Spielberg to it and the opportunity was lost.

The only thing that Stanley couldn't understand about Steven was the speed with which he started and finished producing a film. He was able to plan, make, and distribute a film in less than a year. "How the fuck can you make a film in such a short time?" he often asked Steven on the phone with bewilderment. And when he talked about it to me, he added: "But why doesn't he take more time and carry out more in-depth research?" Stanley got on fine with anyone who took at least two years to make a film. He had always been wary of anyone who was in a hurry to do anything. Most of the directors he admired and spent time with never made more than a one film every two or three years. Cameron, John Boorman, Federico Fellini, and Francis Ford Coppola took all the time they needed to do the job properly.

Thanks to Coppola's Italian name, Stanley often mentioned him to me. Every time he asked me if I knew him, all I said was that there were lots of families with that name in the Cassino area but that I'd never met anyone who had mentioned the director. "How come you're not related?" he kept asking. "Because we're not!" I replied. "Strange," he said, as if he thought it normal that all the Coppolas would work in cinema. If any, I knew those that worked on the land.

He quizzed me about Danny DeVito too, but I didn't know anything about the family. Stanley liked him a lot and often mentioned him. They never actually met, but they respected each other from afar. Once when I was driving, I heard Danny DeVito talking about Stanley on the radio: "I've never met Stanley Kubrick," he said, "but I'd really like to. I admire him enormously, and I love his films. I realize that this will remain a dream of mine, and that we'll never actually meet, but anyway I'd just like to wish him a happy birthday since I know that it's today." I called Stanley from the car immediately: "Were you listening to the radio? Danny DeVito wished you a happy birthday." "Oh, God bless him, thank you very much." When I got home, I asked Stanley if he would like to meet Danny and make his wish come true. He immediately hid behind a hurried "No, no, no!"

One of Stanley's favorite directors was Fellini. Stanley couldn't speak Italian, and so they weren't able to exchange ideas in the same way that Stanley could with other colleagues. This was a constant source of frustration for him. Whenever a new Fellini film came out, it was always at the top of the pile of films to watch on the weekend. Stanley would have spent hours in the lounge talking to Fellini. Instead, he kept me in front of the screen for hours to translate the film while he took notes.

"Emilio, come here. Let's call Fellini," he said, the day after he'd seen Fellini's latest film. He pushed his notepad across the desk to me, and indicated a series of numbers he'd noted down in the Projection Room. "Read him these, and then translate what he says." I hadn't the faintest idea what they were. "Don't worry. Translate exactly what I tell you, then write the answer in Italian to be sure you won't forget it, and then translate it into English for me."

"Why don't you get Riccardo to make these calls?"

"Because you're here and Riccardo isn't. Here, take the phone; it's ringing."

As far as I could make out, these numbers stood for when the music Fellini had chosen for each scene started and finished. Stanley wanted all the details of all the tracks as well as how they had been mixed.

The only thing that I was really sure about was that Stanley was very interested in what Fellini had to say, and that Fellini was more than happy to answer Stanley's questions. Instead of being bored by the awkward silences caused by the translation, he waited patiently and spoke slowly so that I would have time to write down what he said. When Stanley said he was satisfied, and I announced the end of the interview, Fellini asked me to say good-bye to Stanley in the most sincere and affectionate way possible. "Federico says good-bye, 'from the heart,' as we say in Italian." Stanley smiled and gratefully returned the gesture.

"Emilio, before you hang up," added Fellini, "how far has Stanley got with his new film? Has he started shooting yet?"

"The new film?" I repeated, undecided as to whether I should write this on my notepad or not.

"The new film?" said Stanley suddenly. "Don't tell him anything! Say good-bye, say good-bye quickly!" and he tried to grab the phone out of my hands.

"Okay, Mr. Fellini, now I have to say good-bye to you."

Stanley couldn't accept the fact that I didn't watch the films by these directors: "Of course, I've seen them," I answered, "rolled up in the film cans I bring you!" He would have liked me to go to the cinema more often, and wanted me to watch the videotapes he gave me, but I didn't have time.

"When you get home, watch this film with Janette," he said as he gave me a tape of *The Godfather Part II*. "It's a great film with outstanding actors." "When I get home, it's gone midnight, and I get up at six. When am I supposed to watch it?"

The videotape of *The Godfather* is still in my bookcase. It has never been opened.

I didn't even have time to watch Stanley's films. I knew what they were about: I had overheard him talking to the scriptwriters; I'd been on the set every day; I'd met the actors; I'd seen the locations; I'd transported the props; I'd even checked the dailies early in the morning at the laboratory. Even if I'd had the time, after all that, why should I have wanted to watch the film from beginning to end?

Janette used the tickets Stanley gave me to take Jon and Marisa to the cinema in Leicester Square. "Janette went to see *Barry Lyndon*," I told him. "She really liked it, but Jon and Marisa fell asleep." Jon was seven at the time. He'd watched the film attentively for an hour, then he turned to my wife and asked: "When does Dad come on?" The answer disappointed him, and he lost interest.

Before meeting Stanley, I didn't often go to the cinema. I'd only ever gone once in Italy, to an open-air cinema in Cassino. They were showing a western, and I was hypnotized by the vast landscapes. Janette and I had gone to see *Dr. Strangelove* when it came out. We didn't know who the director was. We chose it because it was a Peter Sellers comedy that was having considerable success. I understood hardly anything: the actors talked too quickly, with strange accents, and my English simply wasn't up to it. Janette was disappointed because it wasn't her type of film at all: a war movie with unbelievable dialogues about the atomic bomb. Once, I gave in to Stanley's incessant questioning and admitted that I'd seen *Dr. Strangelove* with my wife. I told him that we had both enjoyed the film. I didn't want to have to face up to another barrage of questions, but sadly, I had opened up new horizons, and there was no saving me now.

"And *Lolita*? Have you seen *Lolita*? And what about *Paths of Glory*?" "No, Stanley. I went to see cowboy films. You know, with John Wayne, Burt Lancaster, Gregory Peck, actors like that. Those are the films I like. The day you make a western, I'll be the first in the queue outside the cinema, I promise."

Even though I hadn't been involved in the production of *A Clockwork Orange*, Stanley still called me to the screening room in Abbots Mead to watch some scenes from the film. At the time, controversy was raging over it in the press and on TV, and Stanley wanted my opinion: "What do you think? Do you find it disturbing?" he said, after he had shown me some violent scenes where Malcolm McDowell and his friends beat up and robbed people. I answered that I didn't think it was over the top, and that I thought it was obvious that nobody should behave like Malcolm did in the film. I also thought, though I didn't tell him this, that it was normal for everyone to behave well and they certainly didn't need a film to remind them to do it. Later I thought something else, and I didn't tell him this either: a film wouldn't make the difference. Bad people stay bad, and good people stay good. When I answered, Stanley scratched his beard, thanked me, and let me go. That was the only time I ever sat in front of a screen showing a film by Stanley Kubrick.

We kept a large skip for trash in the garden at Abbots Mead. We used to throw all the odds and ends from the set into it when a film was finished. Once a week a lorry came to collect it and emptied it at the local dump.

Stanley had hoped that Childwickbury would make it possible for him to keep absolutely everything, but he was wrong. The only thing he actually threw away without hesitating was the film left over after the final editing. I discovered this when he had finished editing *The Shining*. He just asked me to take a few reels to the incinerator and to ask Martin Hunter to help if necessary. Actually, there weren't just a few, there were dozens and dozens of them. Martin and I loaded them into the white Volkswagen minibus and made three trips to the chemical waste incinerator near London before we had got rid of them all.

We tried not to throw away material that was still in good condition, but it wasn't easy. As soon as we made some space, Stanley and Christiane vied for who was going to get to use it. "Don't empty this room to make more space for her," said Stanley, and Christiane retorted: "Emilio, I need more room. Get rid of this stuff." Sometimes, it was enough to drive you mad.

After nearly ten years, there were still thousands of beeswax candles in a room in the Stable Block. They had been commissioned for *Barry Lyndon* and came from a factory near Chelsea. They were beautifully made, and Christiane and Katharina adored them. They had sometimes put them in beautiful candelabra and set them on tables and cupboards to light the house. Instead Stanley hated them, because he was afraid they would start a fire. One day he said to me: "Emilio, get rid of them."

At that time Martin was working at EMI Films. He was cross about the national strike that had been causing power cuts for days. He didn't have to use the editing machines, but work on *The Shining* had just finished and he was trying to clean up and file everything. He needed light, not electricity, so the candles were the solution. We loaded four or five boxes into the minibus and took them to Borehamwood. This still left more than fifty boxes at Childwickbury. We put the candles everywhere Martin had to go: from a room on the ground floor all the way to an office upstairs. As a child, Martin had been an altar boy and so he knew that you could fix candles by dripping a bit of molten wax to use as glue. He put a candle on every other step; each time he knelt down he made the sign of the cross, and laughed.

The strike went on for a couple of weeks, so every day I took a few boxes to Martin, making sure that Christiane and Katharine didn't see me. When Stanley asked me to get rid of them once and for all, Janette suggested I give them to a convent: "Call the Daughters of Charity," she said. She had in mind the institute in Mill Hill where Jon and Marisa had gone to school. "They're bound to need them." At first, the nun I talked to was a bit confused. She couldn't understand why an individual would have hundreds of kilos of candles and thought it must be some kind of joke. In the end I convinced her to give me an appointment, and I found her waiting for me when I arrived at the institute the following day. I got out of Stanley's van, opened one of the boxes, and showed her my riches. She couldn't stop thanking me. "You are doing us an enormous favor. Is there anything we can do to help you?" "No, sister. You're the ones who have done me a favor!"

Years later, as work on *Eyes Wide Shut* was getting under way, Stanley was still fighting a losing battle against the lack of space. He decided to give away some of the books on the ground floor. The books were divided alphabetically and grouped by subject. "Take a few," he said. "I don't need C or Z. but don't touch A. I might still need those." Throwing them away was out of the question, and I didn't want to take then to secondhand booksellers, because so many of the volumes contained Stanley's personal annotations or dedications from who had given him the book. Then I remembered the Daughters of Charity. They were more than happy to accept, and when I arrived with a vanload of boxes, another group of nuns was waiting for me, smiling with gratitude.

A one-meter resin statue of the Sacred Heart of Jesus that Stanley had commissioned for

The statue of the Sacred Heart of Jesus that was commissioned for Full Metal Jacket *but never used.*

Full Metal Jacket but never used was donated to a church in Broadfields Avenue where I went to Mass on Sundays, while the padded chair from Stanley's office in EMI went to Don Fortunato's vestry in the church of Sant'Angelo.

In addition to the leftovers from every film, we were inundated with promotional material: tapes and LPs from record companies, books and novels from publishers, and film equipment catalogs from manufacturers. Everything was addressed "To the kind attention of Stanley Kubrick." I remember that every year he received a catalog from Ferrari UK with all the latest models. Yet Stanley never used a Ferrari in one of his films. Other things arrived with the same frequency: copies of Linda McCartney's calendar with picture of the vegetarian food produced by her company and perfumes from Nina Ricci. With all the people coming and going at Abbots Mead and Childwickbury, seeing your calendar on the wall in Kubrick's kitchen was about the same as having a huge billboard in Piccadilly Circus.

The casting agencies sent hundreds of actors' portfolios to Hawk Films. I put them to one side, and when there were quite a lot, I laid them out on a table with a headshot and the résumé in a closed envelope under the photo. Stanley perused them and said: "Open up," or "Bin that," but mostly "Bin that." Sometimes he asked me if I wanted to choose a few that I liked. "Stanley, do you remember the face you made when I suggested Charles Bronson for *The Shining*? I don't think it would be a good idea." And yet he kept on trying. Even with screenplays from new writers that had been sent to Warner Bros. "I haven't got time," he said, passing it to me, "you read it and let me know what you think." And I put it back on his desk a few hours later.

Strange things arrived in the post every day. Perhaps the strangest of all was a little cardboard kaleidoscope from a certain Bart Winfield Sibrel as a present for Stanley's sixty-fourth birthday. While I was examining it and pointing it at the window, fascinated by the light effects inside, Stanley discovered that this gentleman had made a couple of documentaries to prove that the NASA moon landings between 1969 and 1972 were hoaxes staged with the secret help of Stanley Kubrick, the director of *2001: A Space Odyssey* and expert in "outer space" special effects. "He can go and stick that thing up his arse!" was Stanley's final remark.

12

PIT STOP

IN THE EARLY EIGHTIES, while he was researching the Vietnam War for *Full Metal Jacket*, Stanley was involved in a large number of other film projects. I'd been working for him for ten years, and I was used to seeing him doing a variety of things at the same time. I never actually asked which film he was about to start making, but it was perfectly obvious that all the things he asked me to do couldn't belong to the same project. There were books about artificial intelligence, military magazines, drawings of spaceships, and black and white photos of Nazi Europe. Like a bingo machine that keeps the balls moving even when a number has been extracted, Stanley shifted from one project to another ever after he'd started work on a new film.

Needless to say, carrying out preliminary research into so many different films risked taking away valuable time from the project in hand. This was all the more true after Andros left. I worked full-time to look after the house, the animals, and the other day-to-day tasks, but I certainly couldn't do all the things he used to do concerning film production. Margaret worked with us on and off, and even though Julian had done his best to satisfy all Stanley's new requests, we were still always behind schedule. The new people that Stanley had hired answered the phone, posted letters, and made trips to the library, but though they could start a research project, they certainly weren't able to finish one. There was something special about what Andros had done that Stanley himself now had to provide, and this meant it took even longer to start work on a production project.

Stanley's oldest project was the film about Napoleon Bonaparte. He'd been wanting to make it since the beginning of the seventies and never stopped trying. Every time he finished a film, he went back to *Napoleon* and borrowed more books and talked to historians and university professors to add to this project he had been working on for years.

The story of the greatest European emperor of modern times had fascinated other directors, too. Every two or three years, films were made about Napoleon, and this just delayed Stanley's project even further, because he wanted his to be the definitive film on the subject. The costumes were ready, and in the safe hands of the Queen's Regiment; the books and magazines were meticulously stored in order in cardboard boxes in the Dome Room; the files detailing every day of the emperor's life were arranged in drawers; it was all waiting to see the light. The fact that as the years past, these boxes and filing cabinets were gradually relegated to smaller, more distant rooms was symptomatic of the increasing difficulty that surrounded the project.

However, Stanley didn't lose either hope or interest. While we were location-scouting for *Full Metal Jacket* outside London, he stopped to look at a small hill in the middle of a large area of uncultivated farmland: "I like that field," he said, "but it might not be big enough." He paused and then explained: "I'm looking for a piece of land for *Napoleon*; but it needs to be three or four miles long. If on your travels you come across one with not too many trees and no pylons, make a note of where it is. Then we can contact the owner."

The other big project he started work on in the early eighties was a film about artificial intelligence. This was destined to keep his mind busy for nearly two decades. He had read Brian Aldiss's short story "Super-Toys Last All Summer Long," about a little android's search for maternal love, and saw in it the potential for a spectacular film about the future of the human race and our relationship with computers.

He'd invited Brian to lunch at Childwickbury to talk about adapting his story for the big screen. I went to pick him up at his house in Oxford, and after a day with Stanley I took him home again. On the way back, Brian was much less friendly that he had been that morning. I assumed that the meeting between the two of them hadn't gone at all well, and when I got back to Childwickbury Stanley was anxious to ask me what Brian had said in the car.

"Nothing. Absolutely nothing. He just sat there silently looking cross. Didn't the meeting go well?"

"No, no, it went just fine. I liked the ideas he came up with. Go and get him again tomorrow."

The following day, Brian was once again relaxed on the way and annoyed on the way back. But this time he grumbled: "Who does he think he is? How dare he tell me what I should and shouldn't write? I can decide that for myself!" I kept my eyes on the road and didn't say a word. It went on like this for days. It was rather odd to see this radical change in mood from morning to evening. Brian couldn't restrain himself and commented about everything Stanley had said. This wasn't a particularly astute thing to do because every time I got back to Childwickbury, I found a note on my desk with the same question: "What did Brian say during the journey?" Sometimes I simply wrote: "He slept," when the mental arm wresting match with Stanley had tired him to the point that he just collapsed on the back seat of the minibus. Then there were days when his complaints and comments wouldn't fit on a page. I don't think Brian ever imagined that I was spying on him.

Brian was, as the English say, *short-fused:* he was touchy to the point that a look could be enough to offend him. Stanley and he were the perfect couple. However, they respected each other immensely. Otherwise, they would never have managed to keep on meeting for months. They even managed to start working together again after a row that had estranged them for years.

After all those trips in the car, Brian must have started to become suspicious about my relationship with Stanley. The questions he asked me became more and more wheedling. It was a sign that he was trying to win me over to his side: "Why does Stanley always want to talk about *Pinocchio?*" he asked one evening. "Do you know why?" "Yes," I replied without thinking, stupidly revealing a part of Stanley's plan. Not long before, he had asked me to go to London and buy two copies of all three of the English editions of Carlo Collodi's novel, as well as two videotapes of the Walt Disney cartoon. Katharina's son Alex was a few years old, and I thought that Stanley wanted to give him a present. I would never have guessed that *Pinocchio* was part of the research for *A.I.* When Stanley asked me if I knew *Pinocchio*, I said that I'd read it as a child, and that the moral of the story was a good one: "Having your ears pulled from time to time won't hurt you!" Stanley changed the subject immediately, so I didn't think I was doing anything wrong by answering Brian's question honestly: "Yes. I went to buy the books for Stanley." "Aha!" he exclaimed. What I had told him had confirmed what he already thought. I didn't say another word for the rest of the journey. That was the last time I saw him. Suddenly, Brian's name disappeared from the list of people I had to visit on Stanley's behalf.

The *A.I.* project turned out to be quite complicated, and other writers were called on to help work on the story. The first to arrive was Bob Shaw. He was a stocky Irishman who lived in Lancashire, in the northwest of England. I don't know whether it was due to the long train journeys he had to make or the way Stanley kept changing the direction of the plot, but Bob lasted just over a month.

In 1990 I met the third science fiction writer called to work on the story. Ian Watson was thin, about forty, with not much hair and a small mustache that emphasized his shrewd smile. When I opened the back door of the car for him, he exclaimed in the style of Andros: "Fuck this, I'll sit in the front with you!" I don't know why, but some people manage to put you at ease straightaway. I enjoyed chatting with Ian more than anyone else I'd driven in the Mercedes. I think he must have had just the right character to get on well with Stanley, too. He never took anything too seriously, but he never refrained from making biting remarks. He was as indirect and subtle as Andros had been explicit and irreverent, and totally relied on the perspicacity of his listener, too.

Irony was the only thing that could defuse Stanley's nervousness. There were just two ways to get on with him: tell him he was right all the time or make him laugh when you wanted to contradict him. When, after Brian and probably Bob, the arguments about "Super-Toys" finally got to Ian, he reacted in the best possible way: with a smile. "You certainly are strange," said Stanley. "I get angry with you, and you laugh about it." It was a powerful yet dangerous trick. One day Stanley was so furious that he sent me immediately to Ian's house to take back the fax machine he had lent him: "Enough is enough!" he screamed, banging his fist on his desk before I left. I'd rarely seen him so angry. A couple of weeks later I was on my way back to Ian's to return the fax and bring Ian to Stanley.

Ian lived in Moreton Pinkney, which was much like Sant'Angelo: a small village with fifty houses where everyone knew everything about everybody else. "Pick me up in the Porsche," said Ian. "That way we can have the whole village going!" Actually, the first time I went to Moreton, I had gone in the white Porsche. It wasn't the type of car you could miss in a place like that. Ian had respected Stanley's privacy and never mentioned who had sent for him, but he certainly did get to cause some gossip.

"Emilio, the car . . . I'm not working for the mafia," he said the second time I went.

"What difference does the car make?" I answered. I didn't see what the problem was. "Anyway, I won't even get out. I'll stop in front of your door. You come out, get in, and off we go."

"That's even worse! That way we will look like Mafiosi!"

However, Ian never messed around when he was working. He relentlessly concentrated all his efforts on adapting the story, met deadlines, and was punctual for appointments. When I arrived at his house at the time we had agreed, his wife Judy was waiting at the front door. She waved to me and said: "He'll be down in ten seconds!" And in ten seconds Ian appeared with his briefcase in his hand and a smile on his face. He wasn't in the least discouraged by Stanley's continual changes of tack.

"What did Ian say on the way home?" The usual note from Stanley was on my desk. Most of the time, all I wrote was "He laughed all the time" or "Italian lesson." Ian liked to ask me for some Italian expressions to use in his books, and I couldn't resist the temptation to teach him Andros's mantra too: *"Stanley è nostro zio!"* we repeated together as the Mercedes sped along the quiet English country roads.

"Mmm, lunch," he said as we passed a flock of sheep.

"Ian, never say anything like that in front of *zio* Stanley because he'll fire you on the spot!"

"Why?"

"Because he hates people who ill-treat animals."

"But he's not a vegetarian. He eats meat!"

"When it's cooked and on a plate, it doesn't look like a sheep anymore," I pointed out.

"Okay, lunch isn't a dead animal," he remarked seraphically, pretending to write something in his notebook.

When we were about to arrive at Childwickbury, Ian usually suggested we go to a pub in Luton Hoo for a drink.

"We can't. No way," I always replied.

"Don't worry about driving, I'll drink yours, too."

"It's not just that. See this watch?" And I showed him my wrist. "Stanley has an identical one and he knows exactly where we are. What's more, he knows where we should be in half an hour from now, and it's much closer to Childwickbury than that pub. It's not my job to keep all of you company. I just have to pick you up from home and take you to him. When you get there, you'll find everything you need: if you're hungry, there's food; if you're thirsty, there's water, wine, beer, whiskey, whatever you want."

"But do you always behave like that with Stanley?"

"It's a job, Ian. It's like when you become a priest: you can't change your mind afterwards and get married. You have to give up certain things, such as women."

"Oh, fuck this. I'd never have thought for a moment that priests would give up women."

Was there anything he was able to take seriously?

Ian loved to hear about my life with Stanley. Especially the anecdotes that at first seemed trivial. He found something odd about them, a sort of equilibrium between the surreal and the practical. The one he liked best was about the balls of string. Stanley absolutely adored string. He used to it to tie up just about everything. He couldn't stand it when objects moved or swayed, so he did everything he could to tie them down: chairs tied to other chairs, filing cabinets tied to each other. Even the plywood panels on top of the cabinets to stop the cats from peeing on them had two holes in each side so that they could be fixed in place with . . . string. Things like this, which were of no importance to the world in general but were of vital importance to Stanley, justified a phone call during the night or on those rare Sundays off he gave me.

"Emilio, are you at home?"

"Stanley," I sighed into the phone, "didn't you say that this was my Sunday off?"

"Yes I did, but I need some string. Can you bring me some?"

By that time I had learned a few tricks myself. In the past I would have taken the car, driven to Childwickbury just to go into Stanley's office, open the drawer where I had stored the stationery, and put a ball of string in his hand. But not now.

"Stanley, which room are you in?"

"The Dome Room."

"Okay, stand in front of the bookcase, look at the central shelf, and right there in the middle you'll find a ball of string."

"Okay, thanks. Sorry I disturbed you."

"No, wait. I want you to go there, then come back to the phone, and tell me that you've got it."

"Okay, wait," said Stanley. After a few seconds he added, "I've got it, Emilio. I'm holding the ball of string."

"Okay, Stanley, enjoy the rest of the weekend."

I'd hidden another spare ball somewhere else, just in case the one on the shelf had disappeared. This is what I'd learned about Stanley from experience. I'd hidden the cats' vitamins and dog food all over the place to avoid unnecessary trips back to Childwickbury. Ian always loved to hear the story about the string: "I can't believe it, I simply can't believe it," he kept on saying as he laughed. But then that's how things worked between Stanley and me. I always had to be one step ahead. I had to imagine the unexpected before it actually happened. That was the only way I could avoid going mad.

Another episode that was more practical than surreal, although the opposite could also be true as Ian rightly pointed out, was when we saved a bird that had got stuck down the chimney. Thanks to the cat food and slices of bread that Stanley insisted on throwing out of the window to them because he was afraid they didn't have enough to eat in winter, the birds at Childwickbury had all become obese. This poor starling was caught behind the boards that sealed the fireplace, and as he beat his wings frantically against the wooden planks, Stanley sat motionless and cried, "Call the RSPCA! Call the fire brigade! Call the vet! Call the builders! Call the gardener!"

2–1 to me, Andros.

"I'm not going to call anyone, Stanley!" I explained what I was going to do: I wanted to make a hole in the wood and put a big plastic bag under it to catch the bird.

"How can you be sure that the bird will go into the bag?"

"Because I'll use a clear plastic bag, a large one, and as soon as he drops in, I'll close the bag."

"I don't know, Emilio. It might get hurt."

"Not any more than it will if stays in there while I call the RSPCA and everybody else!"

"Okay, go ahead, good luck."

Holding up my catch, I teased Stanley: "What do you want to do now? Call a bird psychologist?"

"You know, now you come to mention it . . ."

I didn't let him finish his sentence. I went to the window and freed the confused, frightened starling. It flew away clumsily, landed almost immediately in the garden, and started stuffing itself with slices of bread again.

Stanley went off happily to telephone his sister, Barbara, and tell her all about it. Ian took me to one side and confided in a whisper: "Now I see what you mean with that story about the string."

After working with three male writers on the story of the little abandoned android, Stanley felt the need for woman's creative voice. In 1994 he contacted Sara Maitland, a writer who lived in Warton in Northamptonshire. They worked together without actually meeting for some time, and then Stanley asked me to take her an envelope. The place where she lived was off the beaten track down an unsurfaced road and surrounded by groups of little tumbledown cottages. I'd been driving the Mercedes around for a while without finding the house with Sara's number on it, when I met a tall, slim woman with long, straight gray hair followed by a girl who looked and dressed the same. They both shambled decisively towards me and for a moment I thought they were going to ask me for a lift. Then the older of the two called me by name and asked me to follow her. I drove slowly behind them until we reached a little house hidden away behind the others. She made a series of gestures to invite me to park the car. If neither of them was Sara, at least they should know her: somehow they knew who I was.

"Are you Sara Maitland?" I asked the lady before going into the house. It was all rather strange, and I wanted to make sure that I wasn't getting myself into trouble.

"Yes, I am," she said. "Please, do come in," she said insistently.

"Thank you. Do you mind if I ask you a favor? I've been driving for hours, and I wonder if I could use the bathroom?"

"No."

No? Had she really just said no? I looked at her with bewilderment. Sara didn't say anything else. Then before I could get over my surprise, she added, "It doesn't work."

"It doesn't work?" I repeated, in an attempt to fill the silence.

"The valve's broken. You can't flush it."

The way she said this, it seemed like years must have passed since water had last successfully poured into that toilet.

"Don't worry. I'll fix it," I offered, more out of desperation than anything else.

"Do you know how? Are you a plumber?"

"No, but if you work for Stanley, you have to learn to be able to do absolutely anything."

I got to work and managed to repair it. The happy gurgling of water in the bowl could be heard again.

"You're just how Stanley described you," remarked Sara.

None of the four writers working on *A.I.* knew that the others were involved. They were all convinced that they were writing alone. Stanley believed this would lead to better results. He wanted each of them to make a unique contribution without being influenced by the others. He let them read extracts of each other's work without revealing who had written them or when. In addition to Brian, Bob, Ian, and Sara, I think Arthur C. Clarke and David Cornwell (alias John Le Carré) were also involved in this or other projects.

Stanley trusted David implicitly, which was extremely rare. During a telephone conversation I once heard Stanley say these solemn words: "Your word is final." If David was convinced of something, Stanley followed his advice. Full stop. Stanley respected and worked successfully with many writers, but he never went so far as to curtail his own critical thinking.

He always sent me to their homes: "Be kind to these people because I think I need them," he said, and added: "Try to find out what they like." I felt like James Bond in *On Her Majesty's Secret Service.*

In one form or another, film after film, Stanley had always had a group of writers on his payroll. I think he was in touch with anyone who held a pen in England. He had a hundred addresses where he could send novels or stories that he thought were interesting subjects for films. People joined or left this club because of the type of story, their personal commitment, or the results of their previous work. When a new name was being considered for membership, before they received any kind of material, they were subjected to careful vetting by Stanley to see if they were someone he could trust. Who had introduced them? What have they written? Who knows them? What do they say about them? Who are they related to?

Sometimes people were contacted again after years. Perhaps they thought that Stanley had changed his mind about their work, but the truth was it took him years to work his way through the long list of writers who collaborated with him.

Stanley was not discouraged by the fact that he still didn't have a finished screenplay for *A.I.*, and he moved on to the planning and organizing phase.

Unlike the other films, where research aimed to perfectly reconstruct a period of history, an entirely new world needed to be created from scratch for *Artificial Intelligence*. Stanley had hired specialized designers to invent objects, settings, buildings, means of transport, streets, and realistically futuristic machinery. Apart from one young man who was fired after just a few days for trying to get his hands on confidential information, all four of the designers were, rather curiously, named Chris: Chris Moore, Chris Foss, Chris Baker, and Chris Cunningham. They worked individually on *A.I.* and at different times that rarely overlapped. This was another instance of Stanley's strategy to have several people unaware of each other, yet working on the same project.

In 1989, Chris Moore was the first one to be contacted. He worked with Stanley mainly by fax, but their relationship quickly ran aground due to bureaucratic and business issues.

The second to arrive was Chris Foss. He was an elderly gentleman with a round nose. The only time Stanley ever met him was during his interview. He wished Chris good luck with the job and set him up in a room in the Stable Block, where Chris started producing pencil drawings on cardboard. After a while I got to see his work: a beautiful color picture of New York underwater with violent waves breaking against skyscrapers studded with shattered windows. "Put it somewhere safe," said Stanley. "Put it in the Green Room." I had to find a closed space so that I could be sure the cats wouldn't use it as a litter box. The only

Dress rehearsals outside the hangar at Radlett: a member of the *Barry Lyndon* crew offered himself to play an English soldier.

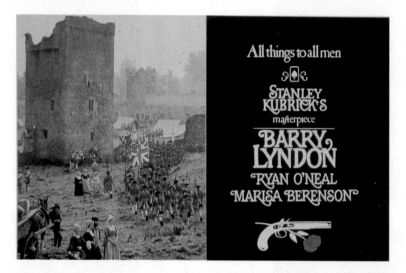

A promotional slide for *Barry Lyndon*. It features the tagline, "All things to all men," a quote from the First Epistle to the Corinthians. The idea was later abandoned.

Ryan O'Neal and me in London.

The label on the folder containing these test shots says, "Farmhouse candle test 21.09.1973." John Alcott and Stanley tested several combinations of lenses and filters to achieve the best result on film when an actor was lit only by candlelight.

Candlelight scenes needed very careful development and printing, too. You can see subtle variations in these two samples from the same footage, printed by different labs.

The editor Ray Lovejoy and me in the Colorado Lounge set. On the table in front of us is the scrapbook with old newspaper cuttings chronicling the dark past of the Overlook Hotel that Alexander Walker created (in vain).

Matthew Modine and me on location during *Full Metal Jacket*.

A scene that was later cut from *Full Metal Jacket*. Stanley told me that he designed this setup because he wanted the Marines to look like small toy soldiers.

Stanley and me at my farewell party in 1994.

Christiane and Janette.

From left to right: Andros, me, Jan Harlan, and Stanley.

Anya, me, Vivian, and Janette.

Christiane and Andros.

Some of the photographs that Stanley took on that freezing night at Mentmore Towers, during a location scouting job for *Eyes Wide Shut*.

Continuity photos of Janette and me from the set of *Eyes Wide Shut*.

Selling a newspaper to Tom Cruise on the set of *Eyes Wide Shut*.

In front of the Caffè da Emilio on the Pinewood back lot.

Tom Cruise and me at the Italian premiere of *The Last Samurai*. This was the first time we'd seen each other again after our sad last encounter in Stanley's Red Room.

place was the bookcase, and this time I had an idea: I moved the shelves closer to each other and left a tiny space where I could slide in Chris's drawing. "Stanley, the drawing is well-hidden in the bookcase." Stanley took a Post-it and made a note of where it was.

Chris Foss didn't create much else, and Chris Baker took his place. He was a reserved and conscientious young man and produced an incredible quantity of drawings. There were always two or three variations on every idea he had after reading extracts of the story. "That guy works hard," I said to Stanley. "Yes, he's really good, incredible," Stanley agreed, but then added: "Don't tell him that. If he's not sure, he'll work harder." That's how it was with Stanley: no news is good news.

Chris Cunningham had been hired to design the robots. He stored these vaguely human-looking creatures in a room in the Stable Block. They were about a meter tall and full of electrical wires and mechanical parts. One of them had actually been finished: the metal parts and colored wires had been covered with a pale, flexible, plastic-like substance. On closer observation, it looked rather like a small child. On its back there was a little door that could be opened to access the electronic control panel. Its skullcap could be opened too; inside there was a tangled mass of colored, luminescent wires. I never really liked going to see Chris because these robots frightened me. They looked like children, but there was something unnatural about them; they seemed to be suffering in some way.

In the first months of 1997, Stanley began looking for a location, and obviously he wanted somewhere near home. For some reason, he was interested in places where car races were held. Bovingdon was an example. It was an abandoned airfield where a group of enthusiasts organized races with old cars. Part of the fun involved crashing the cars into each other and destroying them. I took Stanley to inspect the circuit on a day when it was deserted. A few weeks later he asked me to take him to Halton Airport in Reading, where he wanted to inspect another circuit. He measured the place, took a few photos, and we went back to Childwickbury. I asked him what type of film *A.I.* was: "Are there going to be car chases?"

"No, Emilio, it's something completely different."

"And how long do you think it will take to film it? Will we have to move around a lot?"

"No," he answered, "it won't take long, and we'll stay near home."

He asked me to drive Phil Hobbs around St. Albans so he could do some filming from the Land Rover. Phil had just come back from a trip to the North Sea, where he had been visiting oil rigs. Now he had to film the lampposts along the roads on the outskirts of town. He stuck his head out of the sunroof of the Land Rover and held the video camera at a 45-degree angle so that he could get both the lampposts and the street. I drove at a constant speed: first ten, then twenty, then thirty, until I reached seventy miles per hour. While I went back and forth along the road, Phil filmed the posts that flashed past at regular intervals, and made a note in his notepad of the distance between them and how fast we were going each time. As usual, Stanley told neither Phil nor me why we were doing this.

One day, Stanley said, "Emilio, I need to film a car crash. The car has to crash into a wall at thirty miles per hour. Do you think you can do that?" Thirty miles an hour isn't very fast, and even without an airbag it wouldn't have been all that dangerous as long as I was wearing one of those suits professional motorcyclists use with protective armor. This seemed to reassure Stanley, because he didn't say any more about it for days, but then he said: "Emilio, are you ready for the crash test?" I repeated that I was, if he could guarantee me all the protection I had asked for. "Good," he said, and he didn't mention it again for weeks. When he put the same question to me for the third time, I asked him to explain. "The unions won't give me permission. They say it's too dangerous. If you're sure you can do it, you could drive the car yourself." Once again, I said I would be glad to help, as long as Janette didn't find out about it. But it ended there. I started to think that perhaps the unions had got the better of Stanley this time.

Another of Stanley's projects that lasted for decades was about the Second World War, and more specifically, the Holocaust. He had talked

Some old postcards from Stanley's collection. They were part of the material he was gathering together for the Aryan Papers *project.*

about the problems involved in it with many of the writers that had already worked on other films: Diane Johnson, Michael Herr, David Cornwell, and Riccardo Aragno. Stanley couldn't find a way to channel everything he'd read and studied into a single story. In 1991, Michael Herr suggested that he read *Wartime Lies* by Louis Begley. The book tells the story of young Maciek and his beautiful aunt Tania in Nazi-occupied Poland. Stanley thought he had found a good starting point for the project.

He gave the film the provisional title *Aryan Papers* and worked on it for years. He hired a costume designer, found the leading actors, sent his assistants around Europe to take photos of the towns and villages described in the book, and studied the style and architecture of buildings and interiors of the period with Roy Walker.

Stanley had a boy named Joseph Mazzello in mind for the leading role. He had acted in Steven Spielberg's *Jurassic Park*. After thoroughly questioning Steven about young Joseph's character and qualities, Stanley arranged a meeting. I went to pick up Joseph and his mother at a London hotel and took them to Childwickbury. "See if they speak Italian," Stanley asked before I left, and in fact when I met them, Joseph's mother's face lit up and she asked me where I was from. Even though little Joseph was quiet, he looked lively enough. He was well mannered, too. They stayed with Stanley for a few hours, and then I took them back to their hotel. When I got back to Childwickbury, I was faced with the usual array of questions: "What did they talk about in the car? What did they say about the meeting? What did Joseph's mother say? How did he behave?" I told him that the child played with a video game for the whole journey. "I heard the electronic sounds of the game coming from the backseat while I was talking to his mother, but I don't know what he was playing," I admitted.

"He talked to me about the game during the interview," Stanley said with a smile. "He told me he'd beaten the record. Did his mum tell him off at all?"

"No. Never."

"That's good."

After that first meeting, Joseph and his mother came back to Childwickbury a couple more times. She read Stanley's adaptation of the novel, and Joseph was photographed wearing some forties-style costumes. I think the impression Stanley had after these meetings was that Joseph was perfect for the role, as well as polite, intelligent, and calm, which were three indispensible qualities in his opinion.

In the meantime, Stanley had formulated a production plan that divided the days of filming by actor. In the Bothy, a small outbuilding to the south of the house, he had set up an office where all the drawings, photos, and boxes and boxes of research material were organized. *Aryan Papers* was ready to go.

And yet Stanley faltered. Something strange was happening. It was almost as if he didn't *want* to start work on the film. I don't know what it was: perhaps the story, or that fact that he would have to move to Europe for some of the scenes. Anyway, it was clear that he was not happy about something.

It was around about then that Steven Spielberg's *Schindler's List* came out. Stanley watched it in the Projection Room and then asked me to go to London to see how many people there were outside the cinema when it was released on the weekend. He wanted to have an idea of the number of people who went to see the film without having to wait for the box office statistics that would be available some days later. So I started going around to all the cinemas that were showing *Schindler's List*. I started northwest of London, near Childwickbury and my own home. Most of the population in the suburbs of Edgware, Stanmore, and Golders Green were Jewish, so I often found long queues of people all waiting patiently to see the film. *Schindler's List* was clearly successful in other areas of London, too. When I told Stanley what I'd seen, I thought he would happy to learn that a film dealing with such a delicate subject was so successful. He seemed to be pleased for Steven, but he didn't ask me as many questions as usual. He didn't get angry like he had done when *Platoon* had compromised the release of *Full Metal Jacket*, but then he hadn't even started filming *Aryan Papers*, so it wouldn't have come out for two or three years. There was no way that

Schindler's List could have been a real problem. Nevertheless, I continued to see a new look of perplexity on his face.

The Holocaust wasn't the only aspect of the Second World War that Stanley was interested in. From time to time, he asked me about the battle of Monte Cassino in 1944. Whenever he found an article about it in one of his military magazines, he called me to show me the photographs: tanks, military vehicles, forts, weapons and ammunition, corpses in ditches, and ruins and rubble. "Do you recognize that building?" he asked, showing me a picture of a country house that had been destroyed by a bomb. I explained that I had left my father's house when I wasn't even three years old and that I didn't remember much at all about the village before I left.

I had been evacuated to Calabria in 1944 because our house had been destroyed in the bombing. It was at the end of a road on a hill called Guado del Lupo that dominated the whole valley in the direction of Sant'Angelo. This position made it a strategic target, especially during winter when it wasn't hidden by the leaves on the trees. The bombs had razed it to the ground. When I went back to the village with my family at the end of the year, we had to stay with my mother's family in Fangotti. It was a far less appealing place on the other side of Sant'Angelo in a sort of damp dip in the terrain. Miraculously, that cottage hadn't been damaged, and we all lived upstairs together above the cowshed full of oxen and the donkey.

I have only a vague recollection of the state Cassino was in when we went back. I couldn't say whether it was something I'd seen with my own eyes or the memory of an old photograph. All I know is that I remember a house in the country. It had been half reduced to rubble, but it was still possible to glimpse furniture perfectly in place inside. The ground around the house was a sort of bog with coils of barbed wire sticking out here and there. Stanley had me describe this to him over and over again. He wouldn't accept "I don't remember. I was only three," as an excuse. I told him that for months after we went back, Cassino seemed like a ghost town. The inhabitants had started to clear the rubble from the roads, to remove the wrecks of military vehicles and the branches of fallen trees sodden with rain. But if you turned your gaze to the narrow streets in the center, you could still see heaps of debris, fallen roofing, and upturned tractors covered with dust. I was never happy to go into town, but things in the country were just as gruesome. As the bodies of soldiers who had died in battle gradually surfaced from the fields, they were put in coffins, covered with flags, and left to line the sides of the country roads. I am still haunted by this image.

I told Stanley how I'd met some American soldiers at the end of the war. We waved to them as they drove past in their armored cars, and occasionally they stopped to give us sweets and bars of chocolate. "You see, Stanley: the only thing I really remember well is those bars of chocolate the American soldiers gave us. I ate so much of it that I needed fillings in my teeth." As I told him this, I wondered if it would be useful for his research. "And what do you remember about the bombs?" he insisted. "Not much. I remember that we used to find fragments of grenades on the ground, especially after there had been a storm. The rain washed away the earth and brought the bits of metal to the surface. My friends and I collected them and sold them to the scrap iron dealer when he passed with his cart. We used the money to buy sweets in the village. And then I remember that we used to play in the trenches that the soldiers had dug. They had hidden in them and shot at the enemy, and so did we. We divided into two groups, took up position, and threw stones at each other. The trenches were really deep, or perhaps I was just small."

The thing that fascinated Stanley the most was the bombing of the abbey. The allies were convinced that it was being used to hide German soldiers, and despite repeated denials from the abbot and the German army, they attacked it. It was only after the bombardment that the allies discovered that there had been neither enemy soldiers nor ammunition in the building. Every time we discussed this, Stanley was struck by the breakdown in communication between the two sides. He thought it was grotesque that they had both refused to believe each other and had preferred to act on their relatively unfounded suspicions. Stanley said that strategy during military conflict always ended up ruining that flicker of honesty that humans were occasionally blessed with.

Year after year, his questions became increasingly persistent and precise. I don't think he was actually writing a screenplay, but he always seemed to be reaching further in: he wanted to know how far my house was from the center of Cassino, where the station was, how long it took to get to Rome, how many miles it was on the motorway, and whether there was a military or civilian airport in the area. He never actually told me that he wanted to make a film about the battle, but then he never really told me about his projects, nor did he expect me to ask. And yet the questions he asked me were very much like the ones he asked his assistants when he was location scouting near Childwickbury. He wanted to know all about the hotels in Cassino, too: how many rooms they had, and whether or not there were suites that could be rented for long periods. Everything pointed towards preparations for a film in Italy. He had even found out that near Aquino, a village about ten kilometers west of Cassino, there was an old military airport that had been used during the war as a base for transporting supplies to North Africa. It had been abandoned at the end of the war and was still there. It wasn't far from my house, yet I didn't even know it existed. But Stanley did.

At the end of 1998, one of Stanley's American friends told him he'd seen a TV documentary about the bombing of Montecassino Abbey. The film proposed a different theory from Stanley's, and was based on misunderstandings that the allies had experienced while trying to communicate in English, French, and Polish. The key to this misunderstanding was the word for abbot, *abate*, which sounds almost the same as *abitare* or "live" in Italian. Due to this, the first pilot in the squadron had bombed the abbey instead of the village of Cassino. The others had followed suit, and the abbey had been destroyed. "That's not what I think," said Stanley, "but there might be some truth in this linguistic theory. Tell me more." And he made me talk for hours on end about the differences in pronunciation between *abate, abito, abitato, abitare, abbazia,* and so on.

"Could be," said Stanley, "sometimes a minor glitch leads to a big mistake."

"In Sant'Angelo we say: a grain of salt is all it takes to ruin your broth."

"So true!" exclaimed Stanley, amused at my words of peasant wisdom.

13

A Fleeting Good-bye

On October 28, 1991, I would be turning fifty. As I drew closer to that milestone, I suspected at first, and then began to realize, that the few hours' rest I was giving myself simply weren't enough anymore. The truth really dawned on me one morning while I was carrying a box of books upstairs at Childwickbury. I'd been doing this every day for years and nothing had ever happened, until all of a sudden the weight of the books got the better of me. I felt my heart beat strangely. It was stronger than usual and out of time. All I could do was put down the box and sit on the steps.

I sat out of breath with my head bowed, my elbows on my knees, and my eyes closed. It was only then that I managed to see the events of the previous years all together. Of course, there had been the lengthy task of producing *Full Metal Jacket*, but when I started work on that project I was already exhausted because of the move from Abbots Mead, the restoration work at Childwickbury, and the organization of Stanley's office. Then there had been those winter months spent in the freezing cold at Beckton, and on top of that all the traveling: from one location to another, to and from the laboratories, and to Cambridge with poor Teddy at death's door. I always had a backache; it was like an unwelcome guest that wouldn't go home. And finally there was the death of Jessica, which had used up what little energy I had left.

Not long after all of this, Jon's accident had quite literally devastated me. But I went back to work again at the same frenetic pace. Instead of having a rest to get rid of this exhaustion, I let the usual routine take care of it, but it was an illusion: all I really did was forget how tired I was because I didn't actually have time to think about it. It was only on the weekends, when I managed to get a few hours to myself, that I realized how tired I was.

"What are you doing?" said Stanley, as he came down the stairs. "Do you feel all right?" He looked more surprised than worried. "I felt my heart change beat," I told him. "Here: my heart." And I touched my chest. Stanley reached out, took my hand, helped me up, and told me to follow him. We went into the dimly lit Projection Room and then down a curved passage that led to the door of the Billiard Room. Halfway down this passage, Stanley turned around and asked me to put up my arms. I did as he said, and he started to examine my chest and take my pulse. "Does it hurt if I touch you here?" he said, and I shook my head. "You know that's the first time I've seen you sit down in twenty years. You had me worried."

"I feel better now," I said.

However, the events of that morning left me with a bad feeling and I spent the rest of the day touching my chest to see if my heartbeat was regular. When I went to sleep, I dreamed all night about work, and the following afternoon I called Stanley and asked if I could come up to his office to talk to him.

"Stanley, there's something I have to tell you."

"What is it?"

"I'm thinking of leaving."

It sounds easy, but I had trouble getting those five words out. For once, I sat down at his desk without being asked, and for a few minutes without really coming to the point I blathered about how I had been afraid that morning on the stairs. Stanley kept asking me if I felt okay without really understanding what I was trying to say. When I finally managed to make myself understood, and he realized that I really was resigning, his expression changed: he frowned and sat in silence for a few seconds. I was expecting yet another rapid "No, no, no," but he said nothing. He just sat there with that look on his face that people have when they don't really know what they are dealing with.

November 4th 1991

Dear Emilio,

First of all ......

Happy 50th Birthday.

I am very sad that no-one told me about your suprize party!!

But nevertheless it would give me great pleasure to take you and Janet out for a belated Birthday Suprize Dinner in a really nice Italian Restaurant.

I hope you will allow me this small gesture to show my deep

The letter Vivian wrote me for my fiftieth birthday.

appreciation of your presence in my life for over 20 Years (GULP!) And of course your 50th birthday!!

Love and many Kisses,

Vivian

XXXXXXXXXXXXXXXXX
XXXXXXXXXXXXXXXXXXX

(Please leave me your answer in the Bothy as more than likely if you put it in the main house it will get lost!!)

"It's impossible," he said, finally. And we fell silent again.

"Stanley," I said, "I thought about it all night. I'm tired and I'm getting more and more tired. I don't think I can carry on working for you anymore." He didn't answer, so I continued telling him what I thought. "I want to go home. Back to Italy. My parents are old, and I'd like to spend a bit of time with them before it's too late. I hardly ever see them. I don't even manage to go to Cassino once a year. I miss them." There was still no answer. When I looked up, Stanley had the same incredulous expression on his face, and his eyebrows were closer together than ever. "I miss Sant'Angelo, too," I continued. "I've hardly ever seen the house we bought in the country next to my parents. Janette goes once a year to keep it tidy. I don't even know what furniture there is in it."

Despite his silence, I sensed that Stanley had somehow realized that this conversation was completely different from the others we'd had in his office. He didn't suggest an alternative. He didn't reply with a more fitting analysis. He didn't try to prove that all the variables hadn't been taken into consideration.

"Stanley?" I said. I desperately needed a reaction from him of some kind.

"If you're tired, we can look for some help," he said, finally.

I sighed. "How many times have we tried that? It has never worked. Actually, each time we tried it just got worse."

"I'm sorry," he said, looking me in the eyes.

"So am I, Stanley. So am I."

I sighed again, and so did he. Then I tried to explain better how I felt. I needed him to know all the things I had thought about the night before. "It's as if I felt I was always late. I have to drive faster, walk faster to catch up. I've always been in a hurry, I know. I've always been busy. But this is the first time I've felt late. I'm not just thinking about what I have to do anymore. Can you see the difference? In this way, even an easy job seems like hard work. Until recently it never even occurred to me that I might not be up to it. Now, even before something gets put off until the next day, I think that might happen. It's all different, I don't know how or why, but everything has changed."

All this left me short of breath, and I waited in vain for an answer. "I've done everything I possibly could," I concluded. "Now I think it's time I had a bit of a rest."

Stanley took his time, then he said: "Is there anything I can say or do to make you change your mind?"

"No. I think it's time I go."

"When?" he said, apprehensively.

"In three years."

In the days that followed, Stanley talked about it again. At the time he had said he would have to find a solution, but I hadn't dared to ask whether he meant that he accepted my leaving or that he would have to find a way to convince me to stay. I had talked far too much, and I felt completely drained. Telling Stanley that I wanted to go back to Italy had been more difficult than announcing to Janette's father that I wanted to marry his daughter.

Sometimes he simply said that he would feel bad if I really did leave. At other times he took a much lighter approach and joked: "What are you going back to Italy for anyway?" he said, provocatively. "Here you have the Mercedes, the Porsche. . . . There, what have you got?" "A tractor!" I replied. "I want to work in the fields again, like my father, and my grandfather before the war. I want to stay in the country where it's quiet, and where there isn't any traffic. I think you can perfectly understand that."

I started to look for someone to substitute for me: someone to take care of Stanley after I had gone. None of the people already working at Chidwickbury were suitable. We needed to find someone new. The fact that Stanley paid little or no attention to this suggested that nobody was going to pass the test. I was not so much afraid as sure that he wouldn't let anybody into his offices. In any case, if he wasn't prepared to accept a new factotum, he might at least consent to a new driver. I contacted a man who worked for a minicab company offering services to actors and film producers. I asked him a few questions to see what he was like and Stanley took note of his name and address. Every time I asked Stanley if he'd got in touch with the driver, he answered: "It slipped my mind. I'll do it tomorrow." If Stanley said something like that, he was lying.

The fact that nobody had permission to enter Stanley's offices was turning out to be a mixed blessing. Once I had gone, nobody would know how to find what he needed, be it clothes or research material for a film. Nobody knew where his shirts were, where the film production documents were kept, or which drawer was used for letters from his lawyers. Nobody knew; not even Stanley. I decided to make a comprehensive inventory of everything there was in Childwickbury. It would be an indispensible document for whoever took my place. I used the half hour of overtime I did before going home to open every drawer and every cabinet and write down what was inside.

The three years' notice I gave Stanley was spent pretty much in the usual way. I took people to his house. I looked after the building, the animals, the cars, and his private papers. I saw Childwickbury turn into a film studio for *A.I.*, and I looked on skeptically as a new batch of domestics and secretaries arrived.

Instead, the D'Alessandro household was subjected to substantial changes. We had to move our entire life to another country and leave our son and daughter to live theirs in England. After working at the Biomedic Center for six years, Jon had become deeply involved in mechanics and aeronautics again. He'd found a job in Watford in a factory that assembled fighter planes. Marisa had left the photo studio and gone into business with her boyfriend. Not long after she told us that they were going to live together, her brother did the same. "I'm a bit old-fashioned," said Janette, cautiously, as we sat in the living room with Jon, Sally, and her parents on Boxing Day. "I'm not sure that I really agree." "If that's what makes our daughter happy, then we're not going to stand in her way," said Sally's mother. The times were changing, and it was necessary to change with them. "Fine," said my wife after a moment's hesitation, "so be it. Let's propose a toast!"

Every time I reminded Stanley that I was about to leave for Italy, he changed the subject, played it down, or pretended that he had forgotten. In the meantime, I organized the day-to-day tasks in such a way that there wouldn't be any hitches when I had gone. Tracey was about forty and full of energy and enthusiasm. She'd been hired thanks to an advertisement in the local paper, and I thought she would be the right person to help manage Childwickbury. She settled into the household really well, and I had never seen her taking it easy or wasting time. When she told me that it would be easy for her to deal with some of the things to do in town because she lived in St. Albans and knew the shops there well, I was convinced that she was the one.

A few months later, we put the house in Farm Road up for sale. It had been our first real home. It symbolized economic stability, the birth of our children, their homework spread all over the dining room table, the bedroom where, after hours of work, I fell asleep exhausted in Janette's arms, the runner bean plants I had planted with my father, the cat flap in the back door for Ginger and Rosie, and the wooden posts from Abbots Mead for the fence in the yard. Twenty-six years of our life placed in the hands of a real estate agent.

We started to send out things to Italy with an international courier. After the move from Abbots Mead to Childwickbury, ours was a cakewalk.

There were only six months to go, but Stanley still didn't seem in the least bit worried. The notes he left on my desk never mentioned my departure. All this made me uneasy, because it confirmed my suspicion that he wasn't accepting it. Stanley didn't give me the chance to talk about it, and I couldn't find a way to just bring it into the conversation.

One month left, and no change in sight. Clearly I was going to have to be the one to broach the subject.

"Stanley, we're nearly there. There's less than a month to go. So, what are we going to do?"

"Oh, no. I need at least another three months of you staying here."

"I've sold my house, Stanley! I have no place to live in, don't you see? Everything is gone."

"Gone where?"

"You know where. . . ."

He grunted with irritation, and suddenly he was the same old problem-solving Stanley again. "Okay, rent a house, go in a hotel. I'll pay for everything. Find somewhere to stay for the time being, but for fuck's sake don't leave me now!"

So I rented a house in St. Andrew's Drive, signed a contract for six months, renewed it for another six, and then for yet another six.

At last I got Stanley to accept a date. I was going to leave England definitively on August 18, 1994. Four years had passed since I had told him I was leaving, and I'd been renting the house in Stanmore for eighteen months. Janette knew all too well what Stanley understood by "for the time being." So well, in fact, that she had found a job in a pharmacy and immediately started to look after the garden. In the summer of 1994, the house was in better condition than it had been when we rented it. "It's a pity you're leaving," said the owner. "I don't suppose you could stay another six months?" "Don't you start!" she snapped.

> Dear Emilio and family,
> Good luck & godspeed & joy go with you.
> If I think how I, who don't know you, will miss you, I realize how Stanley & his family will do so from the heart and length of years. Thank you.
>
> Candia

I had telephoned my parents and my brother in Italy to tell them that within a few months I would be back in Cassino. My mother and father were enthusiastic: at last they would be able to spend some proper time with me, not just three or four weeks every couple of years. They were so eager to see me again that they phoned nearly every day, even just to say hello or ask how the day had gone.

But no matter how hard we try to plan life, it always manages to surprise us. One Thursday evening, just before midnight, my niece called. My father was dead. He'd had a heart attack and died in his sleep. He was eighty-six.

I called Stanley to tell him I wouldn't be coming to work the next day. "See what's happened?" I said to him in tears. "I'd been afraid for months that this was going to happen."

At seven in the morning Janette took me to the airport, and in the afternoon of Friday, July 8, I was reunited with my relatives. My mother was very upset, and I was relieved to hear that she was going to stay with my brother for a while. The funeral was on Saturday morning in the Church of Sant'Angelo, and Marisa flew out to be there, too. I managed to put up with the oppressive silence of death for an entire day, and then I decided to leave immediately on Sunday afternoon. I couldn't stand all those people in my mother's living room. I felt like a stranger, distant, from another planet. I got home and called Stanley to tell him that I would be back at Childwickbury on Monday. There was a letter from him waiting for me on the desk at the entrance to the house:

July 9, 1994

Dear Emilio,

I'm so sorry about your father. I know how terribly sad it is. Christiane and I give you our love.

Yours, S

When I actually saw Stanley, all he said was, "Welcome back," and put a hand on my shoulder. He behaved just like any other day. He briefed me about the things I had to do and the trips to London I had to make for him. A few days later, during a break, he came over to me and asked if I was okay. We talked for a few minutes about my father. I told him how I felt and about the funeral in Cassino. For one brief moment, his father, Jack, and mine, Giuseppe, met through our words, within the walls of the Dome Room, beneath the clear light that filtered through the cupola.

It was not long before I was going to leave, but Stanley was unperturbed and continued to act as if nothing was happening. It was becoming ridiculous.

Without saying a word I had continued compiling the inventory: books, toothbrushes, new notepads, used notepads, spare shoelaces, cotton swabs, transcriptions of conversations with writers, spare pens, shirts, stationery, cans of cat food, letters from admirers, blank videotapes, nail clippers, reams of fax paper, socks, scissors, magazine cuttings, and trousers. I stapled the last page, and put the inventory on his bedside table together with a note explaining these three years of work done in secret. I had started to think that not accepting anyone to take my place was part of his strategy: Emilio wouldn't have the heart to leave Stanley to deal with all the impend-

One of the final notes from Stanley before I left.

ing disasters at Childwickbury that rumbled like a distant summer storm.

Less than a week to go. "Emilio, come home about lunchtime. I need you then," he said on the mobile. What did he need, and more importantly for how long? Did ten lightbulbs need changing or did he want to have me around for another ten months? "Okay, Stanley. As soon as I've finished here in town, I'll come straight back." "No, not straightaway, it's not urgent. Come about one, not before."

There was no one to be seen at Childwickbury. No gardeners, no secretaries going to the Stable Block. Nobody. I went into the house and walked towards the kitchen. When I went around the corner I found about thirty people. They all said hello and started clapping. Stanley had decided to organize a surprise leaving party for me. He'd invited Janette, Marisa, Jan and his wife Maria, Julian and Penny, and, of course, Andros. Seeing him there next to Stanley after all those years was moving. Tracey and the other domestics and gardeners shook my hand and patted me on the back. There I was: surprised, confused, excited, and happy.

The warmth of the friendly chatter that surrounded me was comforting and touching, but Andros's shrill laugh reached my ears just in time to help me fight back the tears. It was wonderful: Julian talked to Andros, Janette to Christiane, Marisa showed Stanley the cameras she had brought with her, then we all went out into the garden for soft drinks and sandwiches.

Stanley gave me a letter. It was from Margaret. She wished me all the best and said she was sorry that she couldn't be with us but she had to stay in the office. "Emilio, run for it while there's still time!" said Andros.

For the entire party, Stanley tried to make me change my mind. I hid behind a sheepish smile and made hurried remarks like, "It's all already organized," so as not to encourage him. It was clearly far too late to change my plans, but it was better not to give Stanley a chance. He had

Some snapshots taken at the party in my honor at Childwickbury: left, Stanley and Christiane; above, Andros.

hoped for a surprise, a happy ending to the party, and both Janette and I knew that until we were actually on that ferry, the risk of staying just a bit longer with Stanley was tangible.

Every time Christiane saw us speaking in a corner, she came over quickly. "Stanley, leave him alone!" At the end of the day, when Stanley had realized that he was getting nowhere, he changed attitude and confidently declared that he would be able to manage everything on his own without too much difficulty. The very idea made Christiane laugh out loud.

Andros was by far the most eloquent on the subject. Late in the afternoon, all he said was: "So when are you back—next week?" The only one who didn't laugh openly at this was Stanley. Andros had touched a sore point. For the rest of the party he spared Stanley his ironic remarks, and just made them about me.

In the early evening, all the guests had left Childwickbury. Just like on any other working day, I went round the house to make sure the cats and dogs weren't left out and to see that the doors and windows were closed. When I went inside, Stanley asked me to follow him to the Green Room, where he stopped and looked at me with sad eyes.

"Well then, this is it. . . ."

"Yes, Stanley. It's time to say good-bye."

"Are you really sure you want to go?"

"Yes, I'm sure."

Stanley didn't answer. He just looked down and tried to distract himself by staring at the cats, who were sleeping peacefully on the sofa. "So nobody will be coming tomorrow morning, then?"

"Stanley, don't make it more difficult than it already is."

"And what if you went to work for somebody else? You'd have more free time and you could stay here," he said, clutching at a last faint hope.

"No, you have refused to look for a substitute, and I'm not going to look for another employer. That's how things stand. I'm leaving for Italy. I'm going to take it easy, and I'm not going to get a job. Before you hired me, I worked in lots of different places and I had to deal with disagreements and problems in all of them. But with you, everything's always gone fine. This is the only place where I've felt like one of the family, actually more than family because we've never argued—well . . . with Janette, sometimes—"

"And if you don't get a job, what are you going to do in Italy?" he interrupted, without smiling at my last remark.

"I'm going to rest! And if I start to miss the effort, I'll take the tractor and go and plow the field behind the house."

"Can you have a phone put in the tractor so that I can call you?"

"I wouldn't be able to hear it. The tractor is very noisy. Do you remember how you got angry every time I went out in the Unimog and you tried to page me, but I didn't hear the beeping? The same thing would happen with the tractor."

"I'll buy you a phone that vibrates."

"Stanley, call me at home. You'll see. It'll be just fine."

While we were talking, we had walked past the Red Room, into the Dome Room, along the corridor to the Billiard Room, back to

Stanley's offices again, and then towards the Projection Room, without managing to say good-bye to each other. Neither of us had said a word for ten minutes. We walked slower and slower until we eventually stopped and silence fell. In the middle of the Projection Room, Stanley looked up at me. His eyes were moist, and he didn't know what to say. I just stood there, with the row of seats behind me, and watched Stanley as he started to walk back and forth, covering the full sixteen meters from one door to the other. I didn't know what to do. Then suddenly, as he passed near me, I impulsively grabbed his shirt and squeezed his forearms. "We have to say good-bye!" I told him, looking him straight in the eye. "We have to say good-bye for the last time."

Stanley started to cry. "I didn't think it was true," he said. "Unfortunately it is," I replied, with hardly any voice, and I started to cry, too. We hugged each other, and I felt our sobs shake us. Neither of us seemed able to let go. For a moment our eyes met, and Stanley took a couple of paces back. He raised one arm and, with a sweeping gesture that spanned the entire house, said: "Look at this: this house. This is your house. These rooms will always be here for you. I'll send anyone away to make room for you if you want to come back. Even if you don't let me know in advance, even if you just turn up on the doorstep. Come back whenever you want, but just come back." His voice faltered as he uttered these last words. He looked at me one last time, and hurried away towards the curved passage that led to the Billiard Room. I didn't hesitate, not even for a moment: I turned around and went off in the opposite direction, I walked quickly, taking one step after another until I reached the courtyard, where I got in the minibus and, with a lump in my throat, set off along the road that led to home.

I spent the following two days making the final arrangements for our departure. Janette sorted out the house, and I took care of the documents. I parked Stanley's minibus outside the house for the last time and left the keys on the table. I also left a small present for him and one for Christiane. That's how I said good-bye to him.

Everything was ready. Janette had packed our clothes, the last of the ornaments, and a few plants. I put the suitcases and boxes into the Datsun. We got in, and for the umpteenth time and perhaps the last, I drove towards Dover to take the ferry to Calais. I'd made this trip countless time for Stanley and not often enough for myself. We drove across France towards Switzerland and the Alps. We crossed the Italian border, then passed Milan and Rome. I left the motorway for Naples and drove towards Cassino. On the left, the mountain dominated by the white, rectangular abbey seemed familiar. I drove out of the town, along the narrow country roads better suited to carts than cars like my Datsun, and climbed to the top of Sant'Angelo. We left the village behind us, crossed the river Gari, and followed the line of trees.

My mother heard the sound of the engine as I turned right into the courtyard of the cottage and came out to meet us. We hugged each other, and I saw her smile. It was then that I hoped Janette and me being there would help her get over the death of my father. I unloaded the car and took our bags inside. The furniture we had sent from Farm Road was still wrapped up. Then, the silence of the countryside was broken by the sound of the phone ringing.

"Is everything okay?" said the voice at the other end.

"Yes, Stanley. Everything's fine. We've just this minute got home."

"How are you getting on in Italy?"

"It's a bit early to say, Stanley, don't you think?"

Janette shook her head and tried to concentrate on unpacking our suitcases. It was the evening of August 20, 1994, and I was Italian again.

14

PERSONAL CHEMISTRY

I'D TOLD MYSELF THAT all I needed to get well was a bit of peace and quiet, and it was nice to find out that I was right. As soon as I set foot in my house in Italy, I felt at home and relaxed. I gradually got out of my old habits and made space for new ones that were less urgent and more fundamental: weeding the garden, hoeing the borders so that Janette could plant flowers, collecting the eggs that the hens laid for us every morning, and going into the village to buy anti-parasite spray for the fruit trees.

I certainly hadn't forgotten Stanley. Even if I had wanted to, it wouldn't have been possible. He phoned two or three times a day, every day. For the first week, he kept on asking me how I was settling in to the new house. He was almost obsessive, but I think this was due to worrying more about how he was going to manage without me than me without him. But gradually he calmed down, and our phone calls became friendly chats where we could talk about how things were going. I told him about Sant'Angelo, and he told me about Childwickbury. "It's not as bad as I thought," he said once. "Keeping in touch by phone is easy, and it seems to work." This made me feel less guilty about having left him there with two films on the go.

"Today I went to St. Albans," he said, and specified, "on my own." There was a hint of pride in his voice. "I took the Mercedes. I bought two blue shirts. And I paid by myself. I remembered to take my wallet!" Yes. Stanley was going to get by without me. More or less . . .

"Emilio, where are my socks?" I guided him from a distance. It was a sort of surreal treasure hunt between Cassino and St. Albans. I didn't point out that I'd spent three years compiling an inventory to solve this kind of problem. I thought that perhaps the socks were an excuse to call me or that maybe going through the inventory somehow made him sad. That's what happened to me when, rummaging in my jacket pockets, I came across one of his notes with the shopping list. I stopped and gazed at it tearfully.

Stanley wrote the occasional letter, but he preferred the phone, so I ended up becoming part of his circle of *phone pals.* My chats with Stanley became a regular appointment, and without the constant stress of having to meet deadlines, I rediscovered how pleasant it was to talk to him, how incisive and amusing his remarks were, and how easy it was to be charmed by the way he talked. He was so kind, even now that he didn't have to ask me for anything, it was just impossible to interrupt him and say that I had to go. From time to time, he couldn't resist the temptation to ask whether I'd though about coming back to England. "In a couple of years, Stanley," I said, trying to be as vague as I could. "If the kids organize something then perhaps I'll pop over for a couple of days."

Leaving Jon and Marisa in England hadn't been all that hard. After all, they were adults with their own lives and families. Both Janette and I had always thought that being independent and self-sufficient were precious qualities that helped you grow up. We had brought up our children to know that they could always count on us but were aware that they would also have to make their own decisions. Our house was always a haven—a place they could come back to, where they could talk about their experiences, and perhaps even ask for advice. The fact that we were thousands of kilometers apart didn't change this.

But the first Christmas we spent alone in Italy was terribly sad. My father had warned us about this before we left, but I had simply smiled affectionately and put it down to the way elderly people have of thinking about things. But now I found out it was true. "Emilio, I miss Marisa and Jon," my wife declared. "Janette, we can't have it both ways. . . ." It was obvious that since the phone calls were not enough, we would soon have to find a way to see them again.

We had more land than we needed, so I entrusted it to a farmer who lived nearby. I preferred to use the tractor I'd talked to Stanley about to help my brother cultivate his cornfields. After a year I decided to sell the land and concentrate on my vegetable patch. Time seemed to pass more serenely among lettuce, tomatoes, and potatoes. My father had known all too well that tending one's garden was the secret to happiness.

In Cassino I met friends I hadn't seen since I was a teenager, but at the same time I had the impression that I had lost just as many. I often thought of those I'd left at Brands Hatch and wondered if they ever thought of me. One day, while I was sorting out the trunk where I had kept all the things from my racing days in the attic in Farm Road, I found Trevor Stiles's business card. I used to compete against him at the beginning of the eighties, and I hadn't seen him since I'd stopped racing. I decided to give him a ring.

"Is that Trevor Stiles?" I said rather unconvincingly as I fiddled with his business card. It was, after all, very old indeed.

"Speaking," he replied.

"Trevor! It's Emilio D'Alessandro. Do you remember me?"

"Emilio!" he exclaimed enthusiastically after a moment's hesitation. "Of course I remember; we used to race together! We were always there, head to head, but there was never an accident! I remember, I remember. . . . You used to work for a film director, didn't you?"

Poor Trevor: after all those years he remembered me but he had never known Stanley's name. We talked on the phone for a while. I told him that I'd recently returned to Italy to work on the land and I was surprised to learn that he had set up a farm in Sussex and grew wheat and vegetables. "Now we can compete to see who has the best harvest!" I said with a laugh. "Oh, Emilio, you're my best friend!" You need to have spent time at the circuit to know how sincere Trevor was when he said that.

Not long after I arrived, Stanley's name came up. I had to go to the Town Hall in Cassino to renew my identity card, which had expired in 1960 when I left Italy. When they asked me what job I had done in England, I said I had worked for Warner Bros. The clerk asked me to be more specific, so I added that I had been employed by Hawk Films, an English film production company. "But what exactly did you do?" insisted the clerk, holding a pen and ready to write down a job description that fitted into the established categories acceptable to the document. "A bit of everything, really. Driver, housework, transport of production material and personal documents. I was a plumber, too." But the look on the clerk's face seemed more and more confused. "I was the personal assistant of a film director." The clerk started to write this down and then looked up and asked: "Which director?"

In the days that followed, every time I met someone I knew I was asked the same question: "I hear you used to work for a film director. Who was it?" This went on for days. In the end, exasperated, I gave one of my friends a videotape of *Full Metal Jacket* and admitted: "Stanley Kubrick. I worked for Stanley Kubrick." The next day, everyone in the village knew. I started to get phone calls and visits from people I hadn't seen for decades. "But did you really work for Stanley Kubrick? *That* Kubrick?" they repeated incredulously, and I nodded. "That's impossible!" they all said. "Stanley Kubrick is one of the greatest directors in the world! And you worked for him?" It was a bit embarrassing for me to say, yes, for about twenty-five years I worked for that director, the one whose name makes everyone uneasy. They looked at me doubtfully and asked: "But how the hell did you manage that?" And I didn't know what to answer. It had just happened. I didn't go looking for the job. Actually, Stanley Kubrick had found me and convinced me to leave Mac's Mini-cabs. That was the part of the story that made my friends laugh the most.

When I spoke to Stanley on the phone, I told him about how this news had leaked out: "I didn't want to mention your name, but they wouldn't believe me in the Town Hall, and then all the others kept on pestering me, and so in the end I showed them the letters from Hawk Films. Anyway, in the end they all went mad and wouldn't stop saying how good you are and how great your films are, and that you're the best. One of them even asked me to tell you this, and he said it in English, too: 'Tell Stanley he is the best!'"

"Really?" he said with surprise. "Don't they hate me?"

"Hate you? They're all mad about you and your films!"

"I had no idea. What with all those thing they write in the papers . . ."

"And that's not all. They want to know everything. They ask me questions I can't answer. They know more than I do! They can list all your films, including titles I've never even heard of, and they say they've seen them all more than once!"

"I'm pleased to hear it. Please thank them very much on my behalf."

"And they want to meet you, Stanley! They all say how fantastic it would be to be able to meet you."

"What are they like?" he asked, in a different tone of voice. "Have they mentioned *A Clockwork Orange*?"

"No, Stanley," I reassured him, "they talk about all your films in general. They're people from Cassino and Sant'Angelo. I can't really see them threatening anybody."

"I see. Anyway, be careful just the same."

Faced with this unbridled enthusiasm for Stanley, I was ashamed to admit that I had never actually watched one of his films from beginning to end. Someone lent me them all on VHS, and that's where I discovered Stanley Kubrick's work, in my living room in the country. The only one I never actually watched was *A Clockwork Orange*, because somehow I thought I would be offending him if I did. Every time this film came up when we were talking, Stanley became annoyed. He had never really got over what had happened when the film came out.

On the phone I didn't tell him that at last I'd seen his films. I knew he would be happy, but at the same time I didn't really want to talk about work past or present. I knew that when I had left he was working on *A.I.* and an adaptation of *Traumnovelle*, and every day I wondered how it was going. I asked myself whether he'd found the actors, who was taking him to the studios, and who took the musicians, technicians, and actors to his house. Yet I forced myself not to answer these questions, and I never asked him directly, either. I needed to get away from that world once and for all. When we spoke on the phone, I just asked about Childwickbury, the family, and how Christiane and the girls were doing. I tried to think of Stanley as the best friend I had left in England, the person I had laughed with so many days, cried with for just a few others, the one I had spent the longest hours with, and who had taught me most of what I knew.

It's only now that I really understand why I didn't ask him about the films: I was afraid he would say that it was all different, that things were worse, and that he'd convince me to go back. I knew that he wasn't as happy as he had been. I could feel it. He tried to hide how tired and discontented he was, but a slight difference in his tone of voice or a not very convincing "Everything's fine" was enough for me to realize the truth. These small rifts upset me and were the only things that stopped me from being completely happy in Sant'Angelo. I tried as hard as I could not to think about it. I even declined to go to visit our son and daughter and convinced them to come and see us in Italy instead. And then one day Marisa called to say that she was expecting a baby. Our first grandchild was on the way, and Janette rushed off to book a flight for London.

On April 18, 1996, Janette and I arrived in London for a three-week visit. My daughter's belly was already changing shape under her jumper. I smiled as I remembered when Janette was pregnant. I used to sit and stare at her smooth round belly at night while she slept beside me. Neither Marisa nor Janette seemed particularly overawed by what was happening. Women have a way of being extremely practical at times like this.

On May 1, we went to Childwickbury. Jan had called to find out when I was free. "Come to the house one afternoon; Stanley wants to talk to you." When we arrived, Christiane was in the spacious kitchen where, as usual, a sort of reassuring chaos reigned. She came forward to hug us, and we all greeted each other affectionately. While we were having some tea, I told her how I spent my time in Italy. There wasn't a lot to say. In fact, in two minutes I'd given her all my news. That was the best thing about it. Christiane laughed and then looked behind me. I turned around and saw Stanley standing a short distance away. He spread his arms and smiled: "Welcome back! Let's have a cup of coffee." And with that he put an arm around my shoulder to lead me off to one side. Janette and Christiane went out into the garden, and Jan left us alone, too.

He looked at me and asked, "So, how's it going?"

"You know how it's going. We talk on the phone every day!"

"You're looking good," he said with satisfaction. "I'm glad you're getting some rest. You deserve it."

"You seem to have lost some weight," I said, "but you're just the same as always."

Stanley smiled and turned to look at the garden, where our wives were chatting away. "How are things organized now?" I asked. "Everything's fine," he replied without looking away from the French windows. "Tracey has the ground floor under control. But let's not talk about that," he said drily and turned to face me again. Then with a sincere smile he said, "Do you feel you could help me out on this film starting in the summer?"

No sooner hooked than landed.

"It won't take long. You'll like it," he added to encourage me.

"Is it a new film?"

"No, it's the one I was working on when you left."

"Which, *Traumnovelle*?"

"Yes."

"You haven't started it yet?"

"No, it's called *Eyes Wide Shut* now, but . . ." He stopped. "If you don't come back . . . I don't know . . . I might have second thoughts."

I studied him to see if he was serious. What had those guys in Cassino said? "Stanley Kubrick is a genius!" Could I prefer a tractor to working for a genius? I'd never thought of it in these terms before. If I'd been more intelligent, I would have realized sooner. *If you don't come back, I'll have second thoughts . . .*

"What job are you talking about?" I asked.

"The usual. I've already chosen the actors: Tom Cruise and Nicole Kidman. They are very nice, and I'm sure you'll get on fine, but you won't work for them, and you won't have to do anything for the family either, for Christiane, Anya, Katharine, or Jan. No, you'll work for me. I need you as before for my private daily office work, to take me from home to location, and to be on location in my office for all my private stuff, as usual. You know the drill." And with this explanation, he concluded all the formalities in my contract.

"How long will it take?"

"Sixteen weeks."

"Sure!"

"Sixteen weeks, that is really all it will take, and it's all I've got: I have to respect this deadline; I've made an agreement with Warners and the actors. Cruise is only free for sixteen weeks, but it will be enough. It's a small film."

I didn't believe a word of it. The agreement with this Tom Cruise wouldn't have amounted to much once Stanley had set his production machine in motion. If *Eyes Wide Shut* really was a little film, given that preparations had been under way for some time, with a bit of luck we might have been able to get it finished in two years.

"When do we start?" I asked, and realized that Stanley had noticed the use of the plural, because his face lit up.

"At the end of August."

"I'll have to get the house in Italy organized. Find someone who can pick up the post, pay the bills, that sort of thing."

"Right. Make yourself ready for June."

"No, if we're going to start at the end of August, I can arrive in the middle of the month."

"Okay, say, for that time or a bit before," he said, clinching the deal. "Come with me," he added. "I've got something to show you."

And he went out, took me to the end of the colonnade, stopped in front of the garage door, and asked me to look inside.

"I don't believe it!" I exclaimed. "That's a Rolls-Royce!"

The midnight blue car reflected the light that filtered through the door and gleamed.

"Is it yours?" I asked.

"Yes."

"Didn't you always say that you didn't fancy a Rolls?"

Talking to Stanley about cars, we had agreed that Mercedes were the best: they were solid, with excellent engineering, spacious inside but without looking too big. Rolls were too imposing, and weren't in keeping with Stanley's practical character.

"I know," he answered. "They made me buy it. John Boorman suggested it."

"A mechanic?"

"The director. You know him. You've talked to several times on the phone."

"No doubt . . . And so this Boorman knows about cars, does he?"

"No. Do you know how to drive a Rolls?" he said, fumbling in his pockets and pulling out a black key.

The car still smelled new inside. I sat on the cream-colored leather seat and pulled the door towards me. It closed with a heavy, almost silent click. The Rolls glided out of the garage, and its bodywork glistened in the sun.

"Have you seen what's new?"

"Well, it's a beautiful car," I said insipidly.

"No, I mean, haven't you seen the partition? John Boorman recommended it because the front and back seats are separated. You weren't my driver anymore, and I didn't want anyone else to hear the phone calls I made for work. Anyway, do you like it?"

"No," I replied simply, "I don't like Rolls-Royce. There's no doubt that it looks good, but it's too cumbersome. And then a car like that makes people envious; they all look when you drive past. And you always need to keep it clean, so that passersby can use it as a mirror!"

Stanley started to laugh. "Okay, Emilio, you can let me know what you think when you drive it this summer, all right?"

"I need to talk to Janette first."

We walked back into the garden towards our wives. "Stanley wants me to come back and work for him." I announced. "Fine," said Janette, surprising me, "if it's okay with you, accept." Christiane smiled as if none of this was a surprise to her. Stanley's request, the fact that I accepted, or my wife's reaction.

"I'm pleased," said Janette later as we were driving back. "It gives me an excuse to stay with Marisa now that there's a grandchild on the way." I turned to look at her, and she smiled and added: "I already knew that he was going to offer you a job."

"So did I," I replied. "Then why didn't you say anything?"

"Because you *want* to go back and work for Stanley. And that's fine with me. Let's come back."

That same evening, while we were at my daughter's house for dinner, I got a call from Jan. "Stanley told me you've agreed to come back and work for him," he said cheerfully.

"Yes, in the summer. In August, I think."

"Thanks Emilio! I just don't know how to thank you!"

"Well . . . you're welcome."

"Everything was so complicated without you," he continued. "Stanley was never happy. He could never make up his mind to start work on a film."

"But isn't everything ready? When I left, he seemed to be on the point of starting filming."

"That's true, but then . . . he couldn't make up his mind. There was no way we could convince him."

He told me that Stanley wouldn't accept help from anyone. Not even to go to the supermarket. He drove everywhere on his own. Sometimes he let Christiane take him. That's why the Rolls smelled so new, I thought. Jan confessed that not even Tracey had managed to be granted access to his offices or apartment. Everything was locked.

"Thank God you've decided to come back, Emilio. You've taken a weight off my shoulders! Nobody can substitute the chemistry between you and Stanley."

During the months that followed, we prepared to return to England. We planned to stay away for two years. We didn't take Stanley's estimated sixteen weeks at all seriously. On July 31, 1996, we were back at Heathrow Airport. Once again, Marisa and her ever-more-prominent belly were there to meet us.

Vivian had moved to America, and Stanley wanted us to stay in her house, but Janette and I refused. I explained that it was too big, and Janette added convincingly that it was also too far from Childwickbury. We preferred somewhere in the country similar to where we were in Italy. "Then come and live with me. You can have the Bothy!" exclaimed Stanley. He was already convinced and started to say that it was all ready and all that was missing was the bedsheets. "No thanks, Stanley. We've already had this conversation. We'd rather live on our own."

While Hobby Films was looking for accommodation with a six-month, renewable contract (that's how hopelessly optimistic Stanley was when he was about to start work on a film), we slept for a couple of nights at the Watford Hilton, and then for a week in a room that the domestics had prepared for us on the first floor at Childwickbury. We eventually found a suitable cottage on Bedmond Road in Pimlico, a quarter of an hour from Stanley's house. Stanley paid the rent, and he gave us a white Rover 216. As usual, he looked after all our needs as if he were looking after himself.

Even loading and unloading was a pleasure when it meant using the Unimog. Stanley took this picture.

The Well Farm Cottage was only semi-furnished, so Stanley made sure we had everything that was missing. Jan showed me to the Stable Block. "I'm sorry," he said, opening the warehouse door, "there must have been a misunderstanding, because the workmen have piled up all the furniture here instead of taking it to the cottage. From here on, you're on your own." Welcome back, Emilio. "You can use the Unimog," suggested Jan. The very word was enough to put a smile back on my face. I hadn't seen it or driven it for two years, and I was dying to.

It was in good condition. I don't know who had been looking after it while I was away, but I hoped they'd taken it out to stretch its legs every now and then. I climbed up into the cab, turned the key, pulled the engagement lever, and the Unimog greeted me with a happy roar. Sitting high up in the cab as I drove along the road to the cottage, I felt great: it was just like the good old days.

"I noticed that there are some flower beds around the house," I said to the owner of the cottage a few days later. "If you don't need them, could I use them? I'd like to plant something."

"Aren't you only staying for four months? The agency told me that the rent's paid until December."

"Listen, don't worry. We'll be saying good morning to each other for at least a couple of years."

The farmland was good, and the zucchini, peppers, and beans I put in grew quickly. So did the flowers that Janette planted; they bloomed in just a few days thanks to the summer sun. When the owner of the farm complimented me, all I said was, "We are country folk." And when he asked if I would like to come and work on his farm, I burst out laughing. "The job I'm doing is quite tiring enough, and I don't think I'll be doing it for long. Until I few weeks ago, I thought I was retired."

On the morning of August 7, I started work for Stanley again. I woke up early and at about nine, got in the Rover and drove to Childwickbury. I hadn't received instructions of any kind the previous day.

When I went into the kitchen, Tracey came over to meet me. "Welcome back, Emilio!" It was good to see that she was just as busy as I remember her being when I left.

"Now that you're back, what do I have to do?" she said.

"What you've done up to now," I answered. "Don't mind me. Carry on with your work as you normally would."

"And what about you? Where do you start?"

"With Stanley," I answered impulsively, and headed towards my desk at the entrance to the house. On it I found a closed envelope with an "E." written on it in the usual place. I opened it and started to read:

My private rooms need to be cleaned. Let's meet on the
ground floor in the afternoon, and if possible, you can come
upstairs to tidy up my apartment. Don't go up there now. Wait
until the afternoon. Anyway, I think there's enough to keep
you busy on the ground floor. Sort yourself out. You know the
drill. I'm sorry for the mess I made. Do the best you can.

"I have to clean his rooms here on the ground floor," I announced to Tracey.

"Nobody has ever been in his offices," she confided in a low voice, "either downstairs or upstairs in the apartment."

The cloud of suspicion grew increasingly dense. "I'm sorry for the mess I've made," Stanley's letter confessed.

I was happy to open my cupboards again and find my work clothes just as I had left them two years earlier: boots, long-sleeved shirts, gloves, and the raincoat I wore in the country when it rained. Nothing had been touched. I held a bunch of keys in my hand and hesitated outside the Green Room for a moment. "Nobody has ever been in . . ." Let's have a look.

The large room with green velvet wallpaper didn't exist anymore. Stanley's cats had been left to run wild for two years and had scratched everything within their reach to bits. The sofa was in tatters, its upholstery ripped here and there. There were balls of fur and dust on the floor, as well as crisscrossed threads of unraveled material. The cats must have hung from the walls and dangled from the velvet wallpaper, which was ruined beyond repair.

I cleaned the floor with the vacuum cleaner. Then I dusted down the furniture. Stanley arrived in the afternoon. "Sorry, Emilio," he said quickly, and disappeared in the direction of the Red Room. He closed the door behind him rather too quickly, as if he had something to hide. He opened it again almost immediately, popped his head out, and said: "Don't go upstairs." Then he disappeared again. I carried on cleaning the Green Room.

At six o'clock I called him: "Stanley, it's time for me to go home." We had agreed on clearly defined working hours: from ten in the morning to six in the afternoon, plus half a day on Saturday and Sundays off. "Fine. Thanks for everything," he replied, "and say hello to Janette from me. See you tomorrow." It seemed to work.

The following day I had to deal with the Red Room. As soon as I opened the door I was hit by a pungent smell that I knew all too well. The cats had peed repeatedly on the filing cabinets, and nobody had taken the trouble to clean up after them, or more precisely, nobody had been given permission to do so. Some of the plywood panels on top were covered in patches of greenish mold. I could just imagine Stanley in there: he would move calmly among the piles of paper, and without losing concentration, would wipe away a layer of dust from a book or carefully lengthen his stride to step over some mess on the floor, and all without ever taking his eyes off what he was reading.

The Dome Room wasn't quite so bad. It was stuffed so full of televisions, faxes, computers, photocopiers, and printers that there was not much space left to make untidy. The corridor with the shelves full of LPs was so dirty that you left footprints on the tiles where you passed. I opened one of the two secret storerooms: yards of cobwebs stretched from one corner of the ceiling to another, while others dangled from the walls. There were feathers, whole skeletons of dead birds, dry leaves, and twigs that had fallen down the chimney and rolled or wafted into the center of the room. I expected Christopher Lee dressed as Dracula to appear at any moment.

Stanley, with a seraphic expression on his face but looking slightly embarrassed, pretended he hadn't seen the cobwebs in my hair. Fleetingly, he said: "Thanks, do carry on." And slipped off with the usual warning: "Don't go upstairs." If the Billiard Room had been in the same state as the others, I would never have got out alive. Luckily, it was the cleanest room of all, because it could be accessed from the Projection Room. Tracey and the others, using the excuse that they had to clean the master bathroom, must have secretly swept it out.

In a week I had finished the ground floor, and Stanley looked at me contentedly. It was the first time I'd seen that satisfied smile peek out from underneath his beard since when I had worked together with Andros and Margaret. I had learned to recognize it when we were at Abbots Mead, and it filled me with pride and joy.

"This afternoon you can go upstairs," he said, finally.

"All right. Will I need anything?" I took care to ask.

"You'll see," was the cryptic reply.

"Should I take some detergents?"

"You'll see."

It couldn't be worse than the ground floor. I pushed the door, but it wouldn't open, so I squeezed through the gap and found myself surrounded by paper. It was as if the London Library had been emptied out into the house. I climbed over two cardboard boxes and reached a pile of books with a note on that said: "Start with the ones marked '1.' Number '2' can wait. Nearly all '3' are to throw away." There were numbered Post-its on the top of each pile. That's what Stanley had been doing for the last few days while he kept me away from the disaster. In front of me, there was a narrow, undulating path that led towards the door of Christiane's room. The door to Stanley's office and his bookcase were almost completely blocked. On the other side, with a bit of imagination you could find a way to get into his room, but the corridor leading to the other rooms at the end was impassable. Anyway, nearly everything had "1" on it. There were two years of mail, faxes, letters from Warners, from lawyers, messages from his assistants, books that had been borrowed and never returned, books left open, and books with other books inside them used as bookmarks. I called him on the intercom: "Stanley, aren't you at least going to tell me what I have to do? Shall I get a bulldozer?" "Use your head. Choose. Put what you think is useful in order to one side. Throw away the rest."

When you have to climb a mountain, you should never look at the summit. Keep your eyes on your feet, and take it one step at a time. I started with the post: the brown envelopes were letters from law firms and, generally speaking, had to be kept. I looked for the name of the sender on the white envelopes. If I knew them, I put them in a separate pile; if I didn't, I threw them in the box of things to be burned. It didn't matter if they were fan letters or from other directors asking advice; they wouldn't be much use after two years anyway. I gradually made some space and managed to move forward another half a meter. I found audiotapes, photographs of actors and actresses, and videotapes. Basically, two years of Stanley's life heaped up without rhyme or reason. I found everything apart from the inventory I'd written before I left. The pile of books to take back to the London Library grew slowly but surely. I could already see the expression on the librarian's face when I went to take them back.

I kept on cleaning and sorting things out; I moved forward a yard at a time for over a week. On the first Saturday, I lost track of time and kept on working until the evening. Janette didn't even try to contact me. As usual, she was more shrewd and realistic than me and hadn't put much faith in the idea of regular working hours. In the evening, like on the other days, Stanley said good-bye: "See you tomorrow. Say hello to Janette." On Sunday morning I was at Childwickbury surrounded by Stanley's papers instead of at Brands Hatch, where friends I hadn't seen for years were waiting for me. He didn't miss a chance to have me spend more time at Childwickbury than we had agreed: at ten to six Stanley would call me on the intercom to tell me that this or that needed doing. "Can you take me to St. Albans?" He looked so happy when he left the house and got into the car with me that I just couldn't get cross about the overtime. Yes. I really was working for Stanley again.

During one of our breaks, I told him that I had watched his films when I was in Italy.

"Well, I'm pleased to hear it!" he exclaimed. "Which one do you like best?"

"I really like *Spartacus*," I answered.

Stanley suddenly became very serious and whispered, "Um . . . I don't think much of that."

"What about the others?" he asked. I told him that I had decided not to watch *A Clockwork Orange* because he had banned it. Stanley smiled. Then I told him that I had been enchanted by the elegant atmosphere of *Barry Lyndon*: the crystal-clear skies and green hills of Ireland had brought to mind the months spent with the actors on the set, Ryan O'Neal's charm, and the dignified beauty of Marisa Berenson. On the other hand, *The Shining* had left me a bit disorientated. I remembered how difficult it had been to make the film, and I perceived the tension that there had sometimes been on the set between Jack Nicholson and Shelley Duvall. I couldn't separate reality from fiction.

"I don't know how to explain it, Stanley," I confessed. "It's not easy for me to watch your films as if they were just any old films. My memories get in the way. I can't help thinking about how long it took us to film that scene, or about how foul the weather was when we were working on another. I don't know how you see them," I added. "Are they stories or professional challenges that you have succeeded in?"

"It's about fifty-fifty. It depends," he answered.

"And then I realized that sometimes it wasn't all that easy for me to follow them," I continued. "The story, I mean. I watched *Dr. Strangelove* again, and . . . well, it's not so easy for me to understand your films as, say, a western. There there's always a bad guy who shoots, a good sheriff who goes after him. . . . They're simple stories, and I understand them immediately, but yours . . ."

"You didn't like mine," said Stanley, helping me to finish.

"No, it's not that I didn't like them, it's that—"

"What do you think of *Full Metal Jacket*?"

"Well, *Full Metal Jacket* disturbed me a bit, too."

"Do you mean the violence in the film?"

"No, that wasn't it. In that sense it was no worse than the terrible things I remember seeing when I was a child. It's . . . well, there was . . . too much swearing. A bit of it's no problem, but Lee Ermey was a machine gun! Couldn't you have edited some of it out?"

"The foul language was there because that's how it works in real life."

"You're right. It reminded me of the drill sergeant when I was doing national service. He used to lift these stocky recruits up by their collar, and I was terrified that he would do the same to me: I was only half their size. Lee was identical to him, but . . . Stanley, in the Italian version the bad language was just too much."

"So you think Riccardo and Mario did a good job?"

"Too good, I would say!"

"There, you see? It's *the truth*, and that's how it should be."

"Yes. You're right, as always."

At half past six in the morning on November 17, 1996, Katarina Daniela, our first grandchild was born. It was the third time I'd seen a new born baby in hospital, and exactly the same thing happened as when I had gone to see my own children. I could have stayed there for days, pressed against the glass of the nursery, gazing at Katarina's tiny hands and the thin wisps of hair on her forehead.

Six weeks later, Marisa went back to work, and my wife looked after Katarina. Freelance photographers are busy, especially on weekends with all the weddings and Bar Mitzvahs. Katarina spent the weekend with us at Well Farm Cottage from Friday morning until Monday.

One Sunday afternoon, we decided to take the Rover and go for a drive around the countryside with the baby. Katarina was only two months old, but she was already incredibly curious and was clearly drawn to everything she saw out of the window. She seemed to focus on a colorful cottage, the cows in the fields, and the wooden garden fences. Janette explained everything, and Katarina listened very carefully. "Look at that," said my wife, "isn't it funny? Instead of being lulled to sleep by the sound of the engine like most babies are, she's more wide awake than ever." "She's a D'Alessandro," I commented with pride. "How could she possibly fall asleep in a car?"

It was getting on toward evening when Stanley called on the mobile. He asked if I could stop by his house to pick up some documents to take to Julian. When he found out that Janette and Katarina were outside in the Rover, he asked me to invite them in so that he could see the baby.

"Isn't she beautiful?" he said. "Can I hold her?" He drew her close to him, and Katarina reached out and started playing with Stanley's beard and hair. "What tiny fingers she has, and beautiful eyes, and such smooth hair. God bless you, Katarina," he said, and kissed her on the cheek. She shook all over when his beard touched her and let out a happy little scream because it tickled. We all laughed affectionately. "You have a lovely granddaughter," he said, placing her back in my

My granddaughter Katarina sitting on Stanley's Rolls at Well Farm Cottage.

wife's arms. "Bring her here whenever you want, Janette. Feel free to use the Bothy as if it were you own home."

Stanley was great with kids. He had a very special relationship with Alex, Katharina's oldest child, as well as with Anya's son Sam. The same thing happened with my granddaughter: she learned to recognize him immediately and hugged him tight every time she met him. A couple of years later, when Stanley called home to talk to me, Katarina often answered the phone. She wasn't yet two, but she thought it was a toy. "You are Stanley," she said when she recognized his voice, "here's grand-dad." "My God, your granddaughter already knows how to answer the phone! She even asked me how I was and told me to wait. She's better than a grown-up secretary!"

15

EYES WIDE SHUT

"EMILIO, COME HERE. I want to introduce you to my actors!" said Stanley over the intercom. I knew hardly anything about the film that he was going to start work on in just a few weeks' time, just what he told me when we had met in spring. He was standing in the corridor on the ground floor beside two well-dressed, smiling young people. "Can you take them outside? The driver is waiting for them in the courtyard," he said, withdrawing to his rooms. He had clearly intended to leave us alone. Tom and Nicole asked me if I was married, if I had children, and as usual, what it was like to work for Stanley.

"Just fine," I replied. "Everything has always worked just perfectly."

"But have you really been working for him for over twenty years?" Tom asked.

"Since the end of 1970."

"Congratulations for being with Stanley for such a long time," remarked Nicole.

"And just think, I'd sworn to be faithful to my wife."

"What do you think of the sweet couple?" said Stanley, when I went back to his office.

"Very kind and polite. What do you think?"

"I get on well with them."

Rather late that evening, Stanley gave me a sealed envelope with the script of *Eyes Wide Shut* and asked me to take it to Tom and Nicole. "If they've already gone to bed, lean it against their bedroom door so that when they wake up, it will fall on their feet."

Stanley had rented an apartment for Tom and Nicole on the first floor of a house on the other side of Well End. I knew it all too well: that was where I had seen Stanley's crew at work, surrounded by cats, for a scene from *A Clockwork Orange*, for the very first time, twenty-six years ago. It was like going back to the beginning again.

When I reached the gate of the house, the security guard stopped me. The Cruise family could not be disturbed. When I pointed out that the reason I needed to pass was because Stanley Kubrick had sent me, he replied that his employer, Tom Cruise, had put him there precisely to avoid intrusions of this kind. "Listen," I said, in an attempt to break the deadlock, "I know the owner. Every year I bring him a case of whiskey on Stanley's behalf. I know the house, too. I know it so well that I know which steps of the wooden staircase creak. I could make my way to Tom and Nicole's bedroom door without anyone hearing a sound, and that is where I have to go. Trust me, and trust Stanley Kubrick, who sent me."

The following morning, I found something from Stanley, too. There was a sealed envelope on my desk: "Please stay around because at noon I have to be at Tom Cruise's house. Make sure we take the Rolls." It would be the first time that I had driven the new car.

While the blue limousine glided silently along the streets of Herefordshire, Stanley said apologetically, "I'm really sorry about the partition." "Don't worry about it," I reassured him, "but speak up a bit, will you!"

"You'll see: you're going to like Tom Cruise."

"You choose them, and I drive them," I replied, without really understanding what he meant.

"No, this time you won't have to drive them. Tom and Nicole have their own chauffeur."

"So what do you mean then. What's wrong?"

"You always want actors different from the ones I choose, don't you?"

I suspected that what I had said about *The Shining* might have stuck in his head. "It's just because I don't know them!" I admitted, "I suggested the actors I mentioned to you in the past because I had seen them on TV. In serials, for example."

"People who do soap operas don't work in films," replied Stanley. "It would take tons of makeup to make them credible. But then do you remember Jack Nicholson?"

That was it: Stanley was thinking about what I had said about Jack.

"He didn't need anything. He was ready to act the part. Nothing else needed doing. His eyes were right, his mouth was right. And it's the same thing with Tom."

"All right Stanley. If you're happy with this Tom Cruise, then so am I."

"This time I'm sure you'll like him, too."

When Tom came to meet us in the living room, Stanley asked him if he had read the script.

"Yes, I found it outside the bedroom door. Who left it there?"

"Emilio," Stanley replied.

"But . . . how did he get past the security?"

"Mission *is* possible."

Christiane had regained control of the living room in the clock tower and had filled it with her things, so Stanley had set up camp in the rooms in the Stable Block and had accepted to work for the most part at Pinewood Studios.

He had booked two stages where the set designers had built Tom and Nicole's apartment and the other interiors. The streets of New York had been carefully recreated in the back lot. After the "Vietnam on the Thames" of *Full Metal Jacket*, the decision to shoot a film set in the American city around London hadn't surprised anybody. We parked the Rolls behind one large stage, opposite a two-floor building that housed the production office, laboratories for the technicians, and the actors' dressing rooms.

That's where I saw Margaret again. When Stanley told me he had convinced her to come back and work for him yet again, I had heaved a big sigh of relief. I met her in her office, which as usual was next to Stanley's. The desk she was sitting at was already covered with paper. She was using her shoulder to hold the phone to her ear. Nothing defined the start of work on a new film better than this image. "Here we are, back again," she said with an official air. "The only one missing is Andros," she added nostalgically. "Margaret, the best things in life all end too soon," I said and then added mysteriously, "but who knows what the future holds."

It was a pleasure to take Stanley to the studios and see the same old faces. News of my brief retirement to Italy had spread throughout the Warner Bros. offices, but nobody seemed particularly surprised to see me at his side again.

The work of the set designers was nearly complete. All that was missing were some finishing touches to the furniture. Stanley told me to help them take tables, chairs, cabinets, pictures, and ornaments from Childwickbury. Most of the furniture for Tom and Nicole's apartment came from his home. "Emilio, go to the Stable Block and take some old books," he said. He had in mind the ones he had brought from America and never taken out of their boxes. "Let's air them a bit. Dust them off and take them to the set."

I was convinced that I could transport everything in the Unimog, just like in the good old days, but when I went to get it, I found the exhaust pipe on the roof and the front bumper covered with criss-crossed twigs, leaves, and feathers: the birds in the park had decided to use the Unimog as a nest. "Stay away," said Stanley. "Leave it to the birds, and use another van." The Unimog had finally retired to the country, too.

Stanley went to Pinewood every day to see how work on the set was coming along and to plan the production schedule in his new office. "Can I use your name for a shop?" he asked when we were in the car one morning. "Feel free," I replied, and a few weeks later, while I was walking along the streets of this reconstructed New York, I came across a bar with red blinds that had CAFFÈ DA EMILIO written outside. I remembered what Stanley's parents had said to me when I first met them: on the Avenue of the Stars, downstairs from their apartment in Los Angeles, there was a restaurant called just that. Mr. Emilio was an

My café in the back lot at Pinewood.

Italian immigrant and made excellent coffee. They often stopped to have one on their way home. "Do you like it?" said Stanley, pointing at the writing with a satisfied smile. Then he turned away and gave instructions to the crew.

Stanley wanted me to take him to inspect the buildings that had been chosen as locations, too. He preferred to go in his own car with me at the wheel, so we took the Rolls and followed the location manager, while a van behind us transported the assistant director and the director of photography. Our convoy moved along at a comfortable 50 mph. "Why the hell is he going so slowly?" Stanley exclaimed in irritation. "I need to get there while it's still light out! Emilio, pass him." At the next straight stretch of road, I accelerated to 70 mph and overtook the location manager's car. As I passed, I managed to catch sight of the puzzled expression on his face as he watched us through the window. When we arrived, Stanley got out of the Rolls and started to take an incredible number of photographs. He stuffed roll after roll of film in his pockets. He even put a few in mine.

One of the technicians took me to one side. "How come Stanley let you drive at more than 50 miles per hour?" he asked. "He never lets us do that."

"I have no idea," I said, shrugging my shoulders. "Ever since I've known him, he has always told me to drive at the speed limit because he can't afford to waste time."

The following day we returned to the villa again, but this time there was just Stanley and me. As the days passed, I realized that he asked more and more often to go back to where we had already been with his assistants. He took a light meter with him and said the readings on the display out loud, then he checked the time on his wristwatch and asked me to write everything down on both our notepads so that there were two identical copies, just to be safe. I wrote everything down randomly without having the slightest idea of what the numbers meant, and I asked myself why he hadn't come with someone who knew about photography. But Stanley didn't seem to be at all worried about my ignorance.

Before we left, he insisted on using the Rolls. "Don't you think there's something to be said for all that space?" asked Stanley, as he set up a mobile office in the back of the car, covering the seats with typed documents, colored folders, and a portable computer. Some days later, he passed me a sheet of paper where he had drawn a sort of cuboid wedge shape, with a note of the dimensions for each side. "Take this to the carpenters at Pinewood, please." When they called me to pick up this mysterious object, I immediately realized what it was: Stanley's traveling desk. He put it on his lap, and from the backseat of the Rolls gave orders by phone to his subordinates. He had always done so but never quite as efficiently as now in the Rolls, where everything was close at hand, and pen. "Emilio, give me your mobile," he would say as soon as we got in the car. He used my phone for all his work calls. He didn't want anybody to have his private number. The trouble was that I kept getting calls for Stanley Kubrick. "No, this isn't his number." "No, the director isn't with me." "No, I don't know when he'll be back." However, if someone called my number to talk to me, Stanley was far more abrupt: "He can't answer, he's driving." And he put the phone down.

The filming of *Eyes Wide Shut* was to start at the beginning of November at Luton Hoo, an eighteenth-century mansion house about seven miles north of Childwickbury. The house was one of the locations that Stanley had already chosen before I came back to England, so when he asked me to take him there for a further inspection, the rooms on the ground floor had already been adapted. The electricians were trying to fix nets of tiny lightbulbs to each of the walls as if they were curtains, and a fascinating cascade of lights covered the round staircase in the entrance. Stanley took me down a corridor towards an imposing ballroom. The following week there would be about a hundred walk-ons there, dressed for the Christmas ball that Tom and Nicole attend in the film.

Stanley had summoned the technicians and walk-ons to plan how to frame the scene. It wasn't easy to find the right place for each couple of dancers, and to fill the ballroom uniformly. "Emilio, can you stand here in the middle, please?" Stanley asked, pointing to an empty space in front of him. He called Julia Laeufer, a girl in her twenties who worked in the camera department, and pushed her towards me. "Dance," he said, and gestured to the orchestra to start playing. Julia stood still and looked at me a bit confused. What Stanley asked, had to be done, and so I reached out and drew her towards me: "Sorry," I said, "I'm not much of a dancer, but let's get on with it." Julia smiled, and we started to spin around. I hadn't danced for forty years. The last time had been at a party with Janette before we were married. I didn't know the steps, I didn't know what the music was, so I just swayed here and there and did my best not to step on Julia's feet. Stanley watched us and then looked at the far more able couples who were moving around us. "I think you must be Tom Cruise, and I'm Nicole Kidman," said Julia with a chuckle as she kept on dancing. Stanley called the Steadicam operator and asked her to dance with us and frame us at the same time. After a few seconds, Stanley made everyone stop and moved a few of the couples in the background. When he was satisfied with where we all were, he had some strips of adhesive tape put on the floor so that the actors and cameramen would know where to stand.

I twirled Julia in the center of the ballroom for three hours. By the end of the afternoon, I knew all about her, and she knew everything about my life from Cassino to Childwickbury. Our feet and backs hurt, and we were all in need of a rest, but nobody breathed a word. I caught sight of Jan at the end of the room and I beckoned him over. "Now it's your turn." I said, stepping away from Julia and placing her arms around Jan's waist. I had done enough dancing.

On November 4, Tom and Nicole arrived on the set, and filming of *Eyes Wide Shut* began. The musicians and walk-ons were elegantly dressed for the party, and the Christmas lights on the walls twinkled brightly. The guys from the special effects department used a veil of smoke to make them seem even softer and more enchanting.

A few days later, I met Harvey Keitel, the American actor Stanley had chosen to play the owner of the house who invited Tom and Nicole to the ball. He was wearing black dinner jacket, and there was a blond actress in a tight-fitting, glittering white dress at his side. He didn't look like he was enjoying himself very much. Stanley still hadn't filmed his scene, preferring to do more rehearsals. After five days of basically doing nothing, Keitel had started to talk less and less and was starting to look bored and nervous.

Once he had finally done his scene at the foot of the main stair-case at Lutton Hoo, we moved to Knebworth House, another mansion about ten miles east of Luton. We were supposed to shoot a scene with Tom, Harvey, and another actress. But it all went wrong: Harvey Keitel abandoned the film that same day, and nobody set foot in the house again. I wasn't actually there when Stanley filmed the scene, and I didn't dare ask him what had happened when I went back later to take him home. He just sat in silence on the back seat of the Rolls. It might have been the first trip we had ever made together without saying anything.

As if nothing had happened, the following day the troupe moved to London to the luxurious Lanesborough Hotel in Hyde Park. Stanley had rented the entire third floor. The master suite was to be used as a set, and the actors and assistants stayed in all the other rooms. For himself, he had booked a junior executive suite with an adjoining room where he immediately spread his papers all over the table. Tom had to act with another actress, Jennifer Jason-Leigh. After ten days of filming, the scene was finished and Stanley seemed satisfied again. Then we moved to Soho in the center of London, where Madame Jojo's had been chosen for the pub in New York. We stayed there for six days and it was so tiny inside that it was even difficult to position the cameras.

By the middle of December, we had only completed three small scenes, an actor had left the film, and one of the locations had been canceled. I had been right: it was going to take a long time to finish this. "Two years at least," Margaret had said when she heard Stanley's optimistic forecast of sixteen weeks. She kept on repeating serenely, "It's the usual thing." Warners should have asked *us* for the production schedule, I can tell you!

When the interior sets were ready, *Eyes Wide Shut* moved to Pinewood Studios. My first job there was to look after Stanley's office at the end of the corridor. I knew exactly where he would look for a pencil or which drawer he would open to take out a notepad, so it was easy to make sure everything was in the right place. At about midday, I took his lunch to the set. As usual, he didn't want anything from the caterers and had asked me to cook for him: "You deal with it. Anything will do, even just a bit of boiled meat." I ordered a whole chicken, I cooked it in a saucepan full of water with a little salt, then I removed the bones and skin and took it to Stanley with a few sauces. "It's certainly not Riccardo's cooking, but it's not bad."

Nobody whatsoever was allowed on this set, but as soon as the assistant director saw me arrive he signaled to Stanley, who immediately stopped filming and came over to me. As the weeks passed, I spent more and more time on the set, until in the end I was nearly always there. When I had finished the things I had to do, Stanley asked me to wait for him in his room while he went on filming. Sometimes he asked me to stand in front of the cameras to help with a lighting test: I walked along the sidewalk that had been built in the back lot or stood still under one of the fake lampposts while the technicians adjusted the lighting rigs and Stanley checked the shot on his monitor. I think he just liked to have me around. Within a few months, I had spent more time on the set than anyone else, and the hours I worked that I made a note of in my calendar had started to increase again: one hundred and two hours a week, one hundred and four, one hundred and seven and a half . . .

Despite the fact that my day was always dedicated to Stanley, I didn't feel the suffocating pressure that I had in the past. As promised, he had relieved me of all the duties regarding the production that used to tire me out: "This time, you're my personal assistant," he had said, so now somebody else was taking actors and technicians to and from the set, and even taking the rushes to Dehnam every evening. That afternoon six years earlier when I was sitting opposite Stanley at his desk, I'd had the impression that he really was listening to every word I said. And now I knew that was true.

On the way back to Childwickbury in the evening, Stanley seemed more peaceful than I remembered him being during previous film productions, including *Full Metal Jacket*. He was particularly satisfied with that film and constantly remembered it with pride. In those days, the journeys home were characterized by lively telephone conversations. During *Eyes Wide Shut*, he preferred to rest, sort out his papers, and chat with me.

He rarely made work calls and often spoke to Jack Nicholson to hear how Vivian was getting on. Now that she had moved to Los Angeles, someone else had to call her on Stanley's behalf. He often called his sister Barbara, too, to make sure she was well. Actually, she was the very first person he called from the Rolls, announcing to her cheerfully, "Emilio is back!" The only calls he made about *Eyes Wide Shut* were to Julian or the management at Warners to let them know how the film was coming along. We nearly always went home in the middle of the night, and he often asked with a yawn, "Emilio, if you have a notepad, write that down because I might forget." "How can I write? I'm driving!" I complained. "I haven't got a recorder!" "Good idea," decided Stanley, and the following day he gave me a small, portable recorder: "Switch that on!"

Christmas came, and while Christiane decorated the kitchen windows of Childwickbury with the curtain lights that had been used on the set at Luton Hoo, Stanley gave the crew and actors a few days off. But neither Stanley nor I took a break. He kept going to Pinewood to work on the film and wanted to visit alternative locations for the remaining scenes. We went to Mentmore Towers, an imposing castle in Buckinghamshire about forty minutes from Childwickbury. It was freezing cold but it wasn't damp, and I couldn't see any ice on the road. When we turned into the long avenue that led to the house, Stanley asked me to drive very slowly. He looked at the landscape on both sides to see if it was the right place for the scene he had in mind. He asked me to stop the Rolls before we arrived in the forecourt in front of the house, and then he got out and walked back away from the car. I looked behind me and saw him take out his camera and take several photos of the car with the façade of the house in the background. He stood there, in the middle of the avenue, for a while. I had the impression that he was moving slower and slower. "Everything okay?" I said as I went to join him. "It is quite cold," he replied, and I noticed that his breath had frozen into tiny crystals of ice on the gray curls of his mustache. "How many pictures have I taken?" he asked me in a whisper. *He can't even tell what he just did?* I thought. "You've done enough," I said. "Let's get back in the car. I'll take you to the house. We'll have them let us in so we can warm up a bit." I was worried, and when I took his hand I realized that it was freezing. "Come on, Stanley." I pulled him by his hand. "Let's go and get warm and then go home, shall we?" He nodded and let me lead him. Numb with cold, it took him a long time to get in the car and then to go into the house. Every time I touched him to help him, I shivered, too.

Tom and Nicole proved to be two extraordinary actors. Stanley was always praising their commitment and professionalism. Tom treated me with the honest complicity of a brother but without ever being intrusive. When I arrived at Pinewood early in the morning, I would find him strolling along the paths by the stages that led to the back lot. His children, Isabella and Connor, walked on either side of him and held him by the hand. He smiled and told the children to say hello to me. Isabella, who was four, waved her little hand and said my name. I really appreciated the way Tom was very respectful of Stanley's privacy. He didn't try to go into his office at all costs, he never asked anything more than he needed to know for the part he was playing, and he always waited for Stanley to start a conversation.

Nicole seemed to be even more enthusiastic than her husband, and thoroughly respected all the people on the set. She never behaved like a fickle star. I think she thought of *Eyes Wide Shut* as the most important career opportunity she'd had, and above all as a chance to learn and improve.

May 1997 was the best month of the whole project. Stanley sent me to Culcross Street to pick up a new arrival. "He's a director, but sometimes he likes to act," he had said, and as usual I had to admit that I had never heard of him. I saw a slim man wave to me from the sidewalk. I pulled over, and he knocked on the window of the Mercedes. "I'm Sydney Pollack," he said, opening the door and sitting down on the back seat. That was about the last thing I heard him say. He stared out of the window, and after half an hour of being persistently silent as a clam, all he asked as we were crossing Childwick Green was whether all those houses and the church belonged to Stanley. The umpteenth scene from the script of "Kubrick the evil ogre." But didn't Stanley say that he and Sydney had been talking to each other on the phone for twenty years? Not a word. Sydney only spoke again to politely take his leave of me in the Dome Room. When I met him again in the kitchen

a couple of hours later, he surprised me. He left Stanley to fumble with
the containers of takeout Indian food, came towards me smiling, and
put his hands on my shoulders: "Emilio, I'm sorry. I thought you were
just the driver! Come and have a chat so we can catch up a bit."

As well as being able to film the scenes he hadn't done because
Harvey Keitel had left, Stanley could also eat much better. Sydney was
an excellent cook and made lunch in his trailer for Stanley and Tom.

After about a year, some of the technicians had to leave because they
had other commitments. Peter Cavaciuti, a young Englishman of Italian origin, replaced the Steadicam operator. Stanley had interviewed
him at the end of August and decided to hire him, but without lowering his guard: "Emilio, try to find out what kind of guy this Peter is."

"What do you mean?" I asked.

"He's of Italian origin. Talk to him."

"What has being Italian got to do with it? And what am I supposed
to talk to him about?"

"See if he's a guy who minds his own business. Ask him."

"What kind of question is that? 'Excuse me Peter, Stanley wants to
know if you mind your own business'?"

"Come up with something."

Luckily, Peter himself offered me the solution to the problem. He'd
been on the set for a few days and still hadn't started filming. At first,
things didn't go too well: he tried to move the Steadicam according
to Stanley's instructions, but Stanley kept telling him that his shots
weren't level. From a distance, I watched how the doubts Stanley had
just expressed in his office were being transformed into a sort of psychological battle between him and his new employee. I hoped Peter
would make the right move, which was to hold on. Stanley left him
alone and, in what was yet another perfect exit from a theatrical point
of view, went off a bit cross. Peter looked around and saw me sitting
not far away.

"I hear your name's Emilio. Are you Italian?" he said to break the
ice, and after he had told me that his parents came from the Avellino

area, he asked me what my job was on the set. He said he'd always seen me arrive in a hurry and go straight to talk to Stanley. The trap was sprung, but Peter had got off to a good start: I was expecting him to complain, but he chose to skirt around it. I answered that I worked directly for Stanley, so I wasn't employed by the studio or the production company.

"And how long have you known each other?"

"Oh, I'm just here for this film," I said. In a way, I was telling the truth.

"How do you feel about working for him?" I perfectly understood what he was getting at and appreciated the fact that he didn't come straight out with it.

"Oh, it's fine," I said in as transparent a tone as I could muster. "And what do you do here?"

"I'm the Steadicam operator."

"But wasn't it a woman?"

"I'm the replacement. She had to leave due to other commitments. Where do you live? In Stanley's house?"

"No, no. I've got a flat with my wife not far away. What about you?"

"Muswell Hill."

"Oh!" I exclaimed, recognizing the area.

"Do you know it?"

"Stanley's daughter Vivian lived there, and Andros lives there, too!" I said, letting myself go too far.

"Andros? Andros Epaminondas?"

"Yes . . ."

"I know Andros! His kids go to school with mine! So then, if you know Andros . . . and Stanley's daughter . . ."

I might have given myself away. I never have been much of a liar, and when I heard Andros's name I couldn't help it.

". . . then you've been working for him for a very long time!" Peter concluded.

"Well . . . yes. I worked for Stanley before *Eyes Wide Shut*, too."

"Oh, good," said Peter. I was expecting other questions, but he just smiled, nodded, got up, and walked back to the set a little more slowly than when he had arrived.

"Any news about Peter?" Stanley asked the next day. We were in his office in Pinewood before filming was due to start.

"Everything's fine. He knows Andros! They're friends!"

"Well, damn good!" remarked Stanley. And that was all he wanted to know. When we went to the back lot after sunset, I saw Stanley talking to Peter more calmly, without harassing him as he'd done the evening before. Actually, after that he took every opportunity to congratulate him on his work. "Clever young man, this Peter, he knows his job, all right."

To reward Peter for the patience and discretion he had shown during his first day on the set, I gave him what I considered to be valuable advice about how to get on well with Stanley: "Dedicate yourself to the job as much as you can. Try to do your best, but don't overdo it. Better still, keep something back. That way, when Stanley asks you for more, you'll have it to give to him."

Ten years had passed since Stanley had last made a film, and nothing about his working method had changed. What had changed was the world around him. I'd never before seen so much interest shown in a film being made by Stanley Kubrick. What with the Internet and the general public's growing interest in the private lives of the stars, it was becoming increasingly difficult to defend yourself from the media. Even the passersby were more curious than they had been. They stopped to ask me what all those trailers were doing parked in the streets in London: "Oh, they're filming something for the TV, you know, *Teletubbies*," I said, but I didn't always manage to convince them.

The scene waiting for us at Chelsea and Westminster Hospital was dreadful. It was even worse than the one I had experienced with Ryan. Masses of screaming adolescents were clinging to the barriers and pushing the guards in an attempt to get closer to the entrance. How they had found out that Tom Cruise was shooting a scene from a film there was anybody's guess. Stanley always sent somebody on ahead to the location to avoid situations like this. Depending on what he was told over the radio, he either arrived much earlier or much later than Tom. He used an anonymous-looking car and mingled with the technicians. He had even come up with a trick. When I drove him in the Rolls-Royce, he asked the location manager to come along with us. Stanley left him the backseat and sat next to me. When we arrived, he let the decoy get out first, and as soon as all the eyes and flashing cameras were pointed in the location manager's direction, Stanley would open the car door and quickly slip into the building. "You'll see. They'll think the important person is sitting on the backseat," he had predicted.

The photographers never managed to immortalize Stanley. At least not until May 1997, when a few magazines published unauthorized pictures that had been taken on the set at Pinewood: Stanley Kubrick coming out of Sydney Pollack's caravan; Stanley Kubrick in the studio buggy with Tom Cruise and his daughter; Stanley Kubrick wandering among the production company vans. A photographer had climbed up a tree just outside the studio until he could see over the perimeter wall and aimed his camera at the sheds in the back lot. Stanley was angry and went to complain to the studio management about the lack of security. When they told him that there wasn't much the studio could do about it because the trees belonged to the council, he replied: "Well, one thing is for sure: you can make the wall higher!" And they did. Green wooden panels were added to the top of the fence, and so that he could stop worrying and forget about the whole thing, Stanley hired private security guards to patrol the perimeter near the set day and night.

There was a tangible risk that the public would find out too much about *Eyes Wide Shut* before it came out. After all, there were two superstars in the cast and a huge number of walk-ons who were directly in contact with them. The final dialogue between Tom and Nicole was filmed in Hamleys, a large toy shop in Regent Street right in the center of London. Stanley had devised a way to make sure that none of the walk-ons could hear what the couple was saying. After the shop closed, the film set assistants set up the lights and other equipment and then put some thick black curtains on rails just a few centimeters away from where Stanley had decided to frame the shot. These served to isolate the words whispered by Tom and Nicole. The walk-ons had to walk along a specific route, so they only actually heard fragments of what was being said when they walked in front of the camera where there where no curtains.

My wife and daughter were there too, somewhere among the shelves full of toys. They had come to the set to say hello to me and found themselves following directions from Stanley just like the professional walk-ons hired by Hobby Films. It was funny to see how Janette and Marisa tried hard, and with success I would add, to get lost among the walk-ons. They didn't look at me, they didn't look at Stanley, they kept themselves to themselves. "But how did you two get in here?" a woman asked my wife. "You're not from the agency, and I've never seen you before." "We're here on private business," said Janette, curtly. She had clearly remembered everything I had always said about Stanley's confidentiality. Then Stanley did something that surprised me. He went over to Janette, put a hand on her shoulder, and whispered: "So, do you like it?" "It's wonderful, Stanley," she replied, "I'd never been in a film." Stanley laughed and went back towards the screens he used to monitor the shooting. A horde of women immediately surrounded Janette, but before they could speak, she exclaimed, "We're just friends!" And crossed her arms so theatrically that nobody said another word to her.

Stanley asked Janette to come back to the set many times. She had to walk backwards and forwards at the edge of the frame while Tom walked along the imitation streets of the back lot at night. Stanley was giving us a wonderful gift: at last we could all sit down together at the same table and have dinner every evening.

Eyes Wide Shut was my big-screen debut. At one point in the script, Tom stops to buy a newspaper at a kiosk while a mysterious bald man is following him. On the day when the rehearsals for this scene were

In the role of the news vendor on the set of Eyes Wide Shut.

scheduled, all of sudden Stanley asked me, "Emilio, would you mind going into the kiosk for a moment?" I did what he asked. I sat on a stool and waited for instructions. Stanley looked at me and sized me up: "Perfect!" Then he turned his attention to Tom and to Peter's Steadicam, leaving me there surrounded by papers and packets of cigarettes. For two weeks, for one hour every evening, it was a continual, "Take those gloves," "Get wardrobe to give you another jacket," "Put on that hat," "Take off the hat and put on the earmuffs." Between takes, Tom looked at me and laughed: "Emilio, you look just like a New York news vendor!"

In the summer of 1997, Stanley was about to film a grand masked ball. The year before, not long after I had started work, he asked me if I knew anyone in Venice.

"I've got a cousin there, Raffaele. Why do you ask?"

"I need someone to take some photographs of the carnival masks."

"Well . . . I don't think he's got time."

"In that case, can he find me someone there? You know, because of the language."

It occurred to me that Raffaele had two children, a boy and a girl. They were just over twenty. "Stanley, they might be able to do it, but they're not professional photographers."

"It doesn't matter. I'll tell them what they have to do, and I'll get them a camera if they haven't got one."

When I telephoned my cousin's house, his wife, Edda, answered. Once she had got over the initial shock, Edda listened carefully to the instructions I had been authorized to pass on to her: "Photograph all the masks you can. They're for a masked ball scene; that's all I can say." A week later, she sent us an album of photos taken by her daughter, Barbara. The pictures were numbered, and there were also several pages of notes with details of when the photo was taken, what the mask was called, where it was made, how much it cost, and how long it would take.

"Highly professional. Better than some of the best photographers in London!" said Stanley with satisfaction as he looked through the album.

"As far as I know, Barbara is studying law," I answered with a smile.

Only now did Stanley ask me to call Venice and arrange for the masks to be bought and shipped. It was the first time I had called Edda and Barbara specifically about the film in a year. After they had sent the photos, Edda called from time to time to ask how work on the film was going. She sounded a bit disappointed and wondered whether Stanley had changed his mind or even shelved the whole project. "The film's going ahead," I said. "All I can say is that these delays are perfectly normal for Stanley."

"Tell Barbara to buy the masks with these numbers," Stanley declared at last. And so the phone calls between Childwickbury and the Lido recommenced. In the middle of June, my cousin Raffaele and Edda took Barbara to the various shops. They signed checks and receipts and took the boxes of masks to the courier to be shipped. When the last model was ready to be sent, Stanley asked me if Barbara would like to bring them herself by plane. "There are a lot of masks this time, and I don't trust the couriers. I'd be much happier if she brought them herself. And maybe," he added shortly afterwards, "she might like to come here and visit the set."

Barbara accepted and arrived at Heathrow on a scheduled flight. When I accompanied her to the set the next morning, she was a bit nervous about meeting Stanley, so first I took her for a walk around the back lot along the streets of New York.

We had lunch in the canteen at Pinewood, and just as we were about to stand up, Sydney came in and came over to say hello to me. "This is my niece, Barbara. She's the girl who took the photos of the Venetian masks," I announced. Barbara tried to stay composed and introduced herself. Sydney stopped to talk to us for a while, and when he left, Barbara moved closer to me and said: "Sydney Pollack! How can you manage to work among all these famous people?" "After all these years, you don't notice anymore," I replied. "When I started work as a minicab driver, they were all perfect strangers to me. I only found out later that they were important people!" Then I pointed towards one of the corridors and said. "Look: that guy's Tom Cruise." Barbara was speechless. "Come on, it's time to meet Stanley," I said, talking her by the hand. In the billiard room, Stanley had just finished discussing a scene with Sydney and Tom and was standing in a corner fumbling with his notepads.

"Kubrick is that man down there?" asked Barbara shyly.

"Yes, that's Stanley. Go and say hello to him."

Barbara went towards him, and he turned around. He looked at her over the top of his glasses, and they both stood motionless. I think Stanley was just as nervous about the meeting as Barbara was.

"Congratulations," Stanley tried to say, holding her hand, "you did a very good job."

"But is he really Stanley Kubrick?" Barbara said to me while she was still holding Stanley's hand.

"Sure," I replied, "but don't worry. Talk to him the same way you would talk to your father."

"Nice to meet you," was all she could say, hesitantly.

The orgy scene was going to be filmed in two large country homes, Elveden Hall and Highclere Castle. Elveden was an enormous manor on the border between Suffolk and Norfolk. Here Stanley planned to film the first part of the scene: the long sequence where the models are arranged in a circle, stand up, and get undressed surrounded by a crowd of men. The villa had been deserted for years and was only ever used occasionally as a location for films. The rooms were so vast and empty that it was freezing inside: when I took Stanley to see it for the first time, it can't have been more than fifty degrees. Before we started filming, he made a point of renting a dozen heaters so the actors would be more comfortable; especially the actresses, who had to perform almost completely naked. The heaters were put behind walls and columns, and furniture was used to conceal them. They were left running for an entire week.

Just like the Christmas ball scene at Luton Hoo, the choreography had been carefully prepared. Nevertheless, Stanley insisted on holding rehearsals for days, and just like at Luton, I ended up working as a stand-in: every evening, the walk-ons and the men in the troupe, me included, put on masks and capes. They practiced where they would stand when the girls, who had already rehearsed their movements, came in. In addition to standing us in a circle and getting us to move in and out so that we learned to move together, Stanley wanted to check how the light fell on each and every one of us, so we all had to raise and lower our heads to see how the shadows fell on our masks when illuminated by a powerful overhead spotlight.

The first take was filmed in the evening on September 28, 1997, and everyone was back on the night shift. Work usually started at six in the afternoon and finished at two in the morning. There was nothing particularly unusual about this. It meant eight hours for the actors and about ten for the technicians, who had to assemble and dismantle the equipment. At least it wouldn't have been unusual if I hadn't still had to be at Childwickbury at ten in the morning and never got home until five or six in the morning the next day. It went on like this for over a month: I wrote *total hours* in my calendar, which meant a hundred and twenty-five a week with as many as nineteen per day.

Of course, Stanley did the same. On the way home from Elvenden, we were always both very tired. However, when it rained, Stanley cheered up, moved closer to me and never stopped talking. "Stanley, for Christ's sake, be quiet!" I said. "I've got to concentrate on the road and the directions. You're distracting me!" "But that's exactly why I'm talking to you. To make sure you stay awake." The next day we were stuck at Elveden again. He was worried that I was tired, and so as soon as he came down the steps of his motor home to go to the set, he commanded, "Inside!" And pointed to the open door he had just come out of. "Stanley, I'm just fine here." I added that I would prefer to go for a walk in the park instead of shutting myself in a camper, but he insisted: "No, you need to rest." So I went into the motor home and pretended to sleep. I'm sure he really wanted me to stay there more to look after his stuff than to get my strength back. He never wanted to lock doors: he hated carrying keys around because he was terrified that he would lose them. This applied to the office, the set, the camper, and even his own home. But at the same time he couldn't trust people, so I was his burglar alarm.

In September I decided to run in a charity marathon that Save the Children was involved in. Katarina had been born the year before, and I wanted to collect some money in her name.

"You're mad!" exclaimed Stanley when I told him. "How much training have you done?"

"Training? I'm always on the go. Who needs training?"

"Professional runners train for a whole year before a marathon. It will kill you!"

"Well, thanks for the encouragement," I said with a laugh. "Don't worry, it's not a race to see who comes first; it's more of a walk."

"Don't take part."

"It's done now. I've enrolled. Look, here's my number." And I showed him the thin piece of cloth with 427 printed on it. "Come to think of it, why don't you make a donation? It all goes to charity."

"No. Don't take part," he insisted.

"The money goes to children who are homeless or can't go to school," I replied, without paying attention to what he was saying. "Go on: make a donation."

"Okay. You take care of the money; decide how much: from a pound to a million. Use your head. But don't run!"

"Thanks for the donation, Stanley," I replied simply, and I left him alone.

On September 2 in the morning, I went to pick him up at home. "Emilio, I need you to spend the whole day with me today," he said as he got into the Rolls. I smiled, and I said what we both already knew: "Sorry, Stanley, but today is the day of the London run."

"Put it off, please," he repeated.

"I've got it all planned. I'll take you to the studio, go and run, and then I'll come back to Pinewood to take you home. Don't worry."

"Take your mobile with you so you can call me while you're running."

When I said good-bye before I left, he looked incredibly tense. "Are you sure?" he said for the umpteenth time. I patted him on the shoulder and went out of the door.

Around about dinnertime, I went back to Pinewood. I felt neither more tired nor relaxed than I did on a normal working day. Stanley's office was empty, so I asked Margaret where I could find him. She said he was in the back lot getting ready to shoot a scene with Tom Cruise as soon as the sun went down. "Stanley hasn't got anything done today," Margaret told me. "He's been nervous and distracted the whole time. He kept on changing his mind and disappearing off to go through some papers. I was starting to get worried, and then I remembered that you were running the marathon! Don't do anything like that to him again!"

I went to the back lot and greeted him with open arms. "Here I am!" I announced triumphantly.

"I'm so glad you're back. Are you feeling okay?"

"Sure, Stanley, just fine." And I beat my hands on my chest.

"I don't know how you managed to do it."

"It's like you always say: if you make a real effort, you can do anything."

"You're right," he said and smiled, and then added: "Oh, but sit down. You must be tired, take it easy." He didn't say anything else to me for the whole evening, and he wouldn't let me get up off the chair next to his.

In the middle of the month, Anya was to make her operatic debut in York with an adaptation of Hansel and Gretel. Christiane had designed the scenery, which included a number of triangular wooden angels that filled the ground floor of the house for weeks. When Anya invited her father to come, Stanley gave the *Eyes Wide Shut* crew the weekend off and asked me to drive Christiane and him to York in the Rolls. "If you take us, can Janette stay at our house while we're away?"

"I'm already a babysitter, so I suppose I can be a house sitter, too!" answered Janette without turning a hair.

"Fine," said Stanley when I told him, "What time are we leaving? What way are we going? How long will it take? Are the service stations along the way good?"

"Yes, they are, but let's hope we don't need them, what do you think?"

Stanley and Christiane sat in the back, I put a map on the seat beside me, and we set off for York. We crossed the center of England until we reached Nottingham Forest, where, as a road sign explained, Robin Hood had once lived. The weather was wonderful. The sun was shining, and there wasn't a cloud in the sky; and there was hardly anyone else on the road. Stanley and Christiane chatted happily behind me. "Did you know it's been twenty years since the last time I took you both somewhere?" I said, as I looked at them in the rearview mirror. Christiane laughed and added: "Well done, Emilio! Try to make him see sense!" "You're right," admitted Stanley, "it's so wonderful to go somewhere in the car. We should organize trips like this more often now that you are back in England. As soon as we finish *Eyes Wide Shut*."

At six in the afternoon, we arrived at the hotel where Stanley and Christiane were going to stay. Actually, they were Mr. and Mrs. Harlan, as the register in reception showed.

I set off in the Rolls to return to Janette, but after less than twenty miles, the car started to jolt and make strange noises, and then the engine suddenly stopped. I called the roadside assistance and spent the night sitting furiously in the Rolls as a tow truck towed it towards Childwickbury. When we finally drove through the gates on the Harpenden Road, it was three in the morning. At six I was already on my way back to Stanley in York. I was exhausted. When Stanley saw me arrive in the Mercedes, he asked me if there had been a problem with the Rolls. "Yes, Stanley. The Rolls is at Childwickbury waiting for them to come and take it away. But let's talk about it some other time."

The return journey was pleasant, too. When we arrived home, I asked Stanley, "Would you have gone to York if Janette and I hadn't been here?" "Of course not," he replied simply. And I decided it would be better not to tell him what I had been through.

The second part of the orgy was to be filmed in Highclere Castle, the biggest castle in Hampshire. During the scene, Tom Cruise wanders around the rooms of a stately manor watching groups of people engaged in group intercourse. Stanley had left this scene until last. At the end of January 1998, the troupe filled the square in front of the castle with trailers and vans for fifteen days.

In the weeks before shooting, I was sometimes asked if what was written on the call sheets was true. These papers gave details of the various times actors had to appear on set. I always received them and then passed them on to Stanley. People from the crew told me, "In a few days we'll be having some fun, eh? Lots of girls doing smutty stuff . . ."

"Stanley, I don't know what you are thinking of filming, but I want to stay out of it," I told him before he had the chance to ask me to do anything. "I've heard that there will be . . ." I tried to find a way to rephrase what I'd been told, "there will be sexual activities in the scenes. . . . Please, try not to need me for anything." Stanley looked at me with bewilderment. "Do you remember that time I made a fool of myself because of the condoms for *Barry Lyndon*?" I explained. "Well, when these things are involved, I always end up making everybody laugh, so please, leave me out of it."

16

ASK EMILIO

On February 3, 1998, Stanley announced that the filming of the orgy, and so of *Eyes Wide Shut*, was over. Fifteen months had passed. It was a new record. It was almost as if the frenetic pace of filming had distracted me from everything else, because as soon as the last take was finished, I came down with a terrible bout of flu. It hadn't happened for years: I had a cough, a cold, and my bones ached terribly. I had to stay in bed for four days.

In the two months that followed, I took Stanley to Pinewood nearly every day to prepare the reels of film for editing, as well as to Denham for the print samples. I was starting to feel exhausted again. I had agreed to be available all the time during filming, and now, nearly two years after my return, I was beginning to feel the consequences of that promise. "If you want to take a vacation, feel free," said Stanley, so on April 1, I set off for Sant'Angelo again.

A new friend was waiting for me in Italy. His name was Paolo Morrone. My wife had met him the previous November during the week we spent there once every three or four months to make sure that the house was okay. While I was in England, I had done Paolo a small favor, and he couldn't wait to meet me—partly to thank me personally but also because he was a fervent admirer of Kubrick's films. By then, my employer was an open "secret" in Cassino.

When he came to see me, we sat in the garden to make the most of the beautiful, sunny spring day. In less than two minutes, the conversation turned to my work with Stanley. Paolo told me how Stanley's films were greatly appreciated in Italy and that he was a wonderful director. Paolo described him as "an authentic artist." Whenever a new film of his was due to come out, the wait was nerve-racking, and reactions to his work were always mixed. He never failed to divide both public and critical opinion. It was curious to learn about Stanley's life from a different perspective: a sort of parallel dimension as it were.

"How far has he got with the film?"

"What film?" I answered, evasively.

"The one he's making, *Eyes Wide Shut*."

"So the secret's out already?"

"Well, yes, but only the title and the actors. Tell me more!"

"I can't. I'm sorry."

"At least tell me why you've come back here. Are you on holiday?"

"It's more of a rest than a holiday. I'm waiting for him to call me to go back."

"So the film isn't finished?"

"Paolo, I can't tell you anything."

In an attempt to keep him happy, I offered to show him some of the props I'd kept from Stanley's previous films. I showed him into the living room, and while he looked around with bemusement, I nodded towards the floor: "That's the carpet from *The Shining*." Paolo leaped back, afraid to step on it as if it were a religious relic. "How could anyone believe your story? Someone starts out in the Ciociaria and ends up becoming the personal assistant of one of the greatest directors in the world. I know it's true, but it just seems absurd. It's . . . a fairy tale."

"Well, we need to work to live, don't we?" I said with a laugh. "My job turned out to be this one. Come and have a look in the garage." I opened the metal door and started to rummage among the clothes I used in the garden. Paolo looked on with curiosity. Behind a matted pullover and pair of dusty old trousers, I found a green jacket with lots of pockets and pulled it out.

"Here it is. This is one of Stanley's 'full metal' jackets!" I announced, handing it to him. Paolo didn't really seem to have understood. "It's one of the jackets that Stanley bought for the marines in *Full Metal Jacket*,"

I explained. "There were loads of them when the film was finished. He kept a dozen, and he gave me a couple to use when I'm working in the fields. That's why it's so dirty, but it's authentic. It's original."

"Do you really use it for working in the garden? You shouldn't," he said disconcertedly. "This is . . . it's precious."

"And why?" I asked frankly.

"What do you mean, 'why'?! Because . . . it belonged to Stanley Kubrick!"

"And so? I have no idea how much stuff like this I've got. He gives things to me instead of throwing them away, that way we use them. He does exactly the same."

Over the years I had accumulated a vast quantity of props that I had tried to recycle or reuse in some way. These included Scatman Crothers's jacket from *The Shining*, which was given to Marisa, and the marines' blankets, which I used to protect my gardening tools from the damp. I never really did understand how Stanley chose what to keep and what to throw away. He always wanted to file everything meticulously when he finished a film, and yet it seemed that he couldn't care less about objects, props, and so on. I grew fond of some of the props and tried to find a way to keep them: I gave Matthew Modine's rifle to Jon. I kept Jack Nicholson's red corduroy jacket, but even though it was the right size, I never actually wore it. I kept Sergeant Hartman's hat as way of remembering Lee Ermey. Basically, my house was full of Stanley's stuff. Paolo looked at me as if I had just arrived from another planet. "You have all these things and you don't take care of them?"

Putting the Vietnamese hat from Full Metal Jacket *to good use in the snow at Farm Road with Janette.*

"My way of taking care of them is to use them. Look over here." And I led him outside and around to the garden at the back of the house. "See that table?" I said, pointing at a dark wooden foldaway bench. It was rather low and square-shaped. I'd left some of the vegetables I'd picked in the garden on it. "Do you recognize it?" I asked. "It's the table from *Barry Lyndon*, the one they put the pistols on in the duel scene with Ryan O'Neal. Now I use it for tomatoes."

Then I dealt the final blow. Two years earlier, while I was tidying up the garage, I came across one of the costumes from *Barry Lyndon*. It was made of light blue velvet with tails and large metal buttons. I didn't know what to do with it, so I gave it to Caritas, a charity organization, in Cassino. "Somewhere there must be a tramp dressed as a Prussian officer. What can I say?"

When I said good-bye to Paolo that evening, I suddenly realized how much I had enjoyed telling him about my life with Stanley. Paolo had been discreet. He hadn't insisted when I refused to tell him more about *Eyes Wide Shut*, and he seemed to be so full of admiration for the films I'd been involved in that I didn't feel I was betraying Stanley by sharing a few anecdotes.

Paolo phoned me a couple of times during the next few days. It was good to hear from him. "Stanley called," I said one evening. "I have to go back to him."

"Is it for the film? Is he still working on it?" he asked excitedly.

"No," I said, and then after a carefully calculated pause, "I have to go to Stokenchurch. He's run out of dog food."

"Call me at the last minute when you need me," I had said to Stanley just before I left for my holiday in Italy. And that minute had finally arrived. Despite having spent fifteen months on the set, Stanley had decided to film one scene again. Tom had been asked to come back to the set. Jennifer Jason-Leigh was no longer available, so Marie Richardson, an actress who looked a lot like her, had been called. On May 15, we did the first take of additional photography, and a month later, on June 17, filming of *Eyes Wide Shut* was over. This time definitively.

"Good-bye, Emilio," said Margaret at Pinewood. "Well, that's that out of the way." "It gets worse every time," I said with a laugh, "or maybe we're just getting older, or Stanley is becoming more demanding." "Both!" she replied impulsively. "And anyway, I think I'm going to retire after this one." I didn't tell her what I had talked about with Stanley before I came back to work, but I hoped that the news would help her rethink her decision. Something was about to change.

I spent the summer, the autumn, and most of the winter taking it easy in Italy. Stanley was very tired too. On our last trips back from the set, he nearly always fell asleep. It was only thirty minutes' drive from Pinewood to home, but he regularly dropped off. It had never happened before. When we got home, I secretly watched him drag himself towards the stairs and waited until he was in his apartment before I left. Unlike everyone else, Stanley still couldn't rest. He had to edit the film.

On January 25, 1999, he summoned me again. While I looked after the animals and put back the paintings by Christiane that had been used on the set, he worked nonstop to respect the deadline agreed with Warners. He spent the entire day, and often the night, in the hall that he had renamed the Avid Room. A preliminary copy of the film was due to be delivered to Warners at the beginning of March. Stanley was so tired that I left notes all over the ground floor at Childwickbury instructing the domestics to be as quiet as possible in the morning. I wanted to make sure he had a few hours' peace and quiet before he started work again.

Stanley was pushing himself to the limit. After two years of filming without a break, he kept on working more and more hours each day. The film editor took a copy to America to show to the Warner Bros. executives and Tom and Nicole. But Stanley still didn't stop. On Friday March 5, he organized another private screening of *Eyes Wide Shut* at Childwickbury.

When I took the lady from Warner Bros. back to Brown's Hotel, Stanley called me on the mobile, impatient to know what she had said about the film. I answered that she had spent most of the time asking me the same old questions about my life and that she had seemed pleased with the film. "Good," said Stanley, "let's hope the others like it, too." When I got home, I went to the Dome Room and found Stanley sitting motionless at his desk. He didn't seem to have heard me come in.

"Stanley?" I went towards him and put a hand on his shoulder.

"I can't do it, Emilio."

"Do what?" I asked, worried. He just sat there with his head bowed, swaying almost imperceptibly on the chair.

"I can't get up. I can't pull myself up." He grabbed the armrests, but he still didn't move.

"Stay there, wait," I told him, pulling back the chair. I took him by his forearms and lifted him up a bit, but he seemed exhausted. He was terribly heavy.

"Come on, Stanley," I said to encourage him, and myself, too. "Come on, I'll help you." When at last he was standing up, he looked at me. His eyes were distant and absent.

"Everything okay, Stanley?"

He nodded weakly.

"Go to your room and rest. Forget about the film. Come on, I'll take you as far as the stairs."

We walked slowly and shakily along the corridor. It was as if he had lost control of his limbs for a moment and couldn't get it back. He had reached the absolute limit of physical and mental exhaustion.

Before he started to go up the stairs, he turned around. "Thank you, Emilio. Don't bother to come in tomorrow. Stay home with Janette and Katarina and take it easy."

"No, *you* take it easy, please. I'll be here tomorrow as usual and '*con calma*'—do you remember what Martin used to say?"

Stanley smiled at me.

"I'm going to stay here until I hear you close the door. Otherwise, I'm coming up."

While Stanley struggled up the stairs a step at a time, I tried to focus on the fact that the film was nearly over. We both knew that *Eyes Wide Shut* was almost finished, which would mean the end of all this stress. I kept telling myself that Stanley had always managed to recover. I repeated it over and over again: I'd always seen him bounce back and become again the energetic, victorious fighter I'd come to know. He'd always made it. He just needed some rest.

I thanked God that *Eyes Wide Shut* hadn't been all that difficult to make. It was a good thing that nearly all the scenes had been filmed in the studio. What's more, we'd been able to get most of the props from Childwickbury and work relatively calmly at Pinewood. Stanley had chosen a great cast, too. After two years on the set, they were all still kind, polite, patient, and enthusiastic. Tom had devoted himself impeccably to the film, and as far as Nicole was concerned, Stanley told her, "You've done exactly what I was trying to achieve. There's no need for another take; you've done just what I wanted." We'd been really lucky.

I heard the door of Stanley's apartment close.

The next morning, it was Saturday, March 6. I went to Childwickbury to take care of the animals. There was no note from Stanley on my desk. There was nothing in his office, either. I went back to the Green Room and checked the animals' bowls. I filled them with water and then went out into the garden. I stopped in front of the donkeys' enclosure and looked at the house in the distance: it looked like a terra-cotta and cream-colored rectangle wedged between the green of the damp grass and the vivid blue of the English sky. I stroked the donkeys' noses, and in return they licked my hand. Then I turned to face the portico of the façade lined with columns. The house stood perfectly still. I walked along the east wall that was already bathed in sunlight. I passed by the cats' pen and checked that it was clean. I kept on wandering around Childwickbury without a reason. I made up other areas I had to check or things I had to do. I could still see Stanley sitting there, exhausted. I went back into the house and tidied up his rooms.

The mobile phone rang.

"Hello, Jan," said Stanley's voice.

"Stanley, it's not Jan. It's me, Emilio."

"Oh, I meant to call you."

"You're on the line," I said, a little awkwardly.

"Was there water in their bowls?"

"Yes, I've done the rounds. Everything's okay."

"Are their litters clean?"

"Yes. But . . . didn't you come downstairs last night? I didn't find a note."

"No . . ."

He waited for a moment before saying anything else. I couldn't find the courage to ask.

"Faxes?" he said.

"One for Jan. I took it to his office in the Stable Block."

"Thanks," he said, after a long pause, and hung up.

I spent Saturday afternoon at home with Janette, Marisa, and Katarina. We had dinner together, but I wasn't really in the mood. On Sunday morning I woke up, had breakfast, and went to Childwickbury. There was nothing particularly urgent to do, and yet I set off very early. At six thirty I was already there. I stayed on the ground floor, where I checked that the cats had water and fed the dogs. There weren't any faxes or messages on the answering machine in the Red Room. I left Stanley a note: "Everything is under control: no faxes or messages in the office, the animals are okay, there's no need for you to come down. Stay upstairs until this afternoon. Take it easy. E." I folded it in half, went up the stairs, and slipped it under the door. Then I went home. Janette was making breakfast for Katarina.

At half past four on March 7, the phone rang.

"Emilio, it's Jan."

"Oh, hi Jan," I said automatically, and then I remembered that Jan was in America. Why was he calling? That's all he had said. "Jan?" I checked to see if he was still there.

"Emilio, Stanley's dead."

Janette had felt the silence and turned towards me. She watched as I stood there, motionless with the phone in my hand, and understood everything. I wasn't able to react in any way. Suddenly, I felt emptied out. When my wife touched my arm, I jumped. "What are we going to do now?" I said mechanically. "Let's go to Childwickbury," she said.

We dressed Katarina and went straight to the house. "This is Stanley's house!" our granddaughter exclaimed. I remembered her hands in Stanley's beard and couldn't breathe. Tracey was in the kitchen. She told us that Christiane was in her studio with Katharina. "Can I go and see them?" my wife asked. Tracey said that they were trying to calm her down, and that it might be better if she were left alone. Janette insisted. She put our granddaughter in Tracey's arms and went across the living room towards Christiane's room. I looked at the others and didn't know what to do. I felt hopelessly out of place. Janette put her head around the door and beckoned to me to come in. As soon as she saw me, Christiane got up and ran sobbing towards me. "He's dead, he's dead, Emilio, he's dead," she kept on saying as she sobbed on my shoulder. "I can't believe it," I said, without even knowing why. I couldn't even manage to hug her back. "I found him, he's dead, I tell you," said Christiane, her voice trembling, and that was when I started to cry, too. I held her tight, and she kept on repeating my name.

Somebody said that Jan was on his way back from the United States and would arrive that evening. Vivian was on a flight, too. Anya was already there. Janette stayed in the kitchen holding Katarina, then she told me that she was going to go home and put her to bed. I decided to stay. I had realized that, what with everything, nobody had remembered to feed the animals.

I took some meat out of the freezer and put it in the microwave. I prepared the dogs their bowls and took them out into the garden. The dogs ate in silence. While I watched them, I remembered the way that Stanley had half-smiled at me in the Dome Room the last time I had seen him, when I was helping him stand up. "We'll see each other after the weekend . . . after the weekend." For once in his life he was wrong.

Stanley's body was taken to Luton and Dunstable Hospital for the autopsy. The medical report stated the cause of death was a massive heart attack. Those last months of arduous work had undoubtedly been partly to blame.

I asked Christiane who was going to organize the funeral and the running of Childwickbury. She told me that Katharina's and Anya's husbands, Phil Hobbs and Jonathan Finney, would take care of everything. I met Phil and asked him what I could do. "Nothing," he replied. "You took care of Stanley, and now that he's gone I really don't know what you could do."

I clutched the bunch of keys to the private offices in my hand, and I opened the door of the Red Room. Stanley would never have been in there at that time, but somehow it seemed empty nonetheless. Out of habit, I checked the fax, the answering machine, and tidied up some papers that didn't really need to be moved. I crossed the Dome Room, passed under the pale light that shone through the cupola, and went into the editing room. Everything seemed suspended: the computers were on, and the chairs looked as if Stanley and the film editor had recently been sitting in them. I stopped, surrounded by the buzz of the computers, and couldn't decide whether to continue my rounds or turn back. I went back to the cats. I sat on the sofa and hoped they would climb on my lap. They just looked at me.

The next day I found a note from Phil on my desk. There was going to be a meeting of all the Childwickbury staff at ten. When I arrived in the kitchen, the meeting had already started. Phil was standing up in front of Tracey, the other domestics, the gardeners, the electrician, and all the others. He gave orders with a steady voice, pronouncing each word clearly, and then he started to talk about what would need to be done in the days that followed. Nobody said a word. When he had finished, I broke the silence. "Phil, what do I have to do?"

"Ah, Emilio . . ." he said, a little surprised. It was if he had forgotten until then that I was part of their world. "You do what you want, do what you have always done."

"You've given everybody else orders. You must have something for me to do."

"You were with Stanley, and . . ." he said after a moment's hesitation.

"Yes, but now Stanley's gone, and if I'm not wrong, you're the one giving the orders."

"I don't know. You decide. Try to fit in." He turned to the others again and repeated: "Okay, then that's agreed. Do exactly as I said."

As far as I was concerned, Stanley was still there. He's not dead, I thought, he's here with me and I'll carry on working just as I always have done.

When the funeral was organized, my name wasn't mentioned. During the meeting, I couldn't keep myself from saying something: "Phil, I need to ask you something. Do you know how long I have been working for Stanley? You were just a boy when he hired me. So, since I've been working for him all my life, don't you think I should help out at his funeral, too?"

"Oh, I'm sorry. I hadn't thought of that," he said. "Let me see what I can do. Maybe we can involve you somehow . . ."

Nothing changed. The coffin was to be carried by Phil himself, Jonathan, Tom Cruise, and Jan's three sons. I was given permission to walk behind with a bunch of flowers.

On the evening of March 11, Stanley's body came home. The coffin was taken from the courtyard into the house, through the main entrance of the Avid Room and along the corridor towards the Billiard Room. That's where I saw Stanley again. Jan had come with me. We stood by the coffin in silence. The large room was motionless. I looked at Stanley, but I couldn't believe it. It couldn't be him. It was the end, the end of everything. He'd left me; he'd left me; he had left me.

The funeral was the following afternoon. Shortly after lunch, Janette and I got in the Peugeot 205 and drove towards Childwickbury. Janette was driving; I just couldn't manage it. Despite the pouring rain, there was a large group of journalists and onlookers. They pointed their cameras and video cameras at us, and we were hit by a shower of flashes. I curled up to hide. Thanks to our old secondhand car and Janette's anonymous face, we managed to get though without much difficulty.

When they bombarded her with questions, she had the presence of mind to reply, "No comment," without taking her eyes off the road.

Outside in the park behind the house, large awnings had been set up along the route to the marquee, the large canvas tent above the grave. The perfume of the plants and vases of flowers that lined the way filled the air. The guests arrived in their own cars. Christiane and Jan had invited all the people who were important to Stanley: his friends. Andros, Julian, Michael, Martin, Milena, Sydney, and all the others sat in silence on the rows of wooden chairs in the marquee. In front of them, a green araucaria marked the burial place.

The coffin was lifted up and somebody put a bunch of flowers in my hand. We left the Pine Room and went along the corridor of awnings that protected us from the rain and also from the TV network helicopters that were hovering above our heads. The sound of a cello filled the cold air, and the heavy pale cloth flapped lightly in the wind. We went into the marquee. Everyone turned around to watch the coffin arrive. There was a bunch of red roses on it. The bright orange portrait that Christiane had painted for her husband when they lived at Abbots Mead was on an easel near the araucaria. And there, next to two thin burnished candelabra holding five candles each, the coffin was set down.

I sat on the right, next to Janette, Jon, and Marisa. Behind me, I could hear Julian mumbling prayers in Hebrew.

When the music stopped, Jan went towards the lectern in front of the tree. He made a short speech about the years he had spent working with Stanley and about the projects they had finished together. He mentioned Stanley's kindness, his energy, his strength and determination. "That's what I know about Stanley," he concluded. "If you want to know more, you'll have to ask Emilio." The sound of my name seemed to come at me from a distance. Was that me? My wife put her hand on my knee.

Tom, Nicole, Steven Spielberg, and Terry Semel from Warner Bros. all took turns to speak. They each had an anecdote to tell; they all extolled Stanley's extraordinary qualities. I had the feeling that I didn't know the person they were talking about. Why was I there? Why are they making me stay here, sitting still when I've got loads of things to do? Let me get on with my work. Let me go to Stanley.

Dominic and Ben Harlan played some pieces for clarinet and piano that Christiane and Katharina had chosen for the occasion. Then the coffin was lowered into the grave, and wife and daughter threw the first handfuls of earth onto it. They were followed by Jan, his wife Maria, Anya and Jonathan, then Vivian and me. I suddenly found myself in front of the grave. A few seconds earlier, I had been sitting down, and here I was, on my feet, clutching Vivian's hand. I realized that she had been holding my hand while we took the few paces necessary to reach the coffin. Together we watched the earth fall on the light-colored wood and slide down its sides. Everyone took their turn to say their last farewell. It was there, alongside the graves of his beloved cats and dogs, that Stanley took his leave of the world, wearing one of those military jackets full of pockets he loved so much, stuffed full of diaries, pens, and notepads.

At sunset, we went indoors, and in the large kitchen everybody talked about Stanley and shared their recollections of him. I received numerous handshakes from lawyers, employees of Warners, directors, producers, and numerous famous people whose names I'd always heard being mentioned but had never actually met before. Everyone wanted to offer me their condolences. They told me I was the only person to have stayed alongside Stanley for so many years, and that I had been a leading actor in the film of his life. The pain I felt, exposed to the eyes of all these people, upset me. I didn't want to be there. I missed Stanley. He himself would have felt awkward had he been faced with all those people who had come from goodness knows where just for him. He would have sent them packing with a brisk wave of his hand and an embarrassed smile. Stanley had gone, and yet the kitchen had never been so full of his presence as it was then.

I felt somebody touch my arm. It was Tom. He took me to one side.

"How do you feel?" he asked.

"I don't know, Tom, I'm confused."

"It doesn't seem possible," he whispered, nodding. "It *is* impossible."

He asked me about Stanley's last days, but all I could tell him was what I had seen: how he'd had difficulty getting up the stairs to his apartment, that there was no note on my desk, and that brief, unimportant telephone call. I realized then that he hadn't even opened the note I had left for him on Sunday morning. When I had slipped it under the door of his apartment, he had already gone. I couldn't stop myself from crying. "Now who's going to take care of his office?" Tom asked. I told him to follow me, and I let him into the Red Room. He looked around; he was one of the few who ever got to see inside. "Who's going to take care of all this?" "I don't know. Christiane, hopefully," I replied. We heard Nicole calling us. She wasn't feeling well. She was exhausted and needed to lie down, so I said she could go upstairs to one of the guest rooms. Tom went with her, and I returned to the kitchen.

I couldn't breathe, I couldn't hear anything, and I couldn't feel anything. I repeatedly went back over my last memories in search of a connection, a cause, or a reason. I had always believed that he would make it, that the tiredness didn't count. But no. Maybe I should have done something. . . . I had been worried. "I'm afraid for Stanley," I'd said to Janette and Jan. I'd tried to help him feel better, but it hadn't been enough. He'd pushed himself too far.

Vivian brought me back to earth. I felt a light arm around my shoulders, and then I saw the green grass of Childwickbury again. It was wet with rain. I turned around to look at her and saw that she was devastated. "Shall we go and see Dad?" she asked breathily. We left the hum of the guests behind us and walked along the corridor of awnings to the empty marquee. The chairs were no longer in neat rows, and there was the odd program on a cushion here and there. When we stopped in front of the grave, Vivian asked me how I thought I could manage without her father. "I have to," I answered. "Have you got the strength?" she insisted, her voice trembling. I nodded silently and clenched my teeth. Vivian shook her head as if to say no, then she threw her arms around my neck and burst into tears. Her grief overwhelmed me and dragged me down. We sobbed together, sharing and understanding each other's despair. It was then, as we embraced one another, that I realized we were like brother and sister, that we were both Stanley's children.

"I wasn't there. I wasn't there," said Vivian in tears, holding me tighter all the time. She had her demons to deal with. "I treated him badly." I managed to understand these words through her sobs. "Your father knew that you loved him, and he loved you a lot, too. He can't tell it to you anymore, Vivian, so I will." She cried and cried and looked at my tears and at that heap of earth beside us.

The next morning, I woke up in my bed. It was early, early for a day like that. I should have got up, should have had breakfast, taken the car, and gone to Childwickbury. I should have done . . . done what?

The phone rang. At that time of the morning it could only be Stanley. No, it couldn't be Stanley anymore. It was Andros. His voice was the first I had heard when I had got back home after Jan had told me. Andros had seen it on the TV news. "Why is he dead?" he had said inconsolably on the evening of that wretched Sunday. "Why is he dead?" he had repeated. Neither of us could manage to say anything else. Now, the morning after the funeral, he had the same flat tone to his voice. "I didn't sleep," he said. Neither of us could think of anything to say, so we just stood there, holding the phone in silence for minutes. Then he asked: "What are you going to do now?" "Nothing," I blurted. "I'm not going to do anything." And after a long, long silence, I added: "Once I sort things out, I'm going back to where I came from."

I respected my working hours, and I took care of the animals, especially Priscilla, who was frail but stable. I was even asked to lend a hand with *Eyes Wide Shut*, which was due to be released in the middle of July. After the first few disconcerting days, during which Childwickbury seemed to hold its breath, suddenly everyone started working like mad to make sure the film came out on time. I followed orders without caring who they came from, and I kept on working without ever refusing, and yet it didn't mean anything anymore. I felt insignificant.

One afternoon, as I was going back into Childwickbury, I heard noise coming from one of the rooms in the west wing. I thought it might be the film editor in the Avid Room; the film had to be finished, so it made sense for someone to be working there, but nobody had asked me for the keys. I went to the Green Room, and after I'd got past all the cats, I noticed that there was a light on in the Red Room and saw the shadows of people rummaging through drawers, among papers and notepads, as well as the filing cabinets and Stanley's personal computer. The bunch of keys was still in my pocket, so how had they got in? Someone must have taken the copies from the Key Room and used them to go where they shouldn't.

I staggered towards the courtyard. Someone got out of the Rolls, slammed the door, and walked past me. They wouldn't even leave his car alone. Someone else gave me a dirty look, and I couldn't stop myself from saying, "If you weren't allowed to do certain things before, then you're not allowed to do them now, either!" There was no answer. "At least ask Christiane for permission!" Somebody snorted behind my back. The courtyard was dimly lit by the sunset, and the wind carried the braying of one of the donkeys. It made me think of Rupert, who had died during the night some years earlier. When I went to the enclosure at seven in the morning, the vultures had already pecked his eyes out.

I kept on working every day. I even took Katharina's and Anya's children to school. And then I saw it. The Unimog was in the Stable Block courtyard. Alex's classmates were jumping up and down on the roof and hood. A few weeks later, Phil Hobbs put it up for sale.

"Why should I get rid of them, Emilio?" Stanley had asked on my return to England three years earlier. He was referring to his new collaborators. "At least I know them. I can look after myself." At the time, I didn't see anything wrong with it. Actually, I thought he was right. I'd seen plenty of them come and go over the years. However, the following day I went back to his office. I had a simple but good plan. It was so obvious that nobody had ever thought of it before. "Do you remember what you said to me yesterday?" I began. "Well, it's not true." Stanley looked at me over his glasses. "It's not true that it would be better to keep them." And I continued: "Just because you know what they are like doesn't mean you'll be all right. It simply means that you won't be surprised if there are problems. This isn't a solution, Stanley. Solutions solve problems; they don't justify them." I realized that he had no intention of discussing the subject, but I beat him to it. "And the solution is perfectly obvious: get Andros back!"

Stanley moved on his chair as if to say or do something. "Don't say anything. Wait." I stopped him before he could start grumbling. He was proud, and it still hurt even after all those years. He would have cut off his own hand rather than pick up the phone and ask Andros to come back. "Listen carefully to me. I called him this morning to ask him if he'd like to come back. But I explained to him that it was just an idea I'd had one night when I couldn't sleep and that you didn't know anything about it. Do you know what he answered? 'If the hours are good, why not?'" I smiled, while Stanley continued looking at me and said nothing.

What I would have asked for myself wasn't all that different. I could have split my time between Childwickbury and Sant'Angelo, and kept Janette happy, too. I'd allowed myself to be optimistic: "If you've started a film, we can work together without any time limits. When you've finished, you can give me six months off, or even eight if we can organize the shifts well." Stanley nodded slightly as I explained the clauses and advantages of this new contract. "Time passes for everybody, Stanley. You have to stop working as hard as you have done so far. It's not sustainable anymore, not for anyone, and that includes you." There might have been a reluctant gesture of agreement.

"And let's make Christiane happy, too," I added. "She's been asking you for years to restructure the house! We can take a break, renovate Childwickbury outside and in, as well the people inside. Before you start back on *A.I.*, let's take a break. You can move downstairs while the builders work on the roof. Andros and I can help you take down your books and everything else you need." I couldn't see anything wrong with my plan. Stanley nodded again and seemed more convinced. The idea of changing personnel at Childwickbury was gaining ground. "Right. Let's do that." It was settled. "As soon as we finish *Eyes Wide Shut.*"

But there hadn't been time. The show was over. Now the curtain was closed.

17

BACK TO ITALY

"JAN, I'VE DECIDED TO leave," I announced. Before he could say anything, I added, "Don't worry, I'll sort out Stanley's office. I've already done it once. You don't need to worry about that. But I'm not staying. I can't. My wife's birthday is on August 12, and I want to be in Italy by then." It was easier to explain to Christiane. I went to see her in her studio, where she had remained in solitude for most of the time since the funeral. "I'm sorry," I said, "but I don't feel like staying. If you need help with anything, anything at all, don't hesitate to call me. But now I'd better be going." She understood. Vivian had already gone back to America; she'd made the right choice, too.

I tidied up the documents in Stanley's office on the ground floor. I grouped together faxes and letters, putting the envelopes in order of arrival or by sender. I straightened the contents of the bookcase and shelves. I put writers, lawyers, directors, and vets together. Everything was organized by subject. "Do what Stanley would have done," is all Jan had said, but it was the only method there was. Staying alone in his private rooms again helped me a little. Being surrounded by their familiar silence made me forget what had taken place there a few days earlier. And yet at the same time, I was tormented by anger.

We packed. In Italy, Janette did everything she possibly could to make me feel better. She watched me from afar as I stood still in the vegetable garden and gazed at the mountains around the cottage. Every time we came together, she gently stroked my back with her hand.

In September, Jan invited us to the European premiere of *Eyes Wide Shut* at the Venice Film Festival. "Out of respect for Stanley, I have to refuse," I replied. Jan didn't understand what I meant and insisted, adding that all our expenses would be paid for by Warner Bros. He said that everyone would be there: Tom, Nicole, Christiane, Katharina, and Anya. He didn't mention Vivian. I promised him I'd think about it. I phoned my cousin Raffaele, and he told me that he'd received the same invitation. "I don't know, Emilio. What are you thinking of doing?" I confided in him that it was an awkward situation and asked what his wife had said. "Edda says that if you want to come, you can stay with us." I wasn't in the mood for celebrating, but in the end I accepted. I watched Christiane do her best to stay reserved and neutral. Despite how she was feeling, she somehow managed the interviews and answered the journalists' questions. I understood why she was making this effort to promote the film on Stanley's behalf, and she succeeded with the same style and reserve as her husband. In any case, going back home was almost a relief.

A month later, on October 4, 1999, Marisa phoned to tell us that our second grandchild, Luisa Daniela, had been born. I was a grandfather for the second time, and this managed to cheer me up.

We went back to England to visit Marisa, and on the Sunday I went to Childwickbury. When I called to ask when would be a good time to come, Tracey told me that Christiane would definitely be there in the afternoon. She came through the door under the colonnade to meet us, and we hugged each other. The large kitchen was bathed in sunlight, and as we talked, we did our best not to mention Stanley. Janette enthused about Luisa, and about Jon and Sally's first child, due at the end of the month. But inevitably, we were all thinking about him. In the end, Christiane admitted: "It's all too empty." She stared towards the park and told us about her days spent in solitude in the big house. I realized that she was looking in the direction Stanley's grave. "I'd like to spend a bit of time down there," I said. "Of course, Emilio. There are some chairs. Stay as long as you want."

Christiane stayed in the kitchen to talk to my wife. I went through the French windows, across the grass ruffled by the wind, and towards the group of bushes near the araucaria. I could hear the beating of wings, leaves rustling, and distant birdsong. As always, the sound of nature in the park at Childwickbury somehow amplified the silence.

Ciao, Stanley, I said, with a sigh of emotion. It seemed strange to be sitting in the garden and looking at the ground. There might have been someone else nearby, but I felt alone. I let my gaze wander along the fence and glimpsed the lake through the trees. Then I looked down again. Barnaby came slowly over to me, lay down on my feet, and put his nose on my shoe. I bent down to stroke him and realized that I was close to the white stones that covered the grave.

Pity you went so soon. There was still a lot to do, Stanley. *A.I.*, for instance: it would have been wonderful to help you make it at last, together with Andros and Margaret. I had the feeling that it would have been a great film. It was strange, but I thought it would have been another *A Clockwork Orange*. Not because of the story, but for the effect and the reactions it would have provoked. From the way you talked about it, it must have been an enormous project; it would have echoed everywhere. It would have been another turning point.

Jan gave Steven all the material, and he turned it into a good film. I went to see it at the cinema in Rome. Paolo came with me. The dentist from Cassino, remember? I went to the cinema for the first time in decades. Strange, isn't it? Now that you're gone, I went to the cinema to see one of your films made by someone else. As I was saying, Steven received all the drawings and all your notes and got to work. For a while, Jan called me nearly every day. He wanted to know where you had put all the preproduction stuff. Who knows whatever happened to that Post-it where you had made a note of where the drawing of New York underwater was. Jan never managed to find it. I guided him over the phone, just like I used to do with you. It was another treasure hunt from Cassino to St. Albans. In the end, the film worked out well. At least that's what Paolo said, because, as you know, I don't understand the first thing about cinema.

A few years after *A.I.,* Jan called me for *Napoleon,* too. I don't know if it was for a film or a book; he wasn't really clear about it. That was another treasure hunt. "I can't find the boxes. I just can't find them," he kept on saying. So in the end I sent him a map of the Stable Block by fax. It's not easy to find the treasure if you've never played before.

There's a traveling exhibition of your things, too. It started out in Frankfurt, and it's going all around Europe. When Christiane told me, the first thing I thought about was that poor, unlucky person who had had to deal with all your boxes. I went to see the exhibition in Rome with a group of your admirers from Pescara. I walked along the marble corridors of Palazzo delle Esposizioni and started to laugh: all the things I used to dust down every day were in glass cases as if they were historical artifacts. It was surreal, almost comic. Actually, I started to laugh as soon as I went in, when I saw a piece of frayed string tied to the case of your Eyemo portable camera. I'd put it there to make it easier to carry, and here it was in a showcase, like a relic. "Andros wrote that!" I said, looking at the handwriting in pencil on some signs. "And I went over this one with a pen because it was illegible." Sorry Stanley, but my 20-pence ballpoints have always done the trick, while the ink on some of the letters you wrote with your fountain pens has faded away. When I went into the room with all your equipment, I saw the green-painted metal of the Moviola among all those lenses I used to go and pick up in Freiburg. I couldn't resist the temptation: I trailed a finger across it. "Don't touch," said the museum attendant, and when I blurted out, "Come on, I must have already touched it millions of times!" he looked at me as if I was mad. "If you had any idea how much cat's pee I've cleaned away from under there, you wouldn't stand so close!" It was an interesting afternoon. In the end, I saw the old photos of you when you were young in New York and working on your very first films. I used to find them thrown into cardboard boxes. I never had time to go through them, and now, there they were: framed and hanging on the wall. They really were beautiful pictures.

When I hear that Stanley Kubrick was the greatest film director in the world, it makes me happy and sad at the same time. I think about how he himself was so surprised by the warmth and admiration he received from people he didn't even know because they loved his films. Today I feel lonely, like when Margaret and Andros decided to leave us. He called me to his office so many times just because he wanted to talk: "I'm tired of phoning and writing. Sit down and let's have a cup of coffee." I was so busy back then that it seemed like a waste of time. Now I'd give anything to be able to say to him, "Yes, I'm here with you, let's talk." I would tell him about my parents in Italy; he always liked to hear about them. Or about Marisa's and Jon's jobs, or about car racing. He even went as far as to ask me about the Formula One drivers, because it meant that I would stay with him half an hour longer.

Car racing, my greatest passion, had become part of the family's DNA. Now it was my grandson Elio's turn to make sure the name D'Alessandro stayed in the English driver rankings. Elio had been the most recent happy event during my life in England. He was born on October 29, 1999. Sally was exhausted but happy. As soon as she saw me arrive at the hospital, she exclaimed, "I've given you a racing driver, are you happy?" Jon didn't waste any time. As soon as Elio was eight years old, he enrolled him the karting school, with leave from Sally, who nevertheless grumbled just like Janette had done twenty years before.

One rainy weekend that same October, Jan had asked me to put off going back to Italy for a few days so that I could sort out the things in Stanley's apartment. While I was bending over the papers spread all over the place, I heard Stanley's voice calling me. It was ridiculous, but I kept on hearing it: in my ears and in my brain. I couldn't help looking up from what I was doing and turning to stare at his office. After the umpteenth "Emilio, come here for a minute," I decided to go into the room where he had passed the last years of his life. It was empty. True: the furniture was still there, and there were documents scattered everywhere, and yet it seemed completely empty. The TV was off; the radio was off. It's so silent, I said to myself, so silent. That silent chaos contrasted with what he had always been and what he had always done. Yet that very same chaos had been with him for decades. I'd had the impression that at times he realized how distant and different he seemed to other people. I myself had seen him that way at the beginning. Then gradually, a little at a time, I'd got to know him and to understand his intentions to such an extent that I would justify and defend the way he was. Now that his time was over, and mine had lost all sense, I think I finally grasped exactly what it was that bound us together. We had established an unimaginable and yet stable balance: we had found the place where his intelligence and my ignorance met and worked together in an extraordinary but simple way.

Losing Stanley had hurt me more than losing my own father. His death had been sudden and unfair. That was it: above all unfair and wrong. And I hadn't been ready for it. Going away, and leaving behind all those memories of him, was the only way I could survive.

I sometimes went back to England again to visit my children and grandchildren. Now there were four of them: Marco was born in 2005. And I went to see Andros, Julian, and Peter, too. As Milena once said to me, "We are a family." And then I went to Childwickbury to say hello to Stanley. I still feel him very close to me. I can feel him in my blood. It's difficult to accept that everything in life can change, collapse, and disappear from one moment to the next.

This morning I woke up at dawn again. I sat up in bed, and Janette asked me what had happened. "Nothing," I answered, "I've just remembered that I have to take the Mercedes to Greenford to be serviced, and if I don't go now I'll end up being late." "Emilio," she said without moving, "we're in Italy. Go back to sleep." Nothing has changed yet. I'm still there. I can hear the cock crowing so it's already morning. Then the sound of a distant engine: somebody's already working in the fields. It seems to be coming from behind my house. From my field. I get up slowly so as not to wake Janette and peek through the blind. The tractor really is in my field, it moves towards the house and then away again, following the outlines of the land. There are two people on it. I screw up my eyes, but I can't make them out. The tractor turns again and goes away and the sound of the engine fades. I go downstairs, go outside, and see the tractor turn and come back towards me. One of them calls me, "Emilio! Emilio!" The voice is familiar, the faint blue light of dawn struggles to penetrate the mist hanging above the freshly turned sods of earth, and it's then that I glimpse my father and Stanley sitting shoulder to shoulder and trying to keep the tractor straight. "Emilio!" my father calls out again. Stanley keeps his hands on the wheel and laughs heartily. "What are you two doing up there?" I shout, trying to make myself heard. "You don't even know each other, you only ever met once at Jon's christening!" Stanley answers cheerfully: "These are the most wonderful days of my life, Emilio!" My father laughs again. "Tell Christiane that I feel just fine now. Promise me that you'll tell her." Then Stanley drives the tractor out of the field and towards the road. "No, stop!" I shout. "Don't go on the road, it's dangerous!" But all they do is laugh. "Be careful," I insist, "the bus is coming, you'll get yourselves killed!" My dad reassures me: "Emilio, don't worry. Everything will be all right." Stanley turns into the road and starts to drive away. I begin to run. I run and I run to try and catch up with them, but I can't. I see them turn and wave together, smiling and happy, as the tractor gets smaller and smaller and vanishes into the fog. And while the engine revs louder and Stanley laughs, there is still silence.

AFTERWORD
EMILIO WILL PICK
YOU UP AT THE STATION

IN MARCH 2005, I found an email in the inbox of *Archivio*Kubrick from Paolo Morrone, a dentist in Cassino who was "lucky enough to be a friend of Emilio D'Alessandro, the Italian who was Stanley Kubrick's right-hand man for thirty years."

*Archivio*Kubrick is a website that I started in 1999 as an attempt to make available all the material I'd managed to collect about the films of Stanley Kubrick. Could Emilio D'Alessandro help with the site? That's what Paolo was asking.

Modesty makes it impossible for me to disturb famous people, because I'm convinced that the last thing they want is to be subjected to interviews. I replied to Paolo politely but rather vaguely, saying I'd heard of Mr. D'Alessandro in an English documentary, where he played a small part as the driver who went to pick up Kubrick's collaborators at St. Albans Station. It is difficult for me now to recall what I was thinking of Emilio back then, but I must have had the feeling that there wouldn't be much benefit for my site in that.

Paolo wasn't discouraged at all by my reluctance, though. He persisted in writing me that it would be nice if I could meet Emilio and listen to what he had to say about Kubrick. By the end of July, it seemed rude to keep declining Paolo's invitations, so I agreed to visit Emilio with a group of people from Pescara who wanted to organize a conference about Kubrick, with Emilio as guest of honor together with Christiane Kubrick and Jan Harlan.

The following Saturday, I went to Cassino, and Paolo took me to Emilio's house in the countryside. A small, agile-looking man met us at the gate. He spread his arms wide to welcome us. It was such a spontaneous gesture that it made me smile. We shook hands, and they took me to the kitchen where Janette, Emilio's wife, was preparing lunch. We started to talk, and I immediately felt comfortable there. Not long afterwards, the group from Pescara arrived and time flew. Emilio spoke enthusiastically, and everything he said involved Kubrick in such a real and tangible way that I had the extraordinary feeling of actually being near a person I'd admired for years from afar. It was a revelation, and by the end of the day, strange as it may seem, I found myself thinking of Kubrick as "Stanley." As Paolo was turning the car around, I looked back and saw Emilio waving his arms again just as he had done when we arrived, but this time with one hand raised up in the air.

At the end of September, when Emilio was to be a guest on a Radio Tre program to promote the forthcoming conference in Pescara, Paolo contacted me again and insisted on taking me with him to the recording of the program.

At the RAI (Italian Radio & TV) studios, I sat in the guest room with Janette. She was interested in my work as a researcher at the National Research Council of Italy and in my passion for Stanley's films. When I told her that I'd been to London a couple of times, she insisted on continuing our conversation in English. So we talked about e-commerce, about Piccadilly Circus, and Italian and English cooking. On the other side of the glass, Emilio was telling the story about the cats in Andros's Mini and Stanley's unbridled enthusiasm for electronic gadgets and military vehicles.

A few days later, I received another call from Paolo. Emilio wanted to write a book of his memoirs, and everybody had thought of me. Just like that. I must have babbled something about it being a good idea, not only to show Stanley in a different light from the one perpetuated by the press but also to give everyone a chance to enjoy the emotions that Emilio's words were able to arouse, as I had experienced myself.

"Let's talk about it in more detail. Come next Saturday. Emilio will pick you up at the station." Ah, right.

I spent the following days working on a structure for the book, jotting down ideas, suggestions, and questions I wanted Emilio to answer. It was as if I were preparing myself for a job interview, only when I got there I didn't have a chance to propose anything because I found that it had all been decided beforehand. Emilio and Janette just nodded with knowing smiles and didn't respond otherwise to anything I said. It was as if they already knew exactly what I was going to suggest. After a few minutes, I came to terms with the fact that there was no point trying to "sell" my project. What I had to do instead was get down to work. That same evening, in the pizzeria where we had dinner, I learned more: Janette spoke on their behalf and said that I should think of the book as a gift from her, Emilio, and Stanley. "You don't have to tell us how you want to do it. Whatever you think is fine with us."

On the way back, Emilio did most of the talking but never about the book. He preferred to ask me about my family, about my grandparents' house in the mountains in Tuscany, and if I had any cats. I said I would have loved to have one, but in my place in Rome I didn't have much space. My parents had tortoises in their garden, though. "Oh, I love tortoises!" said Janette. "I had one when I was a child!" After a fairly thorough conversation about tortoises, Emilio asked, rather nonchalantly, "So, will the book be ready by Easter?" It was October 10. Before I could answer, he added, "It has to come out at the same time all over the world." "I think it might take a bit more time than that," I admitted cautiously. "Oh, yes. It always takes longer than you expect," Emilio remarked with a smile. Janette laughed.

I spent the next day with Emilio in his attic opening the trunks where he kept all the things from his life in England. Each of them revealed small treasures: the call sheets from the first day of shooting of *Eyes Wide Shut*, key rings from the Overlook Hotel, faded Polaroids of the set of *Barry Lyndon*, the insurance documents for the Mercedes with Emilio's signature alongside those of the members of the Kubrick family, Christmas cards signed by Christiane, Kubrick's (or rather Stanley's) letters with details of how to manage the house, and the organization of the film being produced at the time. I was surprised by the way Emilio didn't touch anything. He let me do the organizing and cataloguing. All he did was answer my questions when I couldn't work out where a particular object came from. "It's exactly the same as being with Andros," he said after a while, "only you don't swear."

One weekend was not enough to make an inventory of everything. Not least because there was stuff all over the place: in the attic, in the garage, even in Emilio's mother's house. So our research went on after Christmas, after Easter, and after Easter of the following year. Janette interspersed all this with fine lunches, during which we nearly always ended up talking about cats and Emilio casually recounted anecdotes that for me were worth an entire book in my Kubrick library. I needed time to get used to it—to learn to see Emilio and Stanley's day-to-day way of life as normal. Emilio had realized this, and he enjoyed playing with my enthusiasm: "I've got a little surprise for you," he said on more than one occasion when I arrived at the station, and then he showed me some piece of memorabilia in the garage that he had found who knows where—an LP of the *Full Metal Jacket* soundtrack signed by Kubrick, a bunch of keys from Childwickbury, a dusty photo of himself with a mustache in front of the model of the Overlook Hotel.

Sometimes the things he turned up had a profound effect on him. Once he called, his voice shaking with emotion, to tell me that he'd come across a note Stanley had written him after he'd decided to go back to Italy. It had been in one of the pockets of a "full metal" jacket for over ten years. "He wrote that he was really sad I was leaving . . . I'd forgotten about it, this note."

It wasn't easy to decide how much importance to give to each episode. If you asked, and I did want to ask, any random day spent with Kubrick would have been enough to fill a hundred pages. I wanted to convey the idea of the rhythm of those days spent with the director, but at the same time I wanted to remain faithful to Emilio's image of Stanley, leaving mine to one side. For Emilio, Stanley wasn't the genius who had produced some of the undisputed masterpieces of cinema; he was quite simply the best employer you could have, surrounded by the best team of assistants there was. It was both a training course and a school of life. At times, I was worried that I was being too intrusive, and I wondered whether investigating Kubrick's private life was indiscreet. But it was enough to listen to Emilio to realize that he would provide me with facts and impressions, but never secrets.

I needed to understand Emilio before I could start writing his story, but it was difficult to define the real nature of his work, of his presence alongside the director. Emilio was the only person who stayed with him for such a long time, and more importantly, the one who stayed not because he was Kubrick but because he was Stanley. Emilio was beyond being a factotum who deals with and solves the tasks and problems of every day. Nor was he the stereotypical taxi-driver-cum-confidant who wheedles thoughts, fears, and joys from whoever sits on the backseat. There isn't a single word that encapsulates what Emilio did for Kubrick, or what his role was. Calling him an assistant, personal assistant, right-hand man, or one of the family leaves out something essential. Emilio was quite simply there when he was needed, and even when he wasn't—"because you never know." I often thought about Sara Maitland's words in the documentary *The Last Movie*: "[Stanley] was absolutely unaware of the normal frustrations of middle-class-not-particularly-rich life—computers did not break down, why hadn't I got it fixed, why didn't I have a competent fixer, why hadn't I sent for them already, why was my printer not working?" . . . It's true: Stanley knew absolutely nothing about these frustrations, but it wasn't a question of class. It's because all he had to do was call Emilio. The composer Nino Rota had summed up this epiphany better than anybody else while he was chatting with Emilio from the rear seat of the Mercedes on his way back from Abbots Mead: "I wish I'd been as lucky as Kubrick!"

"Filippo," Emilio said once, in a succinct attempt to dispel my doubts, "just write the book the way Stanley would have made a film." Did he want to reassure me or spur me on? I had to make quite an effort not to be terrified by that.

I found that it helped to focus on details that at first seemed unimportant: the radio that was fixed in an instant, the meetings between the two of them over a cup of coffee, the doors of major film companies that had always been closed but were now open, Stanley wanting Emilio around him for no apparent reason. I realized that these images were more meaningful than many of my ruminations. They might even be the answer. The garden in front of the cottage certainly was an answer. It was perfectly kept, and it was only the last in a long line. During the breaks from our interviews, which were not so much for a rest as because it was necessary to feed the hens, I gathered my thoughts in the shade of the portico and looked at the perfectly cut grass, the colorful flowers, and the careful compositions of nearly ripe fruit surrounded by buzzing insects. What else was there to understand? Emilio popped out of the henhouse with a smile and reached out a hand to show me a couple of eggs. And I smiled, too.

Filippo Ulivieri
Rome, July 2012

Acknowledgments

Thanks to Marisa D'Alessandro and Matteo Carnevali for their work on the photographs; to Maurizio Di Meo for his help in Los Angeles, and to all those who have read the many drafts of this book; to Nino Gualdoni for all his advice; to Michele Pavan Deana for being there at the beginning and well after the end, making it twice as much fun; to Nicola Silva for unfalteringly dedicating a vast amount of time to this project.

Filippo thanks Paolo Morrone, without whom this book simply wouldn't have existed; Fabrizio Grimaldi for his limitless generosity and care; and Emilio, Janette, Jon, and Marisa for sharing with him their memories and welcoming him into their family. This, I must say, is the greatest privilege of all.

Emilio and Janette would like to thank everyone who appears in this book, and especially those who have tried without success to find themselves among these pages. You are not here, but you will always be in our hearts.

Appendix

Appreciations

Dear Emilio, I'm still scared of the way you drive, but still love you. Your friend,

Ryan O'Neal

*

Nineteen seventy-one was a momentous year. Rolls-Royce went bankrupt, decimalization came to the UK, Jim Morrison died, Joe Frazier beat Muhammad Ali, half a million people protested against the Vietnam War, and the film *A Clockwork Orange* was released. It is also the year that Emilio D'Alessandro joined the small community of people who worked for one of the foremost creative geniuses of the film industry—Stanley Kubrick. The passion and tenacity with which Emilio embraced every task he undertook guaranteed an impeccable outcome. Over the years it became apparent that, amongst all his other attributes, Emilio's Italian charm and charisma enabled him to sidestep any questions or actions which would come in the way of his loyalty and discretion about all aspects of Kubrick's life to which he was privy. Emilio used all his racing car driver skills and concentration to get through the ever-changing challenges of the next twenty-eight hectic years, which were brought to a sudden halt in 1999 by the untimely death of Stanley Kubrick. This is the story of an incredible life.

Andros Epaminondas, Stanley Kubrick's
production assistant from 1970 to 1980

*

In the frenetic, frantic, fraught life of one of the world's most complex and creative individuals, Emilio brought a sea of calm and order. Nothing was too much trouble or too much of an effort for Emilio. Every task undertaken was completed quickly, quietly, and very efficiently. He never seemed troubled or rushed. . . . Whether driving stars like Jack Nicholson or Ryan O'Neal to and from Kubrick's home or finding the perfect location for Christiane Kubrick to paint (she is a renowned artist), Emilio was always there to make the task so much easier. Always calm and helpful—which, given his racing car driver's background, is not surprising—he became an essential member of a close-knit team. Friendly, wise beyond his years, I truly do think that he took much of the weight off Kubrick's mind in many areas. He was indispensable to us all.

JULIAN SENIOR, VICE PRESIDENT OF ADVERTISING
& PUBLICITY FOR WARNER BROS. EUROPE

*

One afternoon at home in Oxford with my young children I received a telephone call from someone calling himself Stanley Kubrick. I was and still am a private individual who happens to write not at all best-selling books. Of course, I knew at once the call was a hoax. Why would Stanley Kubrick telephone me? The answer, as always with that generous and entirely dedicated man, was in pursuit of something that would contribute to his art, and he briefly thought I might help him re-envisage the story that became *Eyes Wide Shut*. After we had established that this really was Stanley, though I certainly did not feel at all like myself, he said that he would send someone to collect me and bring me to his home and place of work in the English countryside near St Albans.

And so I met Emilio. At once he showed the ease and discretion that are essential for those who work with someone who may be described as a genius. He arrived in a nicely discreet old gray Mercedes—the car of a real person, not a showbiz image creature—and we chatted as he drove. Not everyone can talk and drive without making a nervous passenger even more alarmed.

Emilio spoke of Stanley, about whom I had probably some of the usual wrong ideas—reclusive, moody, difficult—though I find it hard to recall ever feeling like that about someone who not once showed any of that to me. He was a sane man with an overpowering creative vision; the two don't always co-reside in one human personality. The man who emerged from Emilio's conversation was physically brave, emotionally loyal, and unsleepingly devoted to his life's work and his family.

All true.

I became used to, and happily anticipated, these drives through England in the company of Emilio, this kind man who played so practical a part in the workings of what must be, to use the deadening lingo of our times, one of the most fully and richly functional families I've ever had the luck to encounter, that extended family of blood and enthusiasm—and dogs!—in the sprawling organism that is Childwickbury. Emilio spoke frequently of his home in Italy, of his roots. I am prejudiced towards Italy, was raised by Italophone parents in a city full of Italians, Edinburgh, and, being that kind of neoclassical Scot, I was fed by Emilio's "Italianness"; the stories of life in Monte Cassino gave that place new resonances.

Those days are for me long gone, and I was no good at screenwriting at all, but I am still learning from those days as they reverberate in my memory, now that so much has happened to us all. Stanley gone, absolutely not forgotten; and me, bizarrely, half blind, with my eyes suffering an illness that makes them literally "wide shut." No surprise to one who lived with art daily, Emilio, that life imitates it. I wish Emilio love and luck and all good things, and to his family.

He is the perfect companion for a trip into the unknown—kind, reassuring, aware of what is real and important and what is not. Love and work are real, of course; showing off and fancy stuff are not.

That summer of spending time at the heart of the "world of film" taught me that; it is an irony that might not play with all the directors of today. Nor yet with those in their "entourage." It was not an entourage at Childwickbury. It was a family in the best sense, a star under which people might sail under many flags.

CANDIA MCWILLIAM, SCOTTISH AUTHOR,
PRELIMINARY WORK ON *EYES WIDE SHUT*

*

Emilio was my guide, philosopher, and friend during most of 1990 when I was working with Stanley Kubrick on developing the screen story for what became *A.I. Artificial Intelligence*. Nine months of fun and madness! Would I have survived with my sanity intact were it not for Emilio? Given Emilio's many insights, I survived the constant mind-shifts of Stanley, the frequent collapse of the houses of cards of the story, the suggestions that I should maybe work all night and every day—although indeed Stanley was an amiable dictator, with a wry sense of humour, and I felt privileged when he himself finally phoned in person to sever our "relationship" (temporarily, as it turned out).

I lived about sixty kilometers from Kubrick HQ so, for long afternoon brainstorming sessions with Stanley several times a week, Emilio would collect me in the black Mercedes—then later in the white Porsche, which Emilio reactivated especially for me. Emilio and I got on so well during the journeys that I started learning Italian from him. "*Stanley è nostro zio,*" we would chorus on the motorway: Stanley is our uncle. Emilio had refused to drive the low-slung Porsche for three years because he hurt his back shifting tons of Stanley's possessions personally to the manor house; Stanley didn't trust removal men to touch his things. Nor did Stanley trust anyone except Emilio to feed the dogs, even on Christmas Day, requiring Emilio to make a special journey from London; and if, alas, a dog should ever die, to lessen the trauma to Stanley Emilio had hidden away special dog coffins. Of course, Emilio had dutifully started the Porsche weekly, to charge the battery and check the car out, but finally Stanley received a letter from Porsche UK lamenting that he was abusing their fine engineering product by not having the car serviced regularly. Even despite Emilio's best efforts, a minor matter at Kubrick HQ could swiftly escalate into a catastrophe. "Why are you abusing the Porsche, Emilio?" Emilio needed to prevail on the head of Porsche UK (who, of course, had heard of Emilio as Emerson Fittipaldi's former driving partner) to write to Stanley explaining that an unused car didn't need £400 in services.

Emilio revealed many surreal events and mysteries to me—mysteries such as how Stanley could be wearing the same somewhat scruffy clothes every day without those becoming filthy as the months passed. When Stanley liked something, he bought many spares, so he wasn't actually wearing the selfsame jacket and trousers but identical replicas all in the same comfortably used state.

Long-suffering Emilio, whose dearest dream was to retire to his vineyard south of Monte Cassino! When a person was invaluable to Stanley, as Emilio was, it was difficult to escape or to have a life. Since Emilio and I kept in touch long after my stint with Stanley, eventually Emilio told me on the phone, "Ian, I have given notice to Stanley at last. I am quitting."

"What?" I exclaimed.

"Yes . . . I have given him three years' notice."

Naturally, Stanley ignored the three-year warning and Emilio's countdown. One year to go, Stanley. Six months. Three months. "You must pay attention, Stanley—you must make other arrangements." Zero hour came; Emilio had already sold his house. Stanley refused to let him go and rented a house for Emilio to live in for another six months. At long last, Emilio escaped to his vineyard, and to the leisure that would lead to this story of his life (so far!).

IAN WATSON, BRITISH SCIENCE FICTION WRITER,
CO-AUTHOR OF *A.I. ARTIFICIAL INTELLIGENCE*

INDEX OF NAMES